The Poetry of Jack Spicer

For Dorothy

The Poetry of Jack Spicer

Daniel Katz

EDINBURGH
University Press

© Daniel Katz, 2013

Edinburgh University Press Ltd
22 George Square, Edinburgh EH8 9LF

www.euppublishing.com

Typeset in 10.5/13 pt Sabon
by Servis Filmsetting Ltd, Stockport, Cheshire, and
printed and bound in Great Britain by
CPI Group (UK) Ltd, Croydon CR0 4YY

A CIP record for this book is available from the British Library

ISBN 978 0 7486 4098 0 (hardback)
ISBN 978 0 7486 4549 7 (paperback)
ISBN 978 0 7486 7715 3 (webready PDF)
ISBN 978 0 7486 7716 0 (epub)
ISBN 978 0 7486 7717 7 (Amazon ebook)

Contents

Acknowledgements

Writing on Spicer, I've been lucky in my predecessors. While I've tried to mark my debts punctually in this book, my thinking on Spicer has been so thoroughly informed by the work of Robin Blaser, Maria Damon, Michael Davidson, Lew Ellingham, Peter Gizzi, Kevin Killian, and Ron Silliman, that echoes of their writing undoubtedly trespass beyond my delineations; for this, apologies and thanks. And additional thanks to Kevin Killian, for the incredible generosity with which he shared knowledge, materials, and acumen as I wrote this book, responding by email to cascades of queries with alacrity, good humor, and wit; and to Peter Gizzi, for his brilliant sense of Spicer's poetry and its demands, and the energy and acuity with which he engaged me in emails, phone conversations, and the occasional long walk through London in a series of crucial interventions. I can't imagine the book without either of them.

Here at Warwick I've profited from conversation with Nick Lawrence as well as my colleagues in the Modern Commons research group: Thomas Docherty, Ross Forman, and Michael Gardiner. I also thank Jonathan Heron and the Warwick Student Ensemble for the *After Lorca* workshop we conducted together; I hope they learned as much from it as I did. Beyond the Midlands, Richard Sieburth and two anonymous readers for Edinburgh University Press contributed extremely useful readings of sections of the manuscript. David Fussner provided material aid in preparing the manuscript, but more than this, his intelligence, humor, and friendship saw me through this book and much else. Simon Smith's English helped me hear new tones in Spicer, and Miriam Nichols shared her acute insights into the Berkeley Renaissance and vast knowledge of Robin Blaser in conversation in Berkeley.

Preliminary versions of some parts of the book were delivered as talks, and I greatly benefited from feedback received at the University of Sussex, the University of Pennsylvania, Oxford University, the Pratt Institute, the London Modernism Seminar, and Hitotsubashi University in Japan. Thanks to Daniel Kane, the Modernism and Twentieth-Century Studies Group at the University of Pennsylvania, Alexandra Manglis, Christian Hawkey, Suzanne Hobson, and Asako Nakai for helping to make these visits possible. Thanks are also due to some remarkable librarians: James Maynard for indispensable long-distance help with archival material at the University of Buffalo; Peter Larkin at the University of Warwick, for having nurtured over forty years a collection of small press American poetry that would be extraordinary anywhere, let alone the West Midlands; and Anthony Bliss, Susan Snyder, and the entire staff of the Bancroft Library at the University of California, Berkeley, for manifold forms of help during my archival research there.

I thank the Bancroft Library, University of California, Berkeley, and the Poetry Collection of the University Libraries, University at Buffalo, the State University of New York, for permission to cite unpublished work from their holdings. Citations from the published and unpublished writings of Jack Spicer are by kind permission of the Estate of Jack Spicer; from the unpublished writings of Robert Duncan by kind permission of the Estate of Robert Duncan; and from the unpublished writings of Robin Blaser by kind permission of the Estate of Robin Blaser. My thanks to all of the above.

This project also received significant institutional support, for which I'm extremely grateful: an Arts and Humanities Research Council Fellowship provided two terms of teaching relief in 2011, and a British Academy Small Research Grant funded archival research at the Bancroft Library, University of California, Berkeley, in the summers of 2010 and 2011. The book could not have been completed without these crucial forms of aid.

Finally, thanks and love to my family, especially my daughters, Lisa, Daphne, and Esther. The dedication records my greatest debt, and ultimate addressee.

Abbreviations

B   "Jack Spicer Papers," BANC MSS 2004/209, Bancroft Library, University of California, Berkeley.

CP Jack Spicer, *My Vocabulary Did This To Me: The Collected Poetry of Jack Spicer*, ed. Peter Gizzi and Kevin Killian. Middletown, CT: Wesleyan University Press, 2008.

H   Jack Spicer, *The House that Jack Built: The Collected Lectures of Jack Spicer*, ed. and Afterword Peter Gizzi. Hanover, NH: Wesleyan University Press, 1998.

P   Lewis Ellingham and Kevin Killian, *Poet, Be Like God: Jack Spicer and the San Francisco Renaissance*. Hanover, NH: Wesleyan University Press, 1998.

Introduction: "All Is Not Well"

"In his own work, Spicer disturbs," wrote Robert Duncan, introducing his difficult friend to a poetry reading in 1957, "That he continues to do so is his vitality" (*B*). This vitality would remain undiminished throughout the rest of Jack Spicer's life, personally and poetically, testing the limits of his friends, editors, associates, and readers until his death from chronic alcoholism in 1965. Only weeks before his final collapse he began his last poem, addressed to Allen Ginsberg, like this: "At least we both know how shitty the world is" (*CP*, 426). Not long after, he lay dying in San Francisco General Hospital, in and out of coma, but rousing himself for one final proclamation, in Robin Blaser's now legendary telling:

> Jack struggled to tie his speech to words. I leaned over and asked him to repeat a word at a time. I would, I said, discover the pattern. Suddenly, he wrenched his body up from the pillow and said,
>
> *My vocabulary did this to me. Your love will let you go on.*
>
> The strain was so great that he shat into the plastic bag they'd wrapped him in. He blushed and I saw the shock on his face. (*The Fire*, 162–3)

Blaser's portrait is so haunting because while it leaves Spicer literally enveloped in the shit his poetry needed so often to point to, it ends with a no less characteristic ghostly telegram of love. In 1957, Duncan had continued, "Life throws up the disturbing demand 'All is not well' – sign after sign generated of accusation manifest – which it is the daring of Spicer at times in poems to mimic" (*B*). But this shouldn't obscure the social, communal, and ethical dimensions of Spicer's disappointment and rage, as he understood them. As Theodor Adorno put it, "It is part of the mechanism of domination to forbid recognition of the suffering it produces, and there is a straight line of development between the gospel of happiness and the construction of camps of extermination so far off in Poland that each of our own countrymen can convince himself that he cannot hear the screams of pain" (63). For his part, in the context of early gay-rights activism, Spicer wrote: "Homosexuality is essentially being alone. Which is a fight against the capitalist bosses who do not want us to be alone. Alone we are dangerous. Our dissatisfaction could ruin America" (*CP*, 328). It follows that spreading this dissatisfaction, rousing others from torpor, is an imperative in which the ethical and the aesthetic are indissoluble:

> When shall I start to sing
> A loud and idiotic song that makes
> The heart rise frightened into poetry
> Like birds disturbed?
>
> (*CP*, 45)

Spicer had written these lines a few years before Duncan's introduction, perhaps suggesting its terms.[1] That poetry, even as song, had to make space for the discordant and stupid was central to Spicer's poetics, but "idiotic" needs to be read etymologically, as so much of Spicer's vocabulary does, back through the Greek *idios* to the sense of the isolate, private person. "Loneliness is necessary for pure poetry" (*CP*, 150) Spicer wrote, which would be an effective gloss, if only Spicer believed that poetry could or should be "pure," or that solipsistic self-sufficiency was in any way more powerful, or even fundamentally different, from enforced communal conformity.[2] As we shall see, at the very heart of Spicer's disturbances is this: that few if any of the positions he opposes to the targets of his attacks are themselves allowed to stand, intact. At work throughout much of Spicer at his most compelling is a relentless negativity, not only aggressive but also at once self-entrapping, self-consuming and self-fueling: a perverse version of the "beautiful machine which manufactured the current for itself, did everything for itself" (*H*, 5) which Spicer thought the poet should *not* be. If Spicer's "Outside" and its concomitant "dictation" are meant to combat the "idiotic" poet in this sense, they will need to do so by way of idiocy's wily cousin – nonsense, the wrench in the gears of the negative dialectic that opens a tiny breach for love, poetry, friendship, sex: "Being faithful to the nonsense of it: The warp and woof. A system of dreaming fake dreams" (*CP*, 304). Nonsense, which Spicer theorized by way of Dada, is an explicit version of more general dynamics widely in play throughout his work. Spicer's poems, while everywhere crying out petulantly to the reader for understanding, recognition, subtlety, and care, just as frequently thwart the ideal reader they invoke; as Peter Gizzi puts it, they "disrupt even their own procedures by jamming the frequencies of meaning they set up" (*H*, xxiv), thus provoking the betrayal they lament. "I want one true word / With you Jack Spicer / Today tomorrow and every other day" (4) writes Simon Smith, forty years after Spicer's death and from across the Atlantic, capturing beautifully where Spicer leaves his readers: mourning our failure to possess the poet who only wants to give himself to us. In this way, through its incompletion and unanswerable address, Spicer's work often resonates with the prophecy and promise which the last half of Blaser's dictated message from the dying Spicer broadcasts: your love will let you go on, yes, but no less will it force you like Orpheus to look back over your shoulder, at Spicer, in his vocabulary, and where it has left him: "Going into hell so many times tears it / Which explains poetry" (*CP*, 383). Your love, reader, means you will not bring Spicer back: "You can start laughing, you bastards. This is / The end of the poem" (*CP*, 72).

When Jack Spicer died on August 17, 1965, he was largely unknown, especially beyond the San Francisco Bay Area. He had been published in Donald Allen's transformational *New American Poetry Anthology* in 1960 and earlier in the *Evergreen Review*, but had no books out with major publishers, and was not arousing the interest that peers or friends like Creeley, Ginsberg, Duncan, Olson, Levertov, and Ashbery were, or that O'Hara soon would. Recent readings and lectures in Vancouver, however, had been warmly greeted, and Spicer had been offered a position at Simon Fraser University meant to begin in the autumn of 1965. His death ensured that he would forever be remembered as the California poet he was always keen to insist he integrally was, a core poet of first the Berkeley, then the San Francisco Renaissance.[3]

As of this writing, Spicer's general popularity and academic reputation are higher than they have ever been. The critical acclaim that greeted *My Vocabulary Did This To Me: The Collected Poetry of Jack Spicer* on its publication in 2008 is only the most visible sign of a rising wave of interest in Spicer.[4] Up to now a rarely anthologized poet and one often ignored in large-scale overviews of American poetry, it seems likely that henceforth Spicer will figure prominently in both.[5] Explanations for Spicer's tardy reception – belated even in the context of the relative marginalization of the "New American" poets – are not hard to find and indeed, are frequently noted by scholars of his work. Spicer's personal petulance and hostility to those disposed to help him, his ambivalent difficulty in separating success and recognition from selling out or "whorship" as he called it, his principled refusal to exercise copyright over his own work, all contributed to thwart various forms of career advancement available even to the avant-garde. These, combined with his early demise, meant that almost all of his major work was either scantily available or simply unpublished until Robin Blaser's landmark edition of *The Collected Books of Jack Spicer* appeared in 1975, ten years after his death.[6] These circumstantial explanations are important, along with the fact that audiences and readers that did have access to his work – in Berkeley, Boston, San Francisco, or Vancouver – unfailingly responded to its power. But beyond this, the causes of Spicer's long years of relative obscurity can be further probed. In his excellent introduction to Spicer's famous "lectures" on poetics, Peter Gizzi points out that Spicer too can be characterized by the words John Ashbery found to explain the neglect of Frank O'Hara – quite moderate compared to Spicer's – when he dubbed him "too hip for the squares and too square for the hips."[7] Like O'Hara, Spicer fails to fall comfortably on either side of most of the structuring poetic oppositions of his time, but it is striking to see just how far this neither-norness extends in his case, and in how many contexts.

For example, Spicer was an early gay-rights activist and an open, unabashedly gay poet who marked his sexuality throughout his work. However, while he remained largely free of predictable tropes of queer abjection and self-loathing,[8] he was wary of many prevalent gay aesthetic traditions, especially camp, and also had little time for the insistence on gay sex and love as liberating and transformative that is prominent in poets otherwise as diverse as Ginsberg, Duncan, and O'Hara. Tracing idealized visions of gay love back to Whitman (a poet he nevertheless revered) Spicer acidly characterized "Calamus," Whitman's poems on "the manly love of comrades" (272), as: "In the last sense of the word – a fairy story" (*CP*, 56). For Spicer, the erotic is almost always a space of disappointment and frustration, and his take on sex, straight or gay, often seems close to the classic Lacanian formulation, "there is no sexual relation." His work was hardly propitious for a nascent movement of gay affirmation, nor did it seem a telling example of long-buried underground queer traditions.[9]

Similarly, Spicer's offhand demotic tone and fondness for anecdote, recourse to obscenity, rhetorical violence, and interest in jazz can seem similar to prevalent Beat tendencies, while the outpourings of rage, sorrow, and fatigue bear some comparison to the kind of "confessional" writing found in Berryman or Plath. Yet in manifold ways, and most notably through his elaboration of inspiration as alien "dictation" from the Outside, Spicer's poetics work against the precepts of immediacy and personal, subjective authenticity both those schools share.[10] This emphasis separates Spicer from most of the dominant extrapolations of Charles Olson's "projective" position as well, and in some respects leaves Spicer surprisingly close to a poet this self-professed enemy of

"academic poetry" might have been thought to despise, but in
with great care: T. S. Eliot. On the other hand, it is crucial to
the Spicerian form of "impersonality," to use a potentially
shorthand, was in no way consonant with the sort of anti-
strain one might find in contemporaries like John Cage and Asnbery.
Spicer's poems rarely show signs of transcending or foregoing the
subject which they everywhere cross out, and this is why Gizzi's allusion
to Beckett is entirely apt. As in Beckett's case, intimacy is fundamental
to his work in a manner that distances it from much conceptual writing
whose precepts Spicer to some extent shared.

Turning to other significant trends, one might think of Spicer the self-
consciously regional poet and vociferous champion of the local, his work
steeped in the Californian coastal landscape. Again, however, he fails to
find a place within a larger movement: his skeptical, destructive, and
even deconstructive work resolutely rejects the mythological eco-poetics
of a Gary Snyder, to name a poet on the fringes of his circle, or a Robert
Bly, to name one who wasn't. For Spicer, the crashing ocean speaks to
us precisely because it "means / Nothing" (*CP*, 373) not because it offers
the possibility of sense, belonging, harmony, or any of the various forms
of spirituality, often of Buddhist or Native American inspiration, that
are so typical of counter-cultural poetics in the 1960s – especially in the
Bay Area – and which Spicer does not accept. Indeed, Spicer was disillu-
sioned with the 1960s before they even happened, which makes him most
eminently a poet of the 1970s, and it's not surprising that it was during
this decade that his work first came to prominence, if not yet within the
academy, then certainly with poets and artists.[11] That is, Spicer's work
and thought are "untimely" aside from the accidents of publication and
distribution. To some extent, Spicer was simply ahead of his time: his
speculations on Emily Dickinson's manuscript variants and her practice
of embedding poems within letters foretells the path-breaking work of
Susan Howe in the 1980s, while *After Lorca*'s implicit dialogue with
Pound's "Homage to Sextus Propertius" anticipates the sort of theoretical work on Pound as translator which has only come to the forefront
over the last twenty years or so.[12] Likewise, in many ways his late work,
thoroughly informed by linguistics, prefigures the concerns that came to
be received under the broad title of "post-structuralism" in the United
States in the 1970s, and Spicer has been seen as a privileged precursor
by many of the "Language" poets, as well as scholars of their work.[13]
But on another level, Spicer's obsessive assault on what he saw as poetic
expediency or fashion is also an assault on the notion of the "timely"
itself. While wholly identifying with the traditional avant-gardist oppositional stance, as we shall see throughout this study, Spicer's work and

above all his theories of "dictation" and the "serial poem" displace the historicity of both the poet and the poem in ways which trouble the implicitly temporal claims of any avant-garde. One part of the Spicerian emphasis on the ghostly is, precisely, to champion an avant-garde whose time can never arrive.

Spicer was born on January 30, 1925, to upwardly mobile lower-middle-class parents in Los Angeles, where he grew up. After two years at the University of Redlands in southern California he transferred to the more cosmopolitan and more demanding University of California at Berkeley, arriving in 1945. Very shortly thereafter, he met the two friends who would forever remain most important to his life as a poet, to his life: Robin Blaser and Robert Duncan. Born the same year as Spicer, Blaser too was a transfer student and undergraduate at UC Berkeley, but Duncan was a very different proposition.[14] Six years older than Blaser and Spicer, by 1945 Duncan was already widely published and well connected, a rising star in certain bohemian literary circles and well more advanced in life and craft than his two new younger friends. Duncan was also that rarest of things in 1945, an uncloseted gay man. Indeed, Duncan had brought himself out of the closet in the most dramatic and public of fashions, by way of his signed essay "The Homosexual in Society" which had been published in Dwight MacDonald's influential review *Politics* in 1944.[15] The "Berkeley Renaissance" – to use the half-ironic term favored by the poets themselves – which coalesced principally around Duncan, Spicer, and Blaser was also to a very large extent a gay renaissance; sexuality, gender, homosexuality, and queer poetry and poetics were at its core. Meanwhile, if close friendship with an older, successful poet must have been immensely exciting to the undergraduate Spicer, it should be stressed that the impression he made on Duncan was no less powerful: despite his experience of established literary circles on both coasts, Duncan felt Spicer was the first certifiably important poet he had ever met, perhaps a Pound to his Eliot. In February 1947 he wrote: "I treasure most, I suppose, the extreme demand you make upon my poetry. I have never had anyone to write for that could see as much as you do and want as much more than I accomplish. That has been my extreme and rare pleasure. And then, of course, I have leeched upon your poetry. For Jack Spicer, il miglior fabbro" (BANC MSS 78/164c). As well as serious disputes about poetics, crucial to Spicer's vexed relationship to Duncan over the next two decades was his jealousy of the poets who soon came to displace his pre-eminence with him, notably Charles Olson, Robert Creeley, and Denise Levertov.

Spicer studied mostly literature and linguistics at Berkeley and stayed on for graduate work, receiving his MA degree in 1950 but subsequently leaving, as he refused to sign the anti-communist loyalty oath required of all State of California employees (which Spicer technically was, as a teaching and research assistant at the university).[16] He spent nearly two years at the University of Minnesota and then returned to California in 1952, taking part in the activities of the clandestine gay rights organization the Mattachine Society, and supporting himself over the next few years by teaching at UC Berkeley (as loyalty laws had since relaxed) and the California School of Fine Arts across the bay in San Francisco, where he moved in 1954. Through his students there, he became increasingly involved in the Bay Area visual arts community, and was in fact one of the "six" of San Francisco's 6 Gallery, where Allen Ginsberg gave his now legendary reading of "Howl" on October 7, 1955. Spicer missed it; the previous summer he had moved to New York, which he immediately detested, and then on to Boston, having convinced himself that it would be easier for him to make a career as a poet in the publishing and cultural centers of the east coast. Spicer was desperately unhappy in both places (as he had often been in Berkeley and San Francisco, to be fair), though the poets of the Boston scene, especially Stephen Jonas, were crucial in instigating the burst of creativity which came forth from him shortly after his return to San Francisco in 1956, under the added catalyst of the epochal "Poetry as Magic" workshop which he led at San Francisco State University in 1957.

The year 1957 was in many ways a triumph for Spicer: it saw the publication of his first book, *After Lorca*, while the success of the "Poetry as Magic" workshop firmly placed him at the forefront of the San Francisco scene, allowing him to start to emerge from the shadow of Duncan as well as Ginsberg and the Beats, recent arrivals whom Spicer always resented for a variety of reasons, ranging from serious differences in poetics to turf war, misplaced localism, and sexual jealousy. But 1957 is also in some ways the year in which Spicer's biography freezes. From here on in – the eight short years of poetic "maturity" as he himself sometimes saw it – his life is largely his increasingly passionate and difficult reconciliations and squabbles with friends and acolytes; sequential disappointments in love and sex; bitterness, jealousy, admiration, and disdain, in various admixtures and sometimes all together, for the poets he considered his peers, companions and rivals; increasing difficulty holding down increasingly marginal jobs; increasing abuse of alcohol; increasing frustration, anger, sorrow, and despair among those who loved him. The real events are poems and letters, the additional five books he saw published before his death. Yet the details just mentioned are more than only incidental to them: Spicer's often self-destructive and self-defeating behavior, his extreme ambivalence about all forms of success – and above all the literary variety – the distrust and suspicion he felt for rival "schools" and poetic formations all create the context which Spicer needed for his work to be dispatched. His love for the letter as form, his desire that poems and letters each work as the other, testify to this: the catastrophe of his life must also be read as *part* of the work.[17] As has been recognized since serious study began on Spicer, and even more, since groundbreaking investigations by Michael Davidson and Maria Damon in the late 1980s and early 1990s, Spicer's later work cannot be read beyond the contexts of community, coterie, and networks of exchange, within and for which he imagined it.[18] From 1957 onwards, Spicer insisted on poetry (as distinct from the isolated poem as traditionally conceived) as a collective event which might also be an interpellation or a provocation, as the title of his book *Admonitions* attests, but that in every instance must be an assault on the boundaries enclosing subject, object, sender, addressee, poet, and poem according to the logic of the "idios." It is out of these concerns that came into being some of the most unlikely artifacts of the Spicerian archive: the so-called "Lectures on poetics" of 1965, and the theories of the "serial poem" and "poetry as dictation" which they expound.

The "lectures" consist of the recordings of three talks, along with ample question and answer sessions, which Spicer gave during his June 1965 visit to Vancouver, as well as the shorter address to the Berkeley Poetry Conference which he delivered on July 14 of that year – just over two weeks before he was found unconscious in his apartment building elevator and taken to hospital. Although substantially cited and discussed by Blaser in "The Practice of Outside," they remained in their vast majority unavailable to readers until transcribed and edited by Peter Gizzi in *The House that Jack Built* in 1998.[19] These lectures, concerned above all with the theories of the serial poem (also called composition by book) and poetry as dictation, have become almost as important a part of Spicer's legacy as the poems themselves, due no doubt in part to their tantalizingly fragmentary availability over so many years. There are, however, important distinctions to be made between the two theories mentioned.

The "serial poem" or seriality more generally was a long-standing collective concern of Blaser, Duncan, and Spicer, at the heart of the latter's reflections in 1956 and 1957, and extensively explained in his letter to Blaser in the book *Admonitions*.[20] Indeed, in that opus Spicer declares his mature work to begin with *After Lorca* precisely because it was his first work to form a "book" – to move beyond the "poem" as individual, self-enclosed entity. Thus, the theory of the "serial poem" bears an especially heavy burden precisely because of Spicer's own marking of it – within a book of poetry – as responsible for the birth of his truly significant work. As of *Admonitions* of 1957 (published after his death but widely read and disseminated among his coterie) "seriality" and "composition by book" become an essential part of the framework of Spicer's reception within his circle, and thoroughly inform his own sense of the kind of work he wished to produce. Inscribed within venerable and recognizable twentieth-century investigations of poetic form and closure, these theories coalesce at a moment Spicer himself chose to mark as foundational, and for this reason, they are best understood as they emerge from the major problems that inform the "early" work. The discussion of seriality, then, will be largely deferred to Chapter 1, which will examine at length the genesis of Spicer's self-declared poetic break with his "foul" (*CP*, 163) past.

But if "seriality" belongs as much to 1957 as 1965, this can't be said of poetry as dictation. If this idea becomes so dominant in Spicer's late thought that by 1965 "seriality" is in many ways seen as an outgrowth of it, it was also slower to emerge than the theory of the "serial poem," and crucially, less widely shared by his closest circle. To some extent, the theory of "dictation" can be read as a typically hyperbolic Spicerian account of the old story of inspiration, stipulating as it does that the poet should be no more than a radio tuning into and broadcasting an alien message received from "Martians" or the "Outside," or the haunted vessel of an entirely other ghostly voice. In this light, "dictation" is the latest addition to a very long series of speculations about the role of the poet's subjectivity in relation to the art he or she produces, which goes all the way back to Ancient Greece. Certainly, Spicer's poetics can and should be considered in relation to, say, Keats' negative capability, as well as sources demonstrably closer to home: Socratic accounts of divine possession, Blake, or Lorca's *duende*.[21] From such a perspective, many of dictation's claims can seem both familiar and banal. Yet Spicer inflects these potentially tired paradigms to bestow upon them a new violence and force, one sufficient to provoke strong opposition from many recent critics as well as his sympathetic audience in Vancouver and many friends and associates over the years. Crucial here is the sheer extent of Spicer's recusal of the specifically human subject: if dictation insists throughout on the bracketing of the superficially personal or the blatantly volitional, this is not undertaken in order to let a deeper, truer self emerge, as might be the case in Surrealism, Beat immediacy, or Jungian mythopoetics, but rather to give place to something entirely other to the poet, something perhaps entirely other to life and the human themselves. The jokey sci-fi figure of "Martians" as source evokes this anti-humanist strain, and the radio set even more so, leaving the poet no more than a machine: "essentially you are something which is being transmitted into" (*H*, 7).

The poet as radio was suggested by Jean Cocteau's *Orphée*, both play and film (*H*, 7) but especially the latter, in which poems from the underworld are broadcast through a car radio. Still, for Cocteau the radio remains a medium of transmission to the poet, and is not the poet "itself," as in Spicer's more radical version. Spicer's appropriation of Cocteau – a crucial intertextual backdrop to his major work of 1960, *The Heads of the Town up to the Aether* – is also determined by Spicer's deep engagement with the myth of Orpheus, which began before he saw Cocteau's film, and which too was a means for him to work through the questions which came to be considered under the heading of "dictation" and the analogy of the radio set. For it is often by way of Orpheus that Spicer stresses a crucial element of the dynamics of "dictation": that the poet has a privileged relationship to death, not only speaking for the dead and from their world, but even more, only speaking truly when speaking *as* dead, as *After Lorca* will explore, in an investigation carried forward throughout the rest of Spicer's work. Thus, the radio set leads both to the classical underworld by way of Orpheus but also to spiritist tropes of ghostly communication, all of which inform dictation, as Spicer marks at the outset of the first Vancouver lecture, where he presents the spiritist automatic writing experiments of W. B. Yeats and his wife Georgie as a paradigmatic example of dictation and the Outside, linking their practice to Spicer's own "haunting" by Lorca, in his first dictated book.[22]

What "dictation" always stresses in Spicer's account, and what has made it so hard for his listeners and readers to accept, is loss: it is a process of becoming less human, less alive, less distinctive, less oneself: "I really honestly don't feel that I own my poems, and I don't feel proud of them" (*H*, 15), Spicer declares, which also means the traditional property relations between poem and poet no longer obtain, on both the most abstract and most concrete financial levels, in what is also, then, an assault on market exchange. But it is above all the massively anti-expressivist and anti-subjectivist position that provokes dissent throughout the Vancouver lectures, where there is general incredulity at Spicer's repeated insistence of his utter ignorance of and distance from the poems that "speak through" him. At the same time, if "dictation" in general depreciates the role of the poet, now no longer the source of an utterance "projected" outward by the poet's singular voice but rather a receiver attempting to take in and reproduce an alien charge, this does not imply spontaneity, passivity, or freedom from the ego or will. On the contrary, there is effort and violence, in part turned back at oneself: "You have to interfere with yourself" (*H*, 14) in order to make yourself empty and available for the "guest" (*H*, 85) who must inhabit your "house," by which Spicer figures the language, craft, experiences or other "pieces of furniture" (*H*, 85) the Outside will arrange in transmitting a message which, the borrowed furniture notwithstanding, is not "yours." In practical terms, then, Spicer in no way advocates automatic writing but rather a receptive yet disciplined vigilance which includes "censoring" (*H*, 7) elements recognized as originating from the "personal," from "things that you want" (*H*, 7), rather than the Outside: "you don't get the radio program if the radio set has static in it" (*H*, 15). To the extent that poetry is then discipline and self-denial, the "individual abilities" necessary to the poet "are the same as the individual abilities in sainthood" (*H*, 17).

In his call to use discipline, craft (such as rhyme schemes (*H*, 37)), guile, and even subterfuge in order to empty oneself as a "vessel" (*H*, 85) for poetry, Spicer can sound like Rimbaud, an important poet for him, but one he never mentions in these connections. Certainly, dictation echoes Rimbaud's famous slogan "Je est un autre" (250), but Rimbaud's extrapolation of what such an alterity means for the poet takes us even closer. "Si le cuivre s'éveille clairon, il n'y a rien de sa faute" (250),[23] Rimbaud suggests, also likening the poet to "le bois qui se trouve violon" (249),[24] an instrumentality which Spicer's radio upgrades to twentieth-century technology, while inscribing an uncanny distance by replacing the Rimbaldian bugle and violin, which still hark back to inspiration as "breath" or possession as touch, with the impalpable, all-penetrating radio wave. Beyond Rimbaud's own writings, Enid Starkie's account of the Rimbaldian project in her famous biography sounds so uncannily like Spicer, down to the very vocabulary, that a lengthy citation is warranted:

> The outworn conception of the personal writer producing his own work is totally false. The writer is merely the vehicle for the voice of the Eternal, he himself is of no account for he is merely the unconscious expression of someone speaking through him ...
>
> The poet can, nevertheless, of his own accord make an effort to become a suitable wood for the celestial fiddle. To achieve this end he must break down entirely everything that builds up human personality, all that distinguishes it, all the egoism that forms it. He must break it up, just as the soil is broken up by the plough, he must uproot from it all the weeds of habit and prejudice, for only in a soil thus prepared will the seeds of the invisible world grow and flourish. (128–9)

The "invisible world" became a crucial term of Spicer's in the 1960s, naming the alterity that the imperative of dictation asks the poet to tune into, at personal peril and cost: "I am sick of the invisible world and all its efforts to be visible" (*CP*, 342). And aside from the recourse to the

"Eternal," it is hard to imagine a better summation than the above of Spicer's own program of "dictation," which annoyed the Vancouver audiences partially because Spicer insisted that the Outside and dictation be taken absolutely literally, and not as loose figures for useful compositional practices and attitudes. Indeed, the mistake would be to contain Spicer's "theory" as no more than intriguing practical instigations to the writing of good poetry, when the opposite is more to the point: to understand seeming workshop discussions as an allegory for how Spicer wants us to think about what poetry is and does. From this perspective, the echoes of Rimbaud help us to hear Spicer as something other than mystic, mystifier, or self-appointed nuisance to narcissistic models of lyric expression. For in addition to all these, Spicer's erasure of the subject in the theory of dictation must be read as a philosophically considered if not always elaborated or consistent position regarding what might be called the "worldliness" of the work of art. As Hannah Arendt put it, "The artist, whether painter or sculptor or poet or musician, produces worldly objects, and his reification [used by Arendt literally, and outside its negative connotations in Marxist thought] has nothing in common with the highly questionable and, at any rate, wholly unartistic practice of expression. Expressionist art, but not abstract art, is a contradiction in terms" (323). "Dictation" is one of the names of Spicer's desire for an invisibly worldly, or invisible-worldly poetry.[25]

Such a poetry doesn't transcend the subject, but leaves it precisely as the site of error and lack. The Vancouver lectures insist throughout that parapraxis is the mark of authentically dictated poetry, the poem saying the opposite of what the poet "means" or "wants" to say. Yet elaborating on this, Spicer points out that the very word "wants" says two things too, in a passage that is central to both dictation and his work as a whole:

> [Charles] Olson says the poet is a poet when he says what he has to say. Now, you can read that two ways: what he "has" to say, namely "I want to sleep with you honey," or "I think that the Vietnam crisis is terrible," or "some of my best friends are dying in loony bins," or whatever you want to say that you think is a particular message. That's the bad thing.
>
> But what you want to say – the business of the wanting coming from Outside, like it wants five dollars being ten dollars, that kind of want – is the real thing, the thing that you didn't *want* to say in terms of your own ego, in terms of your image, in terms of your life, in terms of everything.
>
> And I think the second step for a poet who's going on to the poetry of dictation is when he finds out that these poems say just exactly the opposite of what he wants himself, *per se* poet, to say. Like if you want to say something about your beloved's eyebrows and the poem says the eyes should fall out, and you don't really want the eyes to fall out or have even any vague

connection. Or you're trying to write a poem on Vietnam and you write a poem about skating in Vermont. (*H*, 6–7)[26]

The Outside speaks not what the ego thinks it wants, but what is wanting to the ego's own sense of its desire. Whence a poetry at once worldly and of the unconscious, rather than from or about it: a poetry of the unconscious not expressed or laid bare, but thrown into the world as one of its events and acts. Which means that the Outside writes a poetry of mistakes through broadcasts, letters, insults, and interpellations. The Outside acts out: "If nothing happens it is possible / To make things happen" (*CP*, 168).

This book will trace what happens with Spicer, moving mostly chronologically through his writing life, but not exclusively so. Chapter 1 will examine his early lyrics, following the evolution of the thinking that led to the theory of the serial poem in 1957, by way of careful analysis of published work and archival material. Here, the addition of a temporal dimension to a predominantly spatial model of poetry will prove decisive. Chapter 2 will focus primarily on *After Lorca* and *Admonitions*, as well as the *Letters to James Alexander*, in an exploration of Spicer's poetics of "correspondence": a punning term which allows him to join the practice of translation to epistolary exchange in the elaboration of a poetics which sees the work as part of an ongoing network across the bounds of life and death, as well as different languages and moments. Here we find a negotiation between a Whitmanian poetics (as mediated by Lorca) of the body, the locality, and the corpus, and what for Spicer becomes a Dickinsonian poetics of the letter, the call, the absent address, and the rant. It is the "admonition," the injunction to the other, which fully translates Spicer's "correspondence" from post-Baudelairean symbolism to an exchange of texts, messages, and desires. Chapter 3 focuses specifically on Spicer's queer poetics, already central to his exchanges with Whitman and Lorca, and their relation to Spicer's more general concerns with community, exchange, and therefore politics – some of the longest-standing concerns in Spicer criticism, stretching from pioneering work by Maria Damon and Michael Davidson to very recent studies by Miriam Nichols and Christopher Nealon. This chapter will examine the recently published "Oliver Charming" papers in the context of Spicer's involvement in the gay rights organization the Mattachine Society and Robert Duncan's stance in "The Homosexual in Society," before reading in close detail *The Heads of the Town up to the Aether*, to see the various genealogies behind and arguments within Spicer's conception of the "city" – a space which, for Spicer, should also be one of argument itself. Chapter 4 examines Spicer's frequent mobilization of classical myth or highly invested medieval topoi such as Arthurian legend, in the context of both Eliot's "mythical method" and post-war "mythopoetics," often Jungian in inspiration. Taking my cue from one of Spicer's letters, I will argue that his interest in these topoi is more "pragmatic" than "mythopoetic," allowing him to bring them into dialogue with the great American poet of "pragmatics" in the linguistic sense of the word: William Carlos Williams. For this reason, Spicer's *A Red Wheelbarrow* will be read alongside *The Holy Grail* and *Helen: A Revision*. Chapter 5 discusses Spicer's last two works, *Language* and the *Book of Magazine Verse*, suggesting that they be seen as in implicit dialogue. In the former Spicer brings to bear on poetry his expertise in linguistics, brought to a new urgency and complexity by his work on an automated children's literacy project at Stanford University, where he was engaged as a researcher during the writing of the book. Examination of archival material related to that project shows its importance in what might be considered Spicer's "poetry of language" in *Language*. Conversely, the *Book of Magazine Verse*, composed of poems expressly written for the very magazines likely to refuse to publish them, can be seen as an investigation into the "language of poetry" – the social and economic structures constraining and defining what "poetry" is allowed to be, and which Spicer doggedly asks them to confront. Most important, however, is that a close look at the books in tandem shows that Spicer did not view these questions as separate, but as fundamentally interrelated. In line with Spicer's interest in poetry as pragmatics, both books are concerned with nothing so much as context – social, historical, regional – of language within and without "poetry." Finally, a brief coda returns to 1958: a key moment in Spicer's trajectory, where the theoretical breakthroughs of *After Lorca* and *Admonitions* are supplemented by the very different but also decisive projects of *A Book of Music* and *Billy the Kid*.

Samuel Beckett famously wrote that "to be an artist is to fail, as no other dare fail, that failure is his world and the shrink from it desertion, art and craft, good housekeeping, living" (*Disjecta*, 145). Spicer's own fidelity to failure, it should be said, extended fully to the last two items on Beckett's list. While Yeats wrote "The intellect of man is forced to choose / Perfection of the life, or of the work" (*Poems*, 296), Spicer chose neither, while insisting on rethinking that very parsing. Surly, grumpy, chronically depressed, sexually frustrated, and alcoholic, Spicer leaves behind a body of work which is remarkably liberating and generative, not only in its re-imagining of the possibilities of poetry, but also in its reticence with regard to the possible as such. Perhaps here more than anywhere else, the late Beckettian imperative to "fail better" finds the voicelessness necessary to carry it into the twenty-first century.

Notes

1. "Disturbance" is a term Spicer employs in his own discussions of poetics, in both *Admonitions* and the "Vancouver lectures," and also figures prominently in critical work on Spicer from Robin Blaser and Jed Rasula. I shall return to this in Chapter 2.
2. In this context, "loneliness," implying lack, also should be distinguished from solitude.
3. Thanks to the brilliant work of Lew Ellingham and Kevin Killian, Spicer's life has been told in illuminating detail. The biographical elements which follow here are drawn mostly from their work and the excellent introduction and chronology in *My Vocabulary Did This To Me*, as well as archival sources. I will of course refer to salient biography throughout this study, but only in moderation, as any reader who wants the full story can easily find it in *Poet, Be Like God*.
4. Another is the existence of the book you are now reading, along with the 2011 collection of articles *After Spicer*, edited by John Vincent, the first academic book solely devoted to Spicer's work. Similarly, it is highly revelatory that a study like Christopher Nealon's *The Matter of Capital* can take for granted both the importance of the San Francisco Renaissance for post-war American poetry and Spicer's central position within that movement; such assumptions would have required some explanation only a few years ago. And if it is less surprising that a book largely on the Duncan circle would have a chapter on Spicer, note that Miriam Nichols' *Radical Affections: Essays on the Poetics of Outside* takes its title from Robin Blaser's crucial 1975 essay on Spicer, "The Practice of Outside" (*The Fire*, 113–63). An overview of twenty-first-century work on Spicer should also include chapters by John Emile Vincent and Michael Snediker in recent books on queer poetics, and Jonathan Mayhew's in *Apocryphal Lorca*, his study of the Spanish poet's reception and appropriation in American poetry. All this activity was spurred by the 1998 publications of Ellingham and Killian's *Poet, Be Like God*, and Peter Gizzi's edition of the "lectures" on poetics, *The House that Jack Built*.
5. Spicer was included in both the original *New American Poetry* anthology, and its successor volume of 1982, *The Postmoderns: The New American Poetry Revised*. He also figured in Eliot Weinberger's 1993 *American Poetry Since 1950: Innovators and Outsiders*, and two anthologies from 1994: Douglas Messerli's *From the Other Side of the Century: A New American Poetry: 1960–1990* and Paul Hoover's *Postmodern American Poetry: A Norton Anthology* of 1994, though he is nowhere to be found in the 2003 third edition of the larger *Norton Anthology of Modern and Contemporary Poetry*, which includes work by Duncan, Creeley, Olson, O'Hara, Levertov, and Gary Snyder. However, David Lehman put him in his *Oxford Book of American Poetry* of 2006, and a chapter on Spicer has been commissioned for the forthcoming *Cambridge Companion to American Poetry*, a further signal of his changing fortune.
6. In this hugely important volume – the only source of Spicer's major works in print until Gizzi and Killian's *My Vocabulary Did This To Me* appeared in 2008 – Blaser also published his glorious long essay on Spicer, "The

Practice of Outside," very recently reprinted in *The Fire: Collected Essays of Robin Blaser*. "The Practice of Outside" remains to this day one of the finest pieces ever written on Spicer, but its inclusion in the *Collected Poems*, the author's close personal connection with his object, and the account of Spicer's death with which I began this introduction, have made the essay the undisputedly privileged critical window for access to Spicer for over thirty years. See Peter Middleton for a fascinating account of its importance in the history of post-war American poetics.

7. Cited in *H*, p. xxi. Gizzi's introduction is illuminating on just how anomalous Spicer's poetics were in their time.

8. Though not according to Robert Duncan, who saw such tendencies behind much of Spicer's criticisms of his work. In this light, it's worth noting that Spicer's legendary rejection of Duncan's *The Venice Poem* was based on very specific grounds: Spicer felt Duncan betrayed his violent masterpiece of jealousy and rage by the addition of an affirmative "Coda," which heals the wounds and leaves the poet restored: "Little cross-eyed king held / secure in the center of all things" (*First Decade*, 107). Lisa Jarnot cites a letter from January 2, 1959, where Spicer writes Duncan that the poem ". . . will knock the Snyderites on their asses. I still disagree with the ending of VP but hell" (183).

9. On these points, Maria Damon's path-breaking work on Spicer's association of gay life with "acute alienation" (*Dark End*, 144) and how that positions him among his peers is extremely helpful, as are John Vincent's interesting speculations on how "being homosexual itself creates difficulties in meaning making" (*Queer*, 153) in Spicer, as well as Michael Snediker's considerations of Spicer and queer "personhood" in *Queer Optimism*. The earliest of these works dates from 1993 and it's not coincidental that sustained study of Spicer as a gay poet begins when queer studies enters an institutionally self-conscious phase. The publication of the "Oliver Charming" papers in *The Collected Poetry* and Kevin Killian's recent archival research into Spicer's involvement with the Mattachine Society ("Spicer and the Mattachine") further enhance Spicer's legibility as a queer writer. Chapter 3 of this study examines Spicer's queer poetics in detail, and in the wake of Killian, Vincent, and Snediker, much more work in this vein is likely to follow.

10. As Gizzi puts it, "dictation also works as a joust with culturally sanctioned myths of poetic authorship that were definitive in Spicer's time, from confessional poetry to the Beat aesthetic. The very process of dictation is one of vigilance, which is both spiritual practice and materialist tedium, placing Spicer closer to the sensibility of Samuel Beckett than to the automatic writing of the dadaists and surrealists, the first-thought-best-thought of the Beats . . ." (*H*, 176).

11. Though academic work on Spicer begins here too, notably with the landmark special Spicer issue of *Boundary 2*, published in 1977. In contrast to the general trend, it should be noted that even before Spicer's death major claims for his work were tentatively suggested by Gilbert Sorrentino in extremely subtle scattered reviews, now collected in *Something Said*. By the mid-1970s Spicer had also attracted considerable attention abroad, notably in England among the Cambridge poets, especially Peter Riley, and

in France where, for example, Jacques Roubaud translated *The Holy Grail* in 1976.

12. Michael Snediker notes "Years before Susan Howe's material accounts of Dickinson's texts, Spicer's own analyses seem no less exacting" (*Queer*, 136). In *The Birth-mark*, Howe herself had stated "... Spicer saw quite clearly, in the late 1950s, the textual problems her letter-poems and poem-letters raise. You don't find this issue mentioned in the endless books now being churned out on Dickinson" (157). The extent to which that last sentence no longer holds shows not only how much Howe has changed scholarship on Dickinson, but also how such changes have made Spicer's interests and methods far more legible than they were twenty years ago. See Chapter 2 of this study for an extended look at Spicer's relationship to Dickinson in terms of epistolary poetics, and to Pound regarding translation.

13. Above all, by Ron Silliman. See Nealon, pp. 107–39, for more on the links between Spicer and the L=A=N=G=U=A=G=E poets. The sense of Spicer's relevance to "post-structuralism" is consistently stressed in the Spicer number of *Boundary 2* of 1977.

14. For biographical information on Blaser, see Miriam Nichols' excellent chronology in *The Fire* (401–10).

15. See Chapter 3 of this study for an extended discussion of this essay and its importance to the Berkeley poets.

16. Among prominent scholars at Berkeley that Spicer studied with are the Americanist Roy Harvey Pearce, the anthropologist Paul Radin, and the poet Josephine Miles. By far the most important for him and the "Berkeley Renaissance" as a whole was the famous émigré Medievalist, Ernst Kantorowicz. See Maria Damon, *Dark End*, and Kelly Holt, for more on the latter.

17. See Chapter 2 of this study for a reading of Spicer's epistolary poetics, and the challenge they pose to traditional parsings of "life" and "work."

18. Crucial here would be his involvement with very local, micro-press journals, such as *J*, which Spicer edited in 1959, and *Open Space*, edited by Stan Persky in 1964 and consistently publishing Spicer as well as polemicizing with him.

19. In addition to Blaser's citations, a fragmentary transcription of the first lecture was published in *Caterpillar* 12 in 1970. Recordings of the three Vancouver lectures in their entirety are now available online at Pennsound: http://writing.upenn.edu/pennsound/x/Spicer.html.

20. The correspondence between the three poets at this time frequently returns to these questions. See Spicer's "Letters to Robin Blaser." Blaser mentions "serial composition" to Duncan in a letter of June 16, 1957 (BANC MSS 79/68).

21. Spicer refers to *Phaedrus* repeatedly from the late 1950s onwards, and *After Lorca* testifies to his interest in the Spanish poet. Spicer also habitually lists Blake among his favorite poets and explicitly lists him as a central poet of dictation (*H*, 5). Blake also used Spicer's vocabulary to explain the process: "I have written this Poem from immediate Dictation ... without Premeditation & even against my Will" (cited in *H*, 43 n. 4).

22. See *H*, 135–6. Spicer is not the only one to link haunting, automatic

writing, and radio or telegraph transmission. See Laurence Rickels' fascinating account of Ludwig Staudenmaier in *The Case of California*, which details how the latter explained his sense of his transformation from a "writing medium" into a "listening medium" by way of metaphors of telegraph and gramophone (14–16).

23. "If the brass comes awake as a bugle, it's not its fault" (my translation).

24. "the wood that discovers it's a violin" (my translation).

25. My reading here closely follows some of the earliest, if long dormant, thinking about dictation in Spicer, as Robin Blaser suggests something similar near the outset of "The Practice of Outside," insisting that for Spicer poetry had to be "an act or event of the real, rather than a discourse true only to itself" (*The Fire*, 113). An enthusiastic reader of Arendt, Blaser later goes further into her vocabulary: "For this reason, Jack would remove himself, as that which is expressed, from his language in order to reopen the worldliness of language" (123); on the serial poem he opines "I call this openness worldly because it measures the I of the poetry and includes the poet in a world" (129).

26. Susan Vanderborg suggests that a similar play on "wanting" is used by Spicer in *A Textbook of Poetry* (58).

Chapter 1

The Early Poetry: Cartography, Seriality, Time

As is well known, it is Jack Spicer himself who offered the most convenient circumscription of his early poems, sketching a clear line of demarcation between his mature work and his juvenilia in a famous letter to Robin Blaser, itself presented *as* a poem in his book *Admonitions* of 1957.[1] There, Spicer explains the fundamental transformation of his practice.

> Halfway through *After Lorca* I discovered that I was writing a book instead of a series of poems . . .
>
> The trick naturally is what Duncan learned years ago and tried to teach us – not to search for the perfect poem but to let your way of writing of the moment go along its own paths, explore and retreat but never be fully realized (confined) within the boundaries of one poem. This is where we were wrong and he was right, but he complicated things for us by saying that there is no such thing as good or bad poetry. There is – but not in relation to the single poem. There is really no single poem.
>
> That is why all my stuff from the past (except the *Elegies* and *Troilus*) looks foul to me. The poems belong nowhere. They are one night stands filled (the best of them) with their own emotions, but pointing nowhere, as meaningless as sex in a Turkish bath. It was not my anger or my frustration that got in the way of my poetry but the fact that I viewed each anger and each frustration as unique – something to be converted into poetry as one would exchange foreign money. I learned this from the English Department (and from the English Department of the spirit – that great quagmire that lurks at the bottom of all of us) and it ruined ten years of my poetry. Look at those other poems. Admire them if you like. They are beautiful but dumb.
>
> Poems should echo and re-echo against each other. They should create resonances. They cannot live alone any more than we can . . .
>
> Things fit together. We knew that – it is the principle of magic. Two inconsequential things can combine together to become a consequence. This is true of poems too. A poem is never to be judged by itself alone. A poem is never by itself alone.
>
> This is the most important letter that you have ever received.
>
> Love,
Jack (CP, 163–4)

This shift from the lyric as compositional unit to that of the "book" or "serial poem," as Spicer came to call it, has been seen as a turning point in Spicer's poetics not only by Spicer himself but by virtually all subsequent critics. Blaser himself titled his 1975 collection of Spicer's work *The Collected Books of Jack Spicer* and omitted nearly all of Spicer's pre-serial work, and when Donald Allen later put out an edition of the earlier lyrics he followed suit, titling it *One Night Stands* and again drawing on Spicer's definition from *Admonitions*.[2] But if this division has been decisive for the editorial and publishing history of Spicer's work as well as the critical legacy, the implications of this rupture and even its very validity remain open to question. Recently, Michael Snediker has taken critics to task for overplaying what he calls Spicer's "renunciation" ("Prodigal Son," 502) of his early lyrics, positing instead a "coherence across a poetic career that from the outset was internally at odds with itself. The turning point, while on some level formally or biographically significant, oversimplifies Spicer's poetic trajectory" (502). Snediker's corrective is useful, and it is true that Spicer continued to write short lyrics well after his "turn" to serial poetry and the "book." However, what Snediker dismisses here under the rubric of "form" and "biography" are in fact some of the most radical and far-reaching aspects of Spicer's poetics, in which it is precisely the categories of "form" and "life" that Spicer urges us to rethink by way of a theory of writing which is also very much a theory of *reading*. That is to say, Spicer's sense of the "book" is not only "formal" in the way that Snediker implies. Certainly, in many instances Spicer makes it clear that he is interested in a looser, more flexible structure, capable of giving amplitude to effects of echo, repetition, digression, and return. But in addition to this are more radical implications: the "book" and "serial poem" also militate more generally for a poetics of deferral, displacement, and spillage of poetry into its historically opposed others, for example, letters and prose, to say nothing of that tricky category referred to as "biography" or "life" – a difficulty Spicer foregrounds in this passage from *Admonitions* by refusing to distinguish poetic artifact and personal letter, work and life, form and biography. Here, the biographical event *is* the poem, which means that "form," interesting or not, is not something susceptible to being assigned a particular "level." In this sense, it is indeed important to oppose a reductive formalism which would assert that Spicer is simply rejecting shorter works in favor of longer constructions, as such a turn would fail to solve the problem that most occupies him: the way in which the "English Department of the spirit" polices the boundaries between "emotion" and "expression," as well as between differing emotions themselves. If the "book" is simply a longer but essentially similar self-identical signifying structure to the lyric, Spicer's objections to the "single poem" will not be answered; the "book" will be judged by "itself alone" as was the poem. His statement here takes on its full force only if "there is really no single poem" also implies "there is really no single book," or at the very least, that the "singleness" of the book is fundamentally different from that traditionally ascribed to the lyric. Spicer asks us to read his "books" as something other than simply longer lyrics, and by the same token, belatedly invites us to read his early works *beyond* the boundaries of the isolated short poem.[3]

In fact, if the letter to Blaser in *Admonitions* hits home with such impact, it is partly because in his previous lyrics Spicer had already been probing the question of borders, boundaries, and limits that he subsequently came to theorize. In his "lecture" on the serial poem from 1965, Spicer declares to his audience of poets, "And you have to go into a serial poem not knowing what the hell you're doing . . . You have to be tricked into it. It has to be some path that you've never seen on a map before and so forth" (*H*, 52). This need to write without a map is important, for the map, cartography, geography, and topographies are among the most prevalent tropes of Spicer's early lyrics, his "one night stands." But it would be hasty to oppose the mapless wandering of the agentless "books" with what might be posited as a programmatic mapping tendency in the "faulty" early lyrics. On the contrary, the drive in the early work to demarcate and chart is what makes possible the troubling of boundaries and borders in the subsequent "books." And of course, if Spicer's letter to Blaser draws a line between the "early" and the "mature" and divides them from each other, that very gesture greatly partakes of the early cartographic poetics from which Spicer is distancing himself. Meanwhile and conversely, by drawing the early poems into an explicit relation with the "books" Spicer also writes them into a larger poetic structure – the very thing they, in their isolation, lacked. In essence, then, I want to suggest that Spicer not only separates the "one night stands" from his later "books" but also, de facto, creates the ghost – to use another of his favored tropes – of an imagined "book of early poems," just as in the letter to Blaser he laments the unborn books his early work might have contained: "Songs Against Apollo," or the "Gallery of Gorgeous Gods" (*CP*, 164). The Blaser letter from *Admonitions* inscribes the early work into *time* – the time of Spicer's writing life. The trap to be avoided is to read this temporality as a teleology, a moment in the poet's "progress" in the evolution to "seriality" and "dictation." On the contrary, it is the very function of time and space in the theories of seriality and dictation to defeat the teleological readings of the English Department. The task, then, is to read this "book of early poems" quite clearly in its status as something which does not exist: as the phantom that foretells Spicer's mature practice, but which also, in its very virtuality, haunts any pretensions the later "books" might have to totality.

*

In the early poems, Spicer's ghostly demarcations very often are concerned with the charting of three sorts of spaces which, if not entirely equivalent, are frequently placed in relation to each other: the body, geographical place or locale, and the poem, sometimes figured as textual corpus. In these respects, Spicer's work is often consonant with the models provided by two older contemporaries who were important to him, Williams in *Paterson* and Olson in *The Maximus Poems*, along with the crucial precedent of Whitman. Like all three, Spicer was very much a poet of place, in his case intent on constructing a specifically Californian, regional poetics, one which would record but also embody local specificities. As Peter Gizzi has shown with reference to particularities such as local pronunciation, much of Spicer's poetics can be seen as "site-specific."[4] Yet almost from the outset, this specificity is disturbed by another factor: that Spicer's sense of the local, the place, the body, and ultimately, the text, was relational and telecommunicational, constitutively structured by absence, transfer, displacement, and mediation. And if this was true generally it was even more so for the crucial site of California, home of cinema and the media, of the virtual, transmissions, and ghosts. When Spicer archly locates San Bernardino as the originary site for Yeats' automatic writing experiments with his wife, it is more than a joke:[5] Spicer saw Yeats' poetics of haunting, dictation, and transcription as exemplary for the "California" he believed in and wanted to create. And if Spicer would eventually conceptualize the serial poem as a structure which can only exceed its own bounds, both falling short of the poetic and going beyond it, from early on the poet is subjected to analogous violence with regard to its traditional role as origin of the poetic product. Beginning with the emphasis on Orpheus, Spicer will figure the poet as in some ways desubjectivized or non-originary, again in a variety of overlapping and sometimes conflicting tropes: as dead or as speaking from death; as irreplaceably singular yet absented from the "big lie of the personal"; as a radio receiver or mailbox; or as a physical network of messages and exchange, from and through which a voice echoes the absence of organic presence or substance. Well before the late 1950s, when Spicer consistently thematizes the epistolary, haunting, and the radiophonic, he is already very much a poet of circulation, and indeed it is as circulatory systems that body, place, and text reflect each other in the early work. In an important graduate school essay, "Donne's Use of Medieval Geographical Lore," Spicer titles one long section "Some Rivers and Waters" and argues the following concerning medieval theories of fluvial correspondences:

> The manner in which these bodies of water were connected was, of course, obvious. Those who understood the doctrine of the microcosm saw immediately that the whole interior of the earth is filled with channels just as the body of man is filled with blood vessels. There is constant circulation in one as in the other . . . This correspondence between the congregation of waters and the congregation of blood was thereafter a commonplace in the later middle ages. (B).[6]

The following citation which Spicer copied from Donne states the theory of the microcosm even more clearly: "The world is a great volume, and man the index of that book; even in the body of man, you may turn to the whole world; this body is a recapitulation of all nature" (B). Thus, it is largely through his own geographic, geological, and cartographic lore that in the early poetry Spicer will write through these already divided sites – body, poet, text, place – both in terms of their internal relations, to the extent that inside and outside are allowed to hold, and in their relations to one another. And it is by way of the microcosm that Spicer attempts to think the circulation of somatic and psychic transits within the individual in their relationship to a world beyond. This is often accomplished in a manner which "Some Rivers and Waters" foretells – by way of oceanic or fluvial imagery. At times, the trope of the microcosm even appears explicitly, as in an early unpublished poem which begins as follows:

> The sea is a mirror to a young microcosm
> Reflecting a portrait in tides, making him monstrous
> His substance becomes his image;
> . . .
> He is divided.

(B)

This poem in many ways rehearses the more elaborate implicit microcosmic identifications of "A Portrait of the Artist as a Young Landscape," which is divided into three numbered sections: "The Indian Ocean: Rimbaud," "The Atlantic Ocean: Hart Crane," and "The Pacific Ocean," ultimately attributed to the poet himself: "For it was I who died / With every tide. / I am the land. / I was the sea" (CP, 10). Interestingly, this geographical parsing of poets and oceans is an extremely late revision – a clean typed manuscript with only a handful of pencil holograph corrections notably cancels and replaces three very different titles for the three sections: "I: Mind as Present Perception," "II: Mind as Past Perception," "III: Mind as Potential Perception" (*B*). If such evidence cautions against reading the first two sections as carefully conceived reflections on Rimbaud and Crane, even more importantly it points to a crucial modulation in Spicer's practice of charting his own identity by projection onto a landscape: the first version used the "ocean" in its ideality to map the different aspects of the poet's own "mind," whereas the second uses different *particular* oceans to map the poet himself in relation to other poets, creating both a cartography of queer poets and a personal identification as specifically Californian.[7]

These two different mobilizations of geographical, microcosmic equivalence will both be important for Spicer throughout his work. Indeed, if the particular modalities are extremely diverse, throughout the early work the "microcosmic" linkages between body, poem, poet, ocean, and an additional crucial element, the labyrinth or maze, are continually parsed and reparsed. For the young Spicer, these are all places that can be entered, penetrated, or breached, but at some peril, for maze-like, they are also spaces where one risks getting lost or imprisoned. Many of the early lyrics extend and literalize one of the governing tropes of Yeats' "The Tower," where we read of Hanrahan's habit of the "unseeing / Plunge, lured by a softening eye, / Or by a touch or a sigh, / Into the labyrinth of another's being" (*Poems*, 243). Thus, the unpublished sonnet "On Falling Into Your Eyes" begins:

> No bastard son of sea-froth deified
> With all his arrows could twist half the pains
> That pinion me as I am swept inside
> And sprawl, half drowning, through your inner veins
>
> (*B*)

The poem subsequently evokes "tides of blood" as "Twin currents on a double circuit" which "flood / My bruisèd fragments towards a source unknown," and shows a crucial valence of Spicer's microcosmic logic: the body for him is less often Donne's "index" than as hectic, chaotic, and uncontained a space as the waterways to which it is keyed. Meanwhile, if "On Falling into Your Eyes" shows the subject as sucked into the roaring torrents of another's pulsating yet invasively smothering body, another short untitled, unpublished lyric posits one's own body as equally unchartable, a maze within a maze: "This angry maze of bone and blood, this body / Wanders in cool formal gardens, dry labyrinths / It is a weeping puzzle . . ." (*B*).

Crucially, a roughly contemporaneous poem suggests that poetry too is a labyrinthine space, and again, one which can be equated with a seductive yet perilous body of water. This untitled poem begins: "Any fool can get into an ocean / But it takes a Goddess / To get out of one. / What's true of oceans is true, of course, / Of labyrinths and poems." It goes on to evoke the risk of drowning "Out in the middle of the poem," and concludes "Any Greek can get you into a labyrinth / But it takes a hero to get out of one / What's true of labyrinths is true of course / Of love and memory. When you start remembering" (*CP*, 23). It is only from a poem written much later that we can see that this early lyric is also a reckoning with Robert Frost. In the posthumously published "book" of 1960, *Helen: A Revision*, Spicer remarks:

> Years ago a kindly English professor told me that Robert Frost had once said in a moment of absolute vision, "Any damned fool can get into a poem but it takes a poet to get out of one."
> I confused this with sexuality and believed it. (*CP*, 245)

Of course, the "confusion" of poetic and sexual spaces that Spicer points to here is structuring throughout much of his work, and reaches a culmination in "Psychoanalysis: An Elegy," as we shall see. But the presence of Frost in the wings of "Any fool can get into an ocean . . ." takes on particular interest when one considers that Spicer uses similar rhetoric and tropes in his early, explicit joust with Wallace Stevens, "A Lecture in Practical Aesthetics," while introducing a crucial element: the map. The poem addresses Stevens by name, and claims "You are an island of our sea, Mr. Stevens, perhaps rare / Certainly covered with upgrowing vegetation," and shortly thereafter suggests: "any island in our sea / Needs a geographer" (*CP*, 14). It closes with a complex network of geographical, corporeal, subjective, and poetic identifications, and is the most explicit dialogue with the essay on Donne found in Spicer's poetry:

> A geographer, Mr. Stevens, tastes islands
> Finds in this macro-cannibalism his own microcosm.
> To form a conceit, Mr. Stevens, in finding you
> He chews upon his flesh. Chews it, Mr. Stevens,
> Like Donne down to the very bone.
> An island, Mr. Stevens, should be above such discoveries,
> Available but slightly mythological.
> Our resulting map will be misleading.
> Though it be drawn, Mr. Stevens,
> With the blood and flesh of both superimposed
> As ink on paper, it will be no picture, no tourist postcard
> Of the best of your contours reflected on water.

It will be a map, Mr. Stevens, a county stiffened into symbols
And that's poetry too, Mr. Stevens, and I'm a geographer.

(CP, 14–15)

This rhetorical paralleling of landscapes, seascapes, bodies, and poems is familiar to us now, but the motif of the map introduces a crucially different element into this poetic constellation by resisting the organicist and ontopological thrust of the figural network within which Spicer operates. A human microcosm might well be a kind of map as well as an index, but a map is not a human. By insisting on a poetry that "stiffens" the real into symbols, Spicer rejects any sense that the poem could be in some way as "alive" as the being that it would extend. He begins to untether the poem from the tropes of body and locus as ground in an affirmation that his rhetoric stresses as contestatory: "And that's poetry too, Mr. Stevens." Indeed, in "A Lecture on Practical Aesthetics" cartography is explicitly portrayed as a form of resistance to a properly cannibalistic microcosmic poetics of incorporation and bodily presence, in which blood and flesh are the ink and paper, and the other that is chewed on is already one's own flesh. Yet as these corporeal elements provide the map itself, the poem also suggests the stiffening into symbol of the physical being as such, the becoming symbol of the most intimate "real." Of course, this opposition is left unstable, as the "geographer" is both the cannibal and the map-maker, and in an ambivalent process the map will be mobilized both as means to and against the body until Spicer's death. One of Spicer's last "books" (as designated by his editors) is the "Map Poems" of 1964, and the motif of the map is as recurrent in the "books" as in the early lyrics.[8]

Among the early poems, however, Spicer's breakthrough regarding these issues comes in "Psychoanalysis: An Elegy," one of the finest poems he wrote in the "Berkeley Renaissance" period of 1945–50. The poem's achievement consists in bringing to crisis the figural exchanges surrounding the mappings of the body, sexuality, the poetic text, and a specifically regional location of the subject that had occupied Spicer up to this point, while re-articulating the debt to Donne in a manner which freed Spicer from the aridity of the metaphysical conceit as seen in some of the early lyrics examined above. What proves decisive here is the framing of the poem as a session of analysis, a move that necessarily foregrounds the subject of enunciation and narrativizes the discourse as it develops, rather than presenting it as a finished demonstration. As in the *Imaginary Elegies*, here Spicer inscribes the discursive voice within time, which both opens the question of seriality and offers him a different, more productive form of irony. This is also one of Spicer's most powerful elaborations of the poetics of address, which will become foundational for his work, and transformational in terms of the figuration of the problems of exchange, transmission, and location that the circulatory microcosmics had attempted to work through.

The poem is framed by a series of five questions from an imagined analyst, all minimal variations on the first: "*What are you thinking about?*" In the first answer, the poet evokes a southern Californian landscape in "early summer," with the "wet hills ... pouring water": "Or the hot wind coming down from Santa Ana / Driving the hills crazy, / A fast wind with a bit of dust in it / Bruising everything and making the seed sweet" (*CP*, 31). This painful, bruising, flowing, sweetening sexuality of a Californian land that doesn't know how to go waste provokes the analyst's next question: "*What are you thinking?*" which elicits from the poet the desire "to write a poem as long as California / And as slow as a summer":

> Do you get me, Doctor? It would have to be as slow
> As the very tip of summer.
> As slow as the summer seems
> On a hot day drinking beer outside Riverside
> Or standing in the middle of a white-hot road
> Between Bakersfield and Hell
> Waiting for Santa Claus.
>
> (31–2)

But in the fiction of free-association the poem indulges, in the next section it is no longer the poem but a woman's body which is likened to the landscape:

> I'm thinking that she is very much like California.
> When she is still her dress is like a roadmap. Highways
> Traveling up and down her skin
> Long empty highways
> With the moon chasing jackrabbits across them
> On hot summer nights.
> I am thinking that her body could be California
> And I a rich Eastern tourist
> Lost somewhere between Hell and Texas
> Looking at a map of a long, wet, dancing California
> That I have never seen.
> Send me some penny picture-postcards, lady,
> Send them.
> One of each breast photographed looking
> Like curious national monuments,
> One of your body sweeping like a three-lane highway

Twenty-seven miles from a night's lodging
In the world's oldest hotel.

(32)

Obviously, the sexual content of the associations becomes increasingly manifest as the poem progresses, culminating with the appearance
of the female body. But it is crucial that prior to this, the second section
projects the fraught, tense California summer not onto the body of
the woman but rather onto that of the poem itself, implying a figural
network in which woman and poem are in some way parallel or even
exchangeable: as both are figures for and figured by the California
summer, each can be a figure for the other too. Still, as the poem
proceeds, the poetic body is clearly superseded by that of the woman
– the paradisal, literally monumental California which the analysand,
a hapless, lost tourist, strives desperately to find, as he makes do with
postcards and maps rather than the unavailable place itself. The poem
ends, however, with a final turn along its associative road:

What are you thinking?

I am thinking of how many times this poem
Will be repeated. How many summers
Will torture California
Until the damned maps burn
Until the mad cartographer
Falls to the ground and possesses
The sweet thick earth from which he has been hiding.

What are you thinking now?

I am thinking that a poem could go on forever.

(32–3)

These lines significantly complicate the previous schema, suggesting
that the "search" that has been meticulously described might also be an
elaborate form of evasion; the roadmap might be likened to a dress, but
clothes *hide* bodies as much as they point to and reveal their forms. If
the cartographer is "mad," cartography might be his ailment: replacing
the object itself with a fixation on its representation and lapsing into the
"idealism" of "the study of images," rather than embracing the "things
that they were emblems of" as Yeats might have put it.[9] The poem
and the session end with maps and therefore dresses burned, and the
"mad cartographer" – now presumably going sane – ready to "possess
/ The sweet thick earth" of the woman's naked body rather than the
diversionary, sublimated substitutions for it. The rich but lost "Eastern
tourist" would finally arrive at his destination, to find his "lodging /

In the world's oldest hotel," the female sexual organ,[10] itself the safe-house of a lyric tradition of erotic landscaping going back to Donne and beyond, but also of a vulgar Freudianism, to which the analytic process has seamlessly led the analysand, step by step, over the series of resistances, diversions, and displacements the poem offers. In such a reading, the poem itself as it emerges in relation to the musings on California would figure as one element in this series, and the free-association would lead the analysand beyond his displaced discussion of poetics into the ultimate sexual "meaning."

But if there is a tendency in the poem to suggest a figural progression from summer to poem to woman to earth – to the grounding of the female body and the female body as grounding – there is much here also which works quite differently. Already, the path sketched above is overly neat. This poem was written in the late 1940s, around the time when Spicer himself was undergoing psychotherapy, as he attempted to sort out an unhappy affair with the heiress Katherine Mulholland, like himself a native of Los Angeles, and a scion of the family whose name itself maps one of that city's most famous streets. The entire poem seems to turn on a submerged pun: this is Spicer's Mulholland Drive, mapping what was almost certainly the only consummated heterosexual relationship of his life, occurring well after he was cognizant of his own homoerotic feelings. Given this, and the utterly frank homosexuality which permeates Spicer's work, the poem can be read as an "elegy" for the repressively normative psychoanalytic institutions of this period, with their insistence on compulsory heterosexuality as the meaning behind every narrative. A few years after writing this poem, Spicer would become active in the clandestine Mattachine Society, one of the earliest gay rights organizations in American history. And indeed, it has been suggested that the line "The sweet thick earth from which he has been hiding" should be read as a reference to homosexuality and not the California-like woman's body at all.[11] That is, should one loosen the figural link between roadmaps and the woman's dress, the poem can be read as ending with the "sweet thick earth" of a very different New Found Land, only accepted when the phantom image of "long, wet, dancing California" is finally abandoned.[12]

However, this figural instability of the purportedly grounding "earth," rather than a hermeneutic problem to be solved, is itself revelatory of everything in the poem which troubles the teleology of destinations in the first place. For the poem does *not* come to its end up to its elbows in sensual dirt, but rather with the reflection "I am thinking that a poem could go on forever." This implies that the possession of the earth is not a figural culmination but just another stop on a road of associations which can have no end point susceptible to cartographic completion or elemental possession. The poem, like psychoanalysis, is posited as interminable, and throughout this text poetry – unlike the female body – is figured not only in terms of space but also time: the poem is not only as "long as California," but also "as slow as a summer . . . as slow / As the very tip of summer." The poem – like the analytic session or a drive along a highway – is something that happens in time and over time, with a particular pace intrinsic to it. Similarly, it is something that is repeated and repeats, again like both the seasons and the psychoanalytic process the poem recounts and mimes: "I am thinking of how many times this poem / Will be repeated. How many summers / Will torture California." All of this suggests that the ending of the poem, like the ending of a session, is no more than provisional; a rest point on a road and in a process occurring in time and space, in which the essential component is drift: of thoughts, of a car wandering over a road, of the days of a season as it unfurls. It is hard to think of a term more apt to describe "Psychoanalysis: An Elegy," than "psychogeographical," and ultimately, in terms of its representations of space and psychoanalysis, it tallies in interesting ways with the Situationist *dérive*. As Guy Debord stresses, the technique of the "*dérive*," or drift, has two complementary purposes. On the one hand, it allows for new forms of cartography, providing "hitherto lacking maps of influences" (66) of the "psychogeographical pivotal points" (66) within a city. But this mapping is only made possible by a concomitant refiguring of the subject's relationship to space itself by means of the *dérive*. Remarking that the primary goal may be either "to study a terrain or to emotionally disorient oneself," Debord continues: "It should not be forgotten that these two aspects of dérives overlap in so many ways that it is impossible to isolate one of them in a pure state" (64). Such considerations lead to these fascinating remarks from Ivan Chtcheglov, appended as a note to DeBord's article: "The *dérive* (with its flow of acts, its gestures, its strolls, its encounters) was *to the totality* exactly what psychoanalysis (in the best sense) is to language. Let yourself go with the flow of words, says the psychoanalyst. He listens, until the moment when he rejects or modifies (one could say *detourns*) a word, an expression or a definition. The dérive is certainly a technique, almost a therapeutic one" (481). Spicer too links the psychoanalytic drift with a geographical wandering which is in turn considered in terms of forms of mapping, however what distinguishes the Spicerian psychogeographical project from the contemporaneous Situationist one is the replacement of the "totality" of the situationist city-space by a potentially non-totalizable California. In the end, it is less a question of deciding whether the "sweet thick earth" is the body of a man or of a woman, but of balancing it against the endlessness to which the poem gestures.[13]

Certainly the temporality of drift in "Psychoanalysis: An Elegy" is counterbalanced by a circular, cyclical temporality of the seasons, recitation, and neurotic repetition, yet what both these conceptualizations share is a resistance to teleological frameworks of progress, arrival and completion. Indeed, the insistence on time, process, and endlessness make "Psychoanalysis: An Elegy" one of Spicer's earliest theorizations of the serial poem, even if it does not yet recognize itself as such. These emphases tend to militate against the poem's equal desire to locate and define, leading to double-binds similar to those traversing Situationist psychogeographical cartography. But crucial to "Psychoanalysis: An Elegy" is that the process of wandering is equated to a speaking which is also an allocution, an address to an other which in itself creates a new erotic frame. As Spicer writes elsewhere: "The relation between the analyst and the patient is the firmest and most hallowed, if the most conventional, sexual relationship in the modern world" (*CP*, 79). Read hallowed here in the strong sense, as erotic haunting is central to Spicer's articulation of another of the main relationships he works through in the early poems: that between the Orphic poet ensconced in death, and the readers his words are meant to transform, a problem foregrounded by a title such as "Poem to the Reader of the Poem." "Psychoanalysis: An Elegy" might imply that for Spicer poetry is mainly about the expression of desire, but this is only true up to a point, as Spicer's insistence is primarily on poetry's power to *produce* desire, with the Orpheus myth as the privileged emblem of poetry as perlocutionary act, something Spicer often calls "song": "Orpheus was a singer. The proudest boast made about Orpheus was not that his poems were beautiful in and of themselves . . . The proudest boast was that he, the singer with the songs, moved impossible audiences – trees, wild animals, the king of hell himself" (*H*, 230). But the Orphic model in which the poet's prime task is to "move" the other points to an additional element implicit in "Psychoanalysis: An Elegy": that the relationship between poet and audience is ultimately one of transference, as the poetic act is predicated on the existence of an audience worth moving, in the absence of which the poet is simply bereft of his task. The importance of community for Spicer and his anguished and frequently hostile relationship to his entourage are informed not only by his own transferences and resistances (notably seen in reference to Duncan and Olson) but even more so by a poetics which is transferential at its core. It is only by way of address and allocution that the poet is put into relation with the enigma of his "own" message and its origin, an origin which for Spicer will increasingly be figured itself as the Outside. However, it must be noted that for Spicer the Outside can also be a form of the inside, as he makes clear in his Vancouver lecture on dictation where he includes among the Outside's privileged figures "an id down in the cortex which you can't reach anyway, which is just as far outside as Mars" (*H*, 5).[14] For this reason, the labyrinthine interiors Spicer often constructs in the early work, especially in relation to the body, are often less in opposition to the Outside of galactic space than a different modulation of it. And while Spicer's psychogeography and psychothalassography dialogue with both the bodily labyrinth of blood and bone and Yeats' "labyrinth of another's being," he diverges from Yeats in that for him the entrapping labyrinth or prison is as likely to be one's own body in its alterity as that of another – a barrier which the song must cross to reach the auditor whose beckoning, in one case at least, explicitly creates it. He writes in "The Song of the Bird in the Loins," "I wait and whisper endlessly / Imprisoned in a well of flesh," soon followed by "I whisper to you through his lips. / He is my cage, you are my source of song. / I whisper to you through a well of stone" (*CP*, 62–3). That intriguing lyric, however, seems overly neat in its symmetries and divisions when compared to another early poem on the body and the voice, on the addressee, its locus, and the desire and message it provokes:

> We find the body difficult to speak,
> The face too hard to hear through,
> We find that eyes in kissing stammer
> And that heaving groins
> Babble like idiots.
> Sex is an ache of mouth. The
> Squeak our bodies make
> When they rub mouths against each other
> Trying to talk.
> Like silent little children we embrace,
> Aching together.
> And love is emptiness of ear. As cure
> We put a face against our ear
> And listen to it as we would a shell,
> Soothed by its roar.
> We find the body difficult, and speak
> Across its wall like strangers.

(*CP*, 22)

This poem turns very largely on the oscillation between the position taken in its first line, and its reformulation in the closing two. At the outset, the poem poses what seems to be a familiar problem of adequation: the body is "difficult to speak," that is, it is difficult for the subject or poet to find words capable of *representing* the body, especially in its desire. But already in the second line, the body presents a difficulty not only for "speaking," or expressing, but conversely for listening, or "receiving": "The face too hard to hear through." This idea of the body as a barrier for a speech that could join two subjects is that on which the poem closes: "We find the body difficult, and speak / Across its wall like strangers." Together, these formulations yield two similar but far from identical representations of the body's relationship to speech: first as a referent which speech cannot communicate, then as a barrier which speech cannot cross, and the poem seems to move from the first position to the second. Indeed, the shift from "to speak" to "and speak" might imply that the body's difficulty is itself the *cause* of our broken speech across it. However, for most of the poem the body is neither that which is spoken, nor that which blocks speech, but that which tries – and fails – to speak something itself: "eyes in kissing stammer" and "heaving groins / Babble like idiots." The syntax scrupulously distinguishes the "we" from "our bodies," and it is the latter which "rub mouths against each other / Trying to talk." This figure, then, does not present speech as a poor substitute for a physical immediacy and proximity which would exceed it, but rather suggests that physicality itself is a poor substitute for a relationship that is of essence linguistic. It is not only that words could never approximate a physical kiss, but also that a kiss cannot equal the speaking of the words of love. If sex is an "ache of the mouth" and love an "emptiness of ear," the fundamental sexual acts seem to be speaking and hearing at least as much as kissing. The physical pressure of the other's face against the ear is not presented as an ultimate cure but only as a "soothing" palliative, roaring in place of an underlying silence which the body cannot break, and which leaves us like "silent little children," literally *infans*: without the speech we crave, in the absence of which we remain strangers, desperately pushing our ears against the dumb bellow of the other's being. The erotics of this poem turn body and speech inside out: by aligning mouth and ear as at once organs of speech and hearing and privileged figures of the body's liminal spaces – orifices allowing entry and exit – physical acts are semiotized while speech and hearing themselves are eroticized as forms of entrance and penetration. Mouth and ear chart the erotic as the nexus where enunciation encounters the body, as the erotic subject comes into being through its *address* to another, a second person whose invocation bequeaths voice onto the desiring subject. However, what the body cannot do, as the pronouns consistently stress, is say "I." In the phantasmatic plenitude this poem mourns, the physical transits of speech – the literal expression from the body of sound and air which enters and fills the other by way of the empty ear – become the ideal model of sexual union, compared to which the material erotic body is horribly inarticulate.[15] But the body's fumbling of a relationship which is in its essence linguistic does not imply that sex is primarily a spiritual affair, sullied by the corporeal envelope. On the contrary, the somatic elements of speech are what eroticize it in the first place, and if we speak "across" the body's walls "like strangers" it is these walls themselves which negotiate erotic exchange. The poem asks how the body can harbor the other as the mind can harbor the other's words, and how a body might reconfigure another as decisively as a sentence, as Orpheus' song. At the same time, the poem demands that the words of love make the body resound. The body's "wall" is not only the "outside" that the Orphic address must breach, but also inside the larger discursive sexual situation, in which bodies are always speaking past each other, in every sense. The problem is not only that words cannot make themselves flesh, but also that flesh, while speaking, can never make itself words or still better, song.[16]

The parallel Spicer plays on here between sex and dialogue is very old, as conventional terms like "intercourse" and "conversation" remind us. And in this poem language is conceived entirely in terms of dialogue and speaking, with no sense of writing whatsoever – in marked contradistinction to the later Spicer, particularly in the book *Language*. However, well before *Language* of 1965, already in 1957 and 1958 in *After Lorca*, *Admonitions*, and *Letters to James Alexander*, Spicer crucially refigures erotic dialogue as "correspondence," to use his own term – a pun which allows him to trope resemblance as exchange and associate the latter with the medium of letter-writing. This also allows a further spatialization of the erotic mappings which occupied him from the start: labyrinths, seascapes, song, and maps are increasingly supplemented by letters, radio waves, and ghostly visitations. As we shall see in the next chapter, Spicer's sojourn in Boston in 1956 was decisive for the next phase of his poetics, and not least his intense engagement with the poems, letters, and manuscripts of Emily Dickinson, some of which he consulted in the Boston Public Library, where he worked from autumn 1955 until he was fired in November of the following year. Just weeks before leaving Boston to return to California for good, Spicer wrote "Birdland, California" in which the Orpheus trope, the emerging postal motif, and the poetics of mapping play against one another in fascinating ways, and show some of the turns Spicer's familiar topoi were taking. Already, the title sounds like a place on a map and indeed it is; however, "Birdland" is not the site of the poem but precisely the elsewhere against which the poem's space is defined: "When will they take all of us back to Birdland?" (*CP*, 61), asks this poem, which, like

"Psychoanalysis: An Elegy," posits California as a lost and promised land of plenitude. The space which the poem does chart in contrast to the title's suggested destination is entirely liminal, less a place properly speaking than a passageway between: an apartment staircase figured as the path up from Hell, traversed not only by Orpheus but also by postmen and butterflies (the latter a frequent symbol of the soul's progress through eternal realms), as the opening lines tell us:

> The stairs upstairs were stairs
> For the sake of ceremony
> If Gertrude Stein had tried them on tiptoe
> She would not have reached the 2nd floor.
> The 2nd floor was a floor
> For the sake of ceremony
> What I mean is
> This is a poem about Orpheus
> Orpheus, he had the weight of Eurydice upon his back
> He tried to carry her
> Up that imaginary stairway.
> Eurydice could be anyone. Is
> I suppose
> Anyone.
> That makes the poem harder.
> This night (Joe Dunn could give a date
> October 1st
> That's Joe Dunn's date)
> But I can't.
> Butterflies transfigure and burn
> In the absences of postmen.

(CP, 60)

Joe Dunn, the dedicatee of Spicer's "Five Words for Joe Dunn on his Twenty-Second Birthday," was one of Spicer's closest friends in Boston, and living with his wife in the apartment next door when this poem was written. He was also a postman.[17] But so is Orpheus in this poem, in which Eurydice becomes a sentence, a message, too heavy to lift out of hell: "Orpheus collapses / Under the weight of the sentence, killing butterflies. / It is already / October 2nd" (CP, 61). Utterance becomes object here, Orpheus no longer a singer but a bearer of a special delivery he is too weak to carry up from below: "An embarrassed Orpheus / Arises / With a heavy Eurydice in his arms" (CP, 61). The word "sentence" in these lines stands out doubly, both in contrast to the "song" Spicer usually attributes to Orpheus and also to the poem itself, whose tonality and idiom is so finely pitched to the phraseology of spoken utterance rather than written syntax. Indeed, the somewhat uncanny feel of the poem comes precisely from its balancing of utterance against the sentence, especially in terms of temporality. The poem presents itself as a single discursive moment of enunciation, yet Spicer stretches this "moment" over several days, negating any particular, cohesive "now" in which this statement could be imagined:

> It is already
> October 2nd.
> October 3rd. Will it ever be important again
> Whether it is October 2nd or October 3rd?
> Have you ever wondered
> What I mean is
> When will they take all of us back to Birdland?
>
> . . .
>
> What I mean is can a poem ever
> Take accidentals for its ultimates?
> It is now October 5th (or 6th)
> English majors
> Can discover the correct date
> (The Yankees used seven pitchers
> That will tell you the day)
> I was lonelier than you are now (or will be)
> October something, 1956.
>
> (CP, 61)

Although Spicer gives us a series of dates, the poem does *not* present itself as a succession of discrete moments now lined up together – for example, a series of journal entries – but rather as a single utterance impossibly slowed down and draped over several days. What is proper to the poem is its irreducibility to the moment of enunciation which nevertheless frames it, not to present it as if in a transcendent timelessness, but rather as ensconced in time yet fundamentally untimely. The moment of poetic enunciation is not datable, even as a fiction, spilling between days in mid-sentence; this renders the research of the English majors transcendentally inconclusive, while the different empirical dates which comprise the poem and which it traverses are the "accidentals" that Spicer is positing as potential ultimates. The dateline is "October something" because Spicer refuses to allow an empirical moment to contain the poem's discursive "now."[18] The final line, however, shunts the poem into an entirely different temporality: not the "now" of "October something, 1956" but rather that "now" conjured by every act of *reading* the poem in its future. In a maneuver which is entirely Whitmanian, this extremely autobiographical or even "confessional" poem throws itself out of the ideal simultaneity (already ironized, as we have seen) of the poet writing what he lives as he lives it and into a "now" that rather belongs entirely to its addressee. The shift from one now to another transforms the auto-biographical index into a ghostly address.[19]

But at the heart of Spicer's entire reflection here is the question of the accidental. What does Spicer mean by "accidentals"? Why is it worth asking if a poem can take them for its "ultimates," and what would be the implications if one did? Certainly, the "accidental" implies chance, the contingent, the non-essential, the unplanned: the openness and avail-ability that Spicer calls for in the letter to Blaser, where he seeks a writing free "to go along its own paths" (*CP*, 163). Indeed, the "accidental" can be seen as a figure for just the sort of intrusion and interruption into a closed circuitry of poetic production that Spicer calls "dictation" and the Outside. Against the idea of "the poet being a beautiful machine which manufactured the current for itself, did everything for itself" (*H*, 5), Spicer consistently champions the Outside not only as dictation and broadcast, but as *event* (the etymological meaning of "accident") and *advent*, as the unforeseen which befalls the poet and unsettles his inter-nal, mechanical ordering of intentions and desire as poet. Whether love would be accidental in this sense is a question which Spicer was ponder-ing around this time. In his play *Troilus* of 1955, the eponymous hero affirms "But people don't fall in love by accident. People die by accident but they don't fall in love by accident," arguing instead that falling in love is something to which the lover must "agree" (92). However, when Troilus and Cressida enjoy their first private meeting, it is immediately after spilling a brimming a glass of wine into her lap that he blurts out, "I love you." Cressida acknowledges to Troilus that she loves him too, before closing Act I by declaring to Pandarus, who enters from the kitchen, "Uncle, there's been an accident" (108). Among other things, "Birdland, California" is a love poem to Joe Dunn, and the reasons why the advent of love is at once an "accident" and the very type of lyric certainty which an accident must come to disturb will become evident in the next chapter, when we examine what Spicer calls "the big lie of the personal." Here, when Spicer asks if accidentals can become ultimates, he is clearly posing a paradox. As Spicer is well aware, to posit an "acci-dental" as an ultimate is to erase it as accidental, rendering it essential. And seriality in Spicer's anti-teleological sense can legitimately be seen as an attempt to solve this problem: only a poem with no finality, no ending as such, could preserve the accident as accident; for Spicer serial-ity is very much an effort to suspend the opposition between necessity and contingency. In "A Birthday Poem for Jim (and James) Alexander," Spicer writes "Poetry seeks occasion" (*CP*, 228); the "accidental" can be viewed as what happens to the "occasional" when it is released into time.

However, the poem's title hints at yet another possible connotation, for if Birdland, California is a neighborhood in San Diego, "Birdland" in and of itself could only evoke to Spicer and his entourage the famous Manhattan jazz club named after Charlie "Yardbird" Parker, which Spicer might have frequented during his short stay in New York City. The poem, then, implicitly maps Boston against both California and New York. Additionally, in music theory an "accidental" is a note that is raised or lowered so as not to be in the signature of the various keys. In the Vancouver lectures, Spicer praised Billie Holiday precisely for singing "off key," going on to state that "any poet who doesn't sing off key ought to be very careful . . . One of the few things we have learned is that you have to learn how to sing off key in some way or another" (*H*, 141). This "off key" singing is one of the most important things Spicer discovered in Boston, where he experimented even more radically with variable line lengths and increasingly achieved a disjunctive coordination between tight lyric fluency, disabused and deflationary colloquial phraseology, and an incisive but prosaic expository sentence unit; song, speech, and the written prose sentence interrupt and disturb each other. One of the finest of the poems where this new mode makes itself heard is, precisely, "Song for Bird and Myself," in which Spicer also devises dazzling, abrupt shifts in pace and timing which would seem to correspond to Parker's signature bebop solos:

> I am dissatisfied with my poetry.
> I am dissatisfied with my sex life.
> I am dissatisfied with the angels I believe in.
>> Neo-classical like Bird,
>> Distrusting the reality
>> Of every note.
>> Half-real
>> We blow the sentence pure and real
>> Like chewing angels.

(CP, 69)

To "blow the sentence" is an apt description of much of Spicer's poetics here, as he begins to think through a "musicality" of poetry (poetry as song) which would derive from the syntax of the sentence's deployment of signification, and not simply be an aural ornament added on to the logos, like a varnish. This is a question he will pursue in both *A Book of Music* and "A Textbook of Poetry." Of course, "blow" also asks to be read two ways, as does "angels" – in her pathbreaking study of Spicer, Maria Damon has emphasized the valency throughout Spicer's writing of "angel" as a slang term meaning a gay man,[20] and that double-meaning drives this exchange between the poet and the musician:

"And are we angels, Bird?"
"That's what we're trying to tell 'em, Jack
There aren't any angels except when
You and me blow 'em."

(CP, 72)

To a significant extent, the poem is built on puns – a trope "The Textbook of Poetry" will examine directly – and relies on a series of terms which condense, relate, and disperse various meanings: the "angel" is also Rilke's, and "Bird" takes us to a story about two birds which make their way into the library, a situation taken in hand by the promisingly named Miss Swift:

Once two birds got into the Rare Book Room.
Miss Swift said,
"Don't
Call a custodian
Put crumbs on the outside of the window
Let them
Come outside."

. . .

But Miss Swift went to lunch. They
Called a custodian.
Four came.
Armed like Myrmidons, they
Killed the birds.
Miss Munsterberg
Who was the first
American translator of Rilke
Said
"Suppose one of them
Had been the Holy Ghost."
Miss Swift,
Who was back from lunch,
Said
"Which."

(CP, 69–70)

Just as "Bird" and the birds rhyme with "Birdland, California," this poem too is concerned with mediations between realms, and what poetry, music and language do in this process. In addition to bird (and perhaps Bird) as Holy Ghost, paraclete, God's mediator, we once again have butterflies: "I knew there would be butterflies / For butterflies represent the lost soul" (*CP*, 70). Yet these butterflies will also be written into the series linking angel (in every sense), "Bird," bird and paraclete:

Have you ever wrestled with a bird,
You idiotic reader?
Jacob wrestled with an angel.
(I remind you of the image)
Or a butterfly
Have you ever wrestled with a single butterfly?

(*CP*, 71)

But as butterflies also "Represent the way the wind wanders / Represent the bodies / We only clasp in the middle of a poem" (*CP*, 70) they come to stand for the entire poetic (and therefore, musical) space in its opposition to where it travels and is received. Butterflies represent the notes and the angels that can only be blown within the song and the poem: "Listen to / The terrible sound of their wings moving"; "Let the wings say / What the wings mean / Terrible and pure" (*CP*, 71).

I've sketched these figural associations not to suggest that the poem constructs a formal argument that can be unpacked and resolved, but rather to emphasize that as counterweight to the speed of its line and its offhand, at times derisory tone one finds a dense and compacted rhetorical network, in its maneuvers still cognizant of the lessons the young Spicer learned from Donne. But the poem's most important structuring device is probably its hectoring, cranky address to the reader, disparaging the laughter it provokes as a comfort to be refused: "But the poem isn't over. / It keeps going / Long after everybody / Has settled down comfortably into laughter. / The bastards / On the other side of the paper / Keep laughing. / Listen. / Stop laughing. / The poem isn't over" (*CP*, 70). Interestingly, the laughter from the other side of the paper is only accepted when the poem is indeed over, and at a moment where it hardly seems a likely response:

Deny
The bloody motherfucking Holy Ghost.
This is the end of the poem.
You can start laughing, you bastards. This is
The end of the poem.

(*CP*, 72)

The poem oddly throws laughter beyond its borders, both spatially ("the other side of the paper"), and temporally – we are allowed to laugh only because "This is / The end of the poem." On the inside, within the space where angelic bodies are available for clasping, is only the "terrible sound" of the butterflies' wings moving and what this moving means, "terrible and pure." And this is a space that the reader as bastard is figured as trying to close down, in an undue haste to get to the end of a poem that only keeps asking to go on, and that finishes reluctantly and with an air of defeat, as if unable to hold out any longer against a burgeoning laughter that we bastards are unable any longer to suppress. In one way, this poem gives us a muddled Orpheus, making his audience laugh when he would have them moved in very different ways. At the same time, it signals what will be an ever-increasing emphasis in Spicer's Orphic mode, as it slides towards the "admonitions" which give their name to one of his books, and Spicer strives not only to move his audience to wonder and transcendence, but equally to self-doubt, annoyance, anxiety, and rage. The song now lashes out at those whose obtuseness would squelch it, bemoans its helplessness against a world that will not receive it. The poem's end is not closure or resolution, but the exhausted defeat of a poem which hasn't yet figured out how not to be over.

In comparison to "Song for Bird and Myself" the "Imaginary Elegies" can seem staid or even tame, but there is no question that Spicer himself gave them pride of place among his early work. Not only did he pointedly spare them from his general criticism in the letter to Blaser from *Admonitions*, he also selected them as his contribution to Donald Allen's *New American Poetry* anthology of 1960, which makes them by a large margin his most widely disseminated work during his lifetime, and probably since.[21] Certainly, part of Spicer's affection must be due to the proto-serial manner in which the "Elegies" are so intensely poems of revision, both in their thematics and in their genesis and elaboration. The first four were written over a period of five years, as their dating in *New American Poetry* indicates, and the fourth is very largely a reflection on the meaning of this interval *within* the poem, and an explicit re-evaluation of some of its earlier statements.[22] Additionally, the first four "Elegies" themselves underwent significant revision between a version Spicer was reading publicly as late as 1957 and that which appeared in *New American Poetry*.[23] But revision has another valency too, as the poems are explicitly about looking and seeing, about the seen and one's own being seen, about the visible, invisible, and the all-seeing eye of God. As such, they are at once poems of desire, recognition, and guilt. They are also elaborate intertextual dialogues with two of the most important poets for the earlier Spicer: Eliot and above all Yeats.[24]

The first "Elegy" begins by identifying poetry with the camera – a device for freezing the evanescent real, capturing a moment that can only be presented in its absence given the temporal interval in which the photograph is developed or the line written. In fact, it seems to be poetry's freezing of the moment that most worries the poet here, as he presents two equally unappealing alternatives – the loss of the moment forever, or its preservation as a simulacrum:

> Poetry, almost blind like a camera
> Is alive in sight only for a second. Click,
> Snap goes the eyelid of the eye before movement
> Almost as the word happens.
> One would not choose to blink and go blind
> After the instant. One would not choose
> To see the continuous Platonic pattern of birds flying
> Long after the stream of birds had dropped or had nested.
>
> (*CP*, 26)

Poetry, to the extent that it is linked to visual memory, is almost depicted as a fascination with death in the poem: "The temporary tempts poetry / Tempts photographs, tempts eyes"; the poet "conjures" his images as if "From photographs," and like the photographer raises the dead: "It is as if we conjure the dead and they speak only / Through our own damned trumpets, through our damned medium" (*CP*, 27). "Elegies" II and III will contrast the shutter-clicking, contingent poetic eye with the vision of God, itself divided between the eye of the moon, evoked in "Elegy II," and that of the sun, found in "Elegy III." In "Elegy II," the lunar eye of God is precisely that which sees everything we do not: "God must have a big eye to see everything / That we have lost or forgotten ... / The moon is God's big yellow eye remembering / What we have lost or never thought" (*CP*, 27). The moon is the opposite of the camera, being the eye to see the properly invisible, the unactualized or unactualizable:

> The moon is not a yellow camera. It perceives
> What wasn't, what undoes, what will not happen.
> It's not a sharp and clicking eye of glass and hood. Just old,
> Slow infinite exposure of
> The negative that cannot happen.
>
> (*CP*, 28)

"Elegy III" begins by reverting to the sun: "God's other eye is good and gold. So bright / The shine blinds. His eye is accurate. His eye / Observes the goodness of the light it shines" (*CP*, 29). However, what emerges as the main concern of "Elegy III" is twilight, the interim space free from both sun and moon, when God's two eyes are closed:[25]

> Most things happen in twilight
> When neither eye is open
> And the earth dances.
> Most things happen in twilight

When the earth dances
And God is blind as a gigantic bat.

(*CP*, 30)

The poem goes on to depict boys basking in the sun by a pool, their "groins . . . pressed against the warm cement," before reaching a powerful and enigmatic conclusion: "Rescue their bodies from the poisoned sun, / Shelter the dreamers . . .":

Splash them with twilight like a wet bat.
Unbind the dreamers.
                              Poet,
Be like God.

(*CP*, 30)

This conclusion is as problematic as it is resonant; indeed, "Elegy IV" will begin with a question many readers might want to ask: "Yes, be like God. I wonder what I thought / When I wrote that" (*CP*, 48). To get a better sense of what Spicer might have thought and what the poem does, we need to look at the figural tradition within which it is working. To a considerable extent, the opposition between sun and moon derives from Yeats, particularly poems like "The Tower," or "The Song of Wandering Aengus," which concludes by tendering the promise of an ultimate reconciliation of the solar and lunar realms, pre-eminent among the list of oppositions the poem rehearses:

Though I am old with wandering
Through hollow lands and hilly lands,
I will find out where she has gone,
And kiss her lips and take her hands;
And walk among long dappled grass,
And pluck till time and times are done
The silver apples of the moon,
The golden apples of the sun.

(*Poems*, 77)

In his article "The Sun and the Moon in Yeats's Early Poetry" from 1952, Spicer's close friend Thomas Parkinson cites these very lines.[26] He is mostly concerned, however, with "Lines Written in Dejection," in which the poet laments having lost "The round green eyes and the long wavering bodies / Of the dark leopards of the moon," to find himself left only with the "embittered" and "timid" sun (*Poems*, 195). In his somewhat schematic account of Yeatsian antinomies, Parkinson stresses that the image of the "holy centaurs" in the poem might function as a symbol of a "composite being," which would represent the "possible resolution" of the "antithetical symbols," sun and moon (50). It is possible that these centaurs are echoed in a composite being Spicer mentions in "Elegy II": the hippogriff, the offspring of a griffin and a mare, combining lion, eagle, and horse. It occurs in place of a long, cancelled passage which seems to take up lines from "Dejection" which Parkinson cited: "All the wild witches, those most noble ladies, / For all their broom-sticks and their tears, / Their angry tears, are gone" (*Poems*, 195). In the earlier version of "Elegy III" is a 25-line passage which begins, "The world is full of watching witches / Bitching the world up," and goes on to scramble phonemically and semantically that statement in a long excursus on "watching bitches / witching the world up," and "witch-hunting bitches / Watching the world upside down" (Killian, "Under the Influence," 138). Parkinson focuses on how the early Yeats conceives of artistic success as deriving from a "marriage of the sun and moon" (53) which establishes the centaur as the emblem of the successful poem, as it were. Perhaps this is why in the revised "Elegy II," the hippogriff appears at the moment when a dialogue with *The Waste Land*, a composite poem if ever there was one, has replaced the long passage on witches:

> Da. I don't remember what I lost. Dada.
> The song. Da. The hippogriffs were singing.
> Da dada. The boy. His horns
> Were wet with song. Dada.
>
> (*CP*, 28)

Parkinson closes by emphasizing how unstable sun and moon imagery is throughout Yeats' *oeuvre* (58). However, the choice to limit himself to the "early" works causes him to omit some of the more important elaborations of the relationship between the two elements. For example, "The Tower," like "Elegy III," invokes the sun and moon in relation to the poet's task. There, Yeats opposes the fanciful moon of poetry and song to "the prosaic light of day" (*Poems*, 241), and sketches the deadly consequences of the madness which mistakes the first for the second. Yet almost immediately thereafter, he declares such a confusion to be his very aim: "O may the moon and sunlight seem / One inextricable beam, / For if I triumph I must make men mad" (242). At the same time, Parkinson neglects an essential element of "The Song of Wandering Aengus": if the poem concludes by evoking a gathering together of sun and moon (and would this be the "madness" that "The Tower" suggests?), it begins by positing their mutual *suspension* as the moment of magical transformation itself: "And when white moths were on the wing, / And moth-like stars were flickering out" (76) is when the magic fish is caught; the "glimmering girl" which the fish becomes disappears at a moment the poem defines with precision – dawn – as she is described as having "faded through the brightening air" (77). "Most things happen in twilight" indeed, the evanescent moment of the girl's apparition before prosaic daylight blots her out. Which brings us to the end of "Elegy III," with its own invocation of twilight: "Splash them with twilight like a wet bat / Unbind the dreamers" (*CP*, 30). Such a call makes a good deal of sense within the figural logic of the poem, but at the same time it seems to imply the very opposite of what "being like God" would mean, as God has been nothing other than the diachronic, stereoscopic vision of the sun and the moon. One might argue that the phrase "wet bat" implies that the poet should be like God is himself at twilight, when he is "blind as a gigantic bat" (*CP*, 30), but such a formulation feels brittle, as the twilight is so insistently defined as an exceptional moment for the Godhead, and not its essence. Unless, of course, that moment of twilight blindness, through its very negation, is the ultimate aspect of both God and Poet. In "The Tower" Yeats explicitly equates poetic creation of beauty and desire with a blindness to *both* forms of light, reminding us that Homer was blind "And Helen has all living hearts betrayed" (242). And Parkinson provides these lines from Martin Hearne, a character in the play Yeats co-wrote with Lady Gregory, *The Unicorn from the Stars*: "We must put out the whole world as I put out this candle. We must put out the light of the stars and the light of the sun and the light of the moon, till we have brought everything to nothing once again. I saw in a broken vision, but now all is clear to me. Where there is nothing, where there is nothing – there is God" (cited in Parkinson, 57). Poet, be like God.

"Elegy IV" continues to extend and investigate these conceits, but no more conclusively: "That two-eyed monster God is still above" (*CP*, 49) it declares, only to eliminate him almost immediately:

> He is the sun
> And moon made real with eyes.
> He is the photograph of everything at once. The love
> That makes the blood run cold.
> But he is gone. No realer than old
> Poetry.
>
> (*CP*, 49)

The poem's refusal to decide if it is God's presence or his absence which is devastating, and its reluctance to delve into this refusal directly, make what is one of Spicer's most elaborately philosophical poems also intellectually disappointing in certain respects. As magnificently desolate as it is, the poet's mournful characterization of his metaphysical scaffolding as a kind of compensatory fable – again reminiscent of "The Circus Animals' Desertion" – is also somewhat predictable:

> What have I gone to bed with all these years?
> What have I taken crying to my bed
> For love of me?
> Only the shadows of the sun and moon
> The dreaming groins, their creaking images.
> Only myself.
>   Is there some rhetoric
> To make me think that I have kept a house
> While playing dolls?
>
> (*CP*, 48)

But the poem recovers its density in returning to problems which Spicer had considered more thoroughly – that of the contours of the poem that tries to hold these very questions within itself, and what is beyond these contours in both time and space. The opening lines prise open the thunderous appeal, "Poet, Be like God," distancing the poet from his earlier work:

> Yes, be like God. I wonder what I thought
> When I wrote that. The dreamers sag a bit
> As if five years had thickened on their flesh
> Or on my eyes.
>
> (*CP*, 48)

These five years separating "Elegy IV" from the three previous are emphasized in repeated phrases which become a refrain – "This much I've learned / In these five years in what I spent and earned: / Time does not finish a poem" (*CP*, 48) – as the poem takes inside itself its distance from itself. Certainly, this opens a space of self-criticism and self-reflection which is eminently Yeatsian, or indeed Wordsworthian, as the "five years" of the "Elegies" recall Tintern Abbey. But what is crucial for Spicer is that this time which divides the poem from itself does not do so in the interests of a greater, dialectical cohesion. The five years function not to complete the "Elegies" but – in theory at least – to rupture or disclose them (to use a term that Spicer will privilege in *After Lorca*), as the poem's end is evoked both temporally and spatially at the elegy's close:

> Above the giant funhouse and the ghosts
> I hear the seagulls call. They're going west
> Toward some great Catalina of a dream
> Out where the poem ends.

> But does it end?
> The birds are still in flight. Believe the birds.

(CP, 49)

The poem ends ambiguously: should we believe that the birds, who have not renounced their quest, know that the poem ends out there, somewhere, or believe that as the birds are still in flight in the timeless "now" of the poem that the latter will never end?[27] Are these birds different from those in "Elegy I," which live on as Platonic image after they themselves have "dropped" or "nested," or are they in fact these very images themselves, still "in flight" because entombed within the poem's Grecian Urn-like temporality? "Time does not finish a poem" only if you can stop time from so doing. This is what Spicer will explore in the "books," and this is why in the letter to Donald Allen cited above, Spicer staked the success of the "Elegies" so heavily on there being more of them. Indeed, "Elegy V" immediately writes a new moment into the series of revisions: "Another wrong turning / Another five years. I can't see / The birds, the island . . ." (*CP*, 230), and the very existence of it along with its successor imply that the "Elegies" can only be conclusively finished with Spicer's death, an ultimate "accidental" which cannot impose ending in a meaningful sense at all; still less so, given Spicer's poetics of ghosts, haunting, and "dead men talking to each other," as we shall see in the next chapter.[28] As the "Elegies" strive to imagine a poetry which wouldn't mimic the camera's static shutter-drop, which could move beyond choosing between what is there and what is not, we see the contours of the project Spicer elaborates in his letter to Blaser: a poetry of process, exchange, and deferral; a poetry which circulates beyond its own borders and sweeps the microcosmic poet into a network that his own circuits can no longer encapsulate. In many ways, Spicer's sense of the serial poem is best summed up by his contemporary, the artist Robert Smithson, here defining a project of his own: "When a *thing* is seen through the consciousness of temporality, it is changed into something that is nothing . . . so that it ceases being a mere object and becomes art" (112). Similarly, one might add that a writer seen through the consciousness of temporality ceases being a mere poet and becomes a ghost.

Notes

1. In Bancroft Library's Spicer archives a handwritten, folded copy of this letter exists, with very minor variants. *Admonitions* was not published during Spicer's life, although by the end of 1957 he had produced complete

typed manuscripts for it, and the material was clearly circulating through readings and as text. A 1957 letter from Robert Duncan to Blaser shows how important this book was for him, above all the letter I cite here (see *P*, 106).

2. Blaser explicitly refers to the *Admonitions* letter in explaining why he excluded the early work from his edition of *The Collected Books of Jack Spicer*: "The point is to keep intact the separation he made between his early poems and the poetry he wanted" (*The Fire*, 129).

3. For more on this, see my *American Modernism's Expatriate Scene*, pp. 119–21, and for a different view, see Joseph Conte, who would probably find my account of the implications of seriality more appropriate for Duncan, as opposed to Spicer, whom he sees as practicing a "finite serial form": "Duncan not only rejects the boundaries of a single poem, but all boundaries . . . Spicer, however, posits the limiting presence of the book" (106). My position is closer to this description of the "serial poem" from Christopher Nealon: ". . . no single lyric was meant to bear the weight of poetic force because each poem was part of a serially realized – and perhaps unrealizable – poetic 'whole,' with no author" (32). This "unrealizable," provisional quality of seriality in Spicer seems to me crucial. In terms of the statement itself, John Vincent examines Spicer's rhetoric of relationship critically, reminding us that one-night stands are not necessarily "meaningless," and indeed, can be read as a form of seriality themselves (*Queer*, 151). Michael Snediker extends these reflections with an examination of the bath house within gay culture, and goes on to ponder what kind of erotic relationship seriality might imply, given Spicer's recusal of "personal need" in his poetics more generally (*Queer*, 146–50). Finally, much of this chapter will proceed in the spirit of Vincent's recent assessment of the statement as something other than an outright condemnation of the early work, given the ironic potential created by its contextualization *within* a "book" ("Before *After Spicer*," 6–7).

4. Gizzi refers to regional pronunciation in the context of punning (*H*, 199); his section on California in his afterword to *The House that Jack Built* is an excellent account of Spicer's regionalism (pp. 199–206), as are the analyses by Michael Davidson in *The San Francisco Renaissance* and Maria Damon in *The Dark End of the Street*.

5. "He [Yeats] was on a train back in, I guess it was 1918. The train was, oddly enough, going through San Bernardino to Los Angeles when his wife Georgie suddenly began to have trances, and spooks came to her . . . And she started automatic writing as they were going through the orange groves between San Berdoo and Los Angeles" (*H*, 4). In *A Vision* Yeats only locates the event as happening on a train "somewhere in Southern California" (9) and specifies that this was when Georgie began dictating the voices to Yeats, rather than writing down their utterances herself. Spicer omits the earlier history of Georgie's own automatic writing, which Yeats discusses in detail.

6. In addition to the essay, the Bancroft archive also contains a thick file of notecards containing citations from Donne, as well as much material pertaining to the theory of the microcosm, such as this citation from John Johnston's *The Constancy of Nature*: "Man is the epitome of the

world, a marriage of Superior and inferior bodies, a Microcosme of a Macrocosme."

7. Spicer's revision here also has other implications: already we see in germ and action a version of Spicer's poetics of dictation and haunting, as the names Rimbaud and Crane come to take possession of texts that were not consciously written to be about or "belong" to them. The poem takes on its final form through a gesture which could seem arbitrary, or extraneous to the concerns that dominated its production (provided the scholar has access to the archives backstage). But astonishingly, the seascapes in question *become* figures for Rimbaud and Crane simply by having these names tethered to the texts beneath them, a fact which testifies to the contingent and unreliable nature of rhetoric, certainly, but just as much to its properly uncanny, magic ability to create meaning beyond the logos, something Spicer will investigate carefully in "A Textbook of Poetry." These two valencies are not simply opposed. Michael Snediker insightfully argues that "magic" for Spicer is always also that of "smoke and mirrors," a not entirely believable "compensation": "Spicer in some fundamental way doesn't believe in poetry and that, again, makes his poetry all the more transforming" ("Prodigal," 498). Or as Cressida describes the ocean in Spicer's play *Troilus*: "Just a cold dark fact that no metaphor could make significant. It didn't even mean to be meaningless" (143), a problem, as we shall see in Chapter 5, that returns as central in *Language*.

8. "Come back to California, come back to California every mapmaker, every mapmaker is pleading to James Alexander" (*CP*, 205) Spicer writes in *Letters to James Alexander*, while the sequence *A Fake Novel about the Life of Arthur Rimbaud* gives us this: "A metaphor is something unexplained – like a place in a map that says that after this is desert. A shorthand to admit the unknown" (*CP*, 294). Meanwhile, the *Homage to Creeley* section of the same book features a lyric titled "The Territory is Not the Map," followed by a note which needs to be heard in terms of Spicer's extended dialogue with Yeats: "This is a poem to prevent idealism – i.e. the study of images. It did not succeed" (*CP*, 254).

9. I refer here to Yeats' "The Circus Animals' Desertion," where regretting his fascination with his own "masterful images," Yeats laments: "Players and painted stage took all my love / And not those things that they were emblems of" (*Poems*, 394). In a letter to Graham Mackintosh, Spicer stresses the map as a figure of containment which proscribes any real exploration or encounter: "They have made maps of every square inch of the world and imprisoned us inside those maps. Let's escape" ("Letters to Graham Mackintosh," 100).

10. "The Scrollwork on the Casket" reinforces such an association: "A short story is narrower than a room in a cheap hotel; it is narrower than the wombs through which we descended" (*CP*, 24).

11. For this reading, and several other suggestions and interpretations which tally or dialogue with my account, listen to the fascinating discussion between Al Filreis, Rachel Blau DuPlessis, Julia Bloch, and C. A. Conrad, "Poem Talk 28: Jack Spicer's 'Psychoanalysis: An Elegy'" at: http://poemtalkatkwh.blogspot.com/2010/02/spicer.html.

12. "New Found Land" refers to John Donne's Elegy 19, "To His Mistress

Going to Bed," a poem which almost certainly informs Spicer's own "Elegy" here. Donne refers to his lover's body as "O my America, my new found land," and the final section is a paean to the revelation of the naked body: "Full nakedness, all joys are due to thee. / As souls unbodied, bodies unclothed must be" (125).

13. In terms of the temporality of the development of Spicer's own poetics, the poem is also divided. While the work almost certainly originates in 1949 or 1950, archival evidence suggests that the final section on the "mad cartographer" was a late addition, composed in Boston in 1956 around the same time as the equally pivotal "Song for Bird and Myself."

14. Geoffrey Hlibchuk helpfully cautions against the "temptation to sharply demarcate" Spicer's Outside from "the interiority of subjectivity." I don't think it follows, however, that "dualities such as inside and outside become essentially meaningless" (311) in Spicer. On the contrary, it is only because they continue to mean that Spicer can refold them as he does.

15. A short, contemporaneous fragment emphasizes these aspects: "Flesh fails like words to translate or to touch / Each others [*sic*] starkness, / Like files we rasp and rub, / Each other's flesh against the darkness . . ." (*B*).

16. In some respects, this poem would be a fine example of what Miriam Nichols has defined as a primary goal for Spicer: "to make words point to the flesh that suffers their imprint" (14). I would only add that such an imprint thrills the flesh too.

17. For Spicer's time in Boston and friendship with Joe Dunn, see *P*, pp. 69–77; for the latter's job in the postal service, see p. 125.

18. Of course, this does not lessen one's gratitude to Gizzi and Killian for confirming that it was indeed on October 5 that the Yankees used seven pitchers in a World Series loss to the Dodgers (*CP*, 444). (The World Series, which determines the yearly champion in American baseball, is awarded to whichever of the two finalists wins four games out of a "series" which can be as long as seven (as there are no draws). The 1956 series featured two of the most iconic baseball teams, the New York Yankees and the neighboring Brooklyn Dodgers, with the Yankees winning what in the UK would be called a "derby" in seven games. The Dodgers moved to Spicer's hometown of Los Angeles in 1958, the same year the New York Giants relocated to San Francisco to become Spicer's favorite team and allow him to attend major league baseball games on a regular basis).

19. Whitman's "Crossing Brooklyn Ferry" is very largely structured by an uncanny voice which posits itself alternately as within the "now" of a ferry crossing and the "now" of any particular reading of it.

20. See Damon, *Dark*, pp. 155–70 for an illuminating account of the implications of Spicer's use of the term.

21. In unpublished correspondence with Donald Allen, Spicer first proposes *Billy the Kid*, but subsequently assents to what must have been Allen's preference: "Sure print the 4 elegies" (*B*, letter of September 2, 1959). At the same time he defines the "Elegies" in terms implicitly serial: "Either I'm right and there will be a lot more or I'm wrong and they don't belong. I'd know in six months." Sometime in 1960 he sent Allen "Elegies V and VI" and announced that as he was now working on "something else" there probably wouldn't be more for awhile; in fact, there were to be none.

22. Allen dated every contribution to the anthology, but the time span attributed to the "Elegies" was Spicer's idea: "I guess you'd better call the years of composition 1950–1955 although, as you know, it was re-furbished later" (*B*, letter of September 9, 1959).

23. A recording of an April 11, 1957, reading by Spicer of the earlier versions is available on PennSound (http://writing.upenn.edu/pennsound/x/Spicer.html). Kevin Killian provides a transcription in "Under the Influence."

24. In terms of their rhetoric and insistence on the figures of the sun and moon, they often echo Robert Duncan's "Heavenly City, Earthly City," though ultimately I don't believe they share that poem's concerns. Still, its opening lines cannot but be resonant for any reader of the *Elegies*: "Beauty is a bright and terrible disk. / It is the light of our inward heaven / and the light of the heaven in which we walk. / We talk together" (*First Decade*, 34).

25. Miriam Nichols has recently provided an interesting reading of the "Elegies" which tallies with mine in important ways, particularly regarding Spicer's concern with the "eternal" and "temporary" (152). Likewise, she stresses the importance of the "twilight zone" in Spicer's schema, but differs significantly on how she reads the significance of the sun and the moon, focusing on distinctions between "cognition and perception" and "the mechanisms of language and the becoming of a universe" (155). See pp. 153–8 for the entirety of her argument. For an analysis of the God of the "Elegies" in relation to Spicer's tendency to "vacillate between gnosticism and Calvinism" (162), see Norman Finkelstein.

26. Thomas Parkinson and his wife Ariel were two of Spicer's closest friends, especially during his student years at Berkeley. Spicer would have been in constant conversation with Parkinson, for whom he was also a teaching assistant, in the years leading up to this article, which were also those when Spicer composed the first drafts of the "Elegies."

27. Spicer's revision increases this uncertainty; the early version casts the birds as flying "To where all poems end," and answers its ultimate question with this final line: "The birds believe it's there. Believe the birds" (Killian, "Under the Influence," 140).

28. John Emil Vincent also reads the "Elegies" as largely concerned with the "problem of closure" (*Queer*, 163), focusing especially on "Elegies" V and VI (163–4).

Chapter 2

Correspondence and Admonition

"Sentiment is not to the point. A dead letter is there because it has no longer real addresses."
> Jack Spicer, "Chapter II: The Dead Letter Office," in "A Fake Novel about the Life of Arthur Rimbaud" (*CP*, 293)

In June 1955, a restless Jack Spicer somewhat surprisingly left the San Francisco Bay Area to seek his fortune on the east coast of the United States. His first stop was New York City, for which he quickly developed a near pathological hatred. By the autumn he was in Boston, and with the help of Robin Blaser, then working across the Charles River at the Widener Library of Harvard University, he secured a job as a librarian at the Boston Public Library. By the time Spicer was dismissed from this post in November 1956, he was well ready to return to California and did so, arriving with striking new poems such as "Song for Bird and Myself," but few financial prospects. However, Robert Duncan helped arrange for Spicer to get work teaching at San Francisco State College, most notably the legendary "Poetry as Magic" workshop, which heralded Spicer's return to the scene and re-established his eminent position within it, despite the explosion of popularity of the Beats, a development which occurred very largely during Spicer's absence.[1]

Indeed, if Spicer's sojourn back East had largely been unhappy, both he and his entourage felt that his time in Boston, combined with the intense communal exchanges instigated by the "Poetry as Magic" workshop in San Francisco, had been transformative for his poetry.[2] In addition to Blaser, Spicer had associated with poets Joe Dunn, John Wieners, and above all Stephen Jonas, who became an important friend and inspiration for him. Writing to Blaser very shortly after his return to California, on December 21, 1956, he explained why he wanted to dedicate his translation of García Lorca's "Ode to Walt Whitman" to Jonas: "It's going to be dedicated to Steve Jonas as he taught me how to use anger (as opposed to angry irony) in a poem" ("Letters to Robin Blaser," 38). And in fact, the "Ode" – with dedication as promised – came to form the centerpiece of Spicer's first book, *After Lorca*, the work taken by Spicer himself along with his entourage and subsequent critics to be the inauguration of his mature poetics and major work. Begun just after his return to California, Spicer's book of "untranslations"[3] is his most critically discussed work, for a variety of understandable reasons. Not only did Spicer himself designate it as marking his discovery of serial poetry and the "book" as form, he also used one of its "letters" as his "statement on poetics" for Donald Allen's *New American Poetry* anthology. Moreover, the way it charts a proto-poetics of "dictation" and the Outside through tropes of haunting and above all translation make it one of the most fascinating dialogues with the poetics of Yeats, and even more so, Pound, produced by any American poet of his generation. Indeed, Spicer is arguably the first major poet to take Pound's translation practice as something other than an idiosyncrasy, establishing a kind of dialogic, collaborative originary translation text as an enduring trope of American poetics;[4] *After Lorca* is undoubtedly a central work in the venerable tradition of modernist translation outlined by Steven Yao.[5] Finally, its figuration of itself as a homoerotic collaboration between "Lorca" and "Jack" and its outline of the dynamics of queer poetic transmission through the Whitman-Lorca-Spicer network it establishes, render it a crucial work of queer poetics.[6]

It is Spicer's peculiar genius to use the trope of translation to weave together all these aspects at once: "dictation" and a relationship to the Outside, poetry as collaboration, and queer poetic genealogies and exchanges. However, the overriding trope of translation in the work has to some extent obscured another which is of perhaps even greater importance for Spicer's subsequent poetics: that of letter writing and the epistolary poem. Of course, *After Lorca* is at pains to present these two figures as connected or in parallel. Not only is the book composed entirely of a set of (at times fictive) verse translations of poems and another set of (fictive) prose letters, but it uses a single term to define them both: "correspondence," which designates *both* the finding of any English term to translate a Spanish one, *and* the imaginary exchange of letters between "Lorca" and "Jack." Thus, the "correspondence" between "Jack" and "Lorca" must be said to correspond to and translate the accompanying "translations," in a rhetorical economy in which the translations correspond to and translate the letters too. Such "correspondences" have been noted for some time; however, less attention has been given to the fact that such a framework makes *After Lorca* "correspond" to and with Spicer's subsequent book, *Admonitions*, itself framed as a series of letters or messages, and in many ways an explicit extension and revision of *After Lorca*.[7] Both these books point to a postal motif which will be important to Spicer until the end of his life, especially in "A Fake Novel About the Life of Arthur Rimbaud" from *Heads of the Town up to the Aether*, along with a work closely related to it, the *Letters to James Alexander*. As it is meditations on poems as letters and the "postoffice" as locus of transmission and exchange that lead Spicer towards the switchboard and radio as privileged figures for a poetic circulation occurring both through and beyond the poet, it is safe to say that the epistolary model is indispensable for the development of the theories of both the serial poem and dictation. Moreover, it is within these epistolary books that Spicer will rearticulate and disturb an entire series of oppositions which are central to the new poetics he elaborates at this time: public/private, pure/impure, personal/impersonal, poetry/prose, poem/letter. In this process, his most important instigation might be an obscured ghost of *After Lorca*, who without appearing could very well lie behind them all: Emily Dickinson.

Spicer found himself working at the Boston Public Library when one of the most important works in the history of American literature was published: Thomas Johnson's three-volume variorum edition of the poems of Emily Dickinson. Spicer had been interested in Dickinson since highschool, but the Johnson edition was the first reasonably reliable printing of her work ever to appear, revealing an even more daring and brilliant poet than the one Spicer had long known, as well as opening a window onto Dickinson's manuscripts and compositional practices. As the Public Library happened to own around eighty of the manuscripts on which Johnson had worked, Spicer took advantage of the occasion to study the manuscripts himself and review the Johnson edition for the *Boston Public Library Quarterly* of 1956.[8] While Spicer queries Johnson's readings of the manuscripts in several places, much of his concern falls on the larger issue of Dickinson's letters and her practice of embedding poems within them, and the questions which ensue:

> One of the most difficult problems of the editor has been the separation of prose from poetry. This may come as a surprise to some readers. The only surviving prose Emily Dickinson wrote occurs in her letters, and, in their published form, the poetry in them is always neatly set off from the prose. In her manuscripts, however, things are not so simple. She would often spread out her poetry on the page as if it were prose and even, at times, indent her prose as poetry. (*H*, 232)[9]

Although Spicer shows himself generally favorable to the project of extracting poems from their prose surroundings, he also proves constantly attentive to the damage done to poems when read outside the context of the letter in which they appear, or in the absence of "key prose passages" (*H*, 232). Such concerns finally lead him to the following suggestion:

> The reason for the difficulty of drawing a line between the poetry and prose in Emily Dickinson's letters may be that she did not wish such a line to be drawn. If large portions of her correspondence are considered not as mere letters – and, indeed, they seldom communicate information, or have much to do with the person to whom they were written – but as experiments in a heightened prose combined with poetry, a new approach to both her letters and her poetry opens up. (*H*, 234)

The link to *After Lorca* is clear, as in addition to being structured through its six letters from Jack to Lorca, it is precisely the distinctions between poem and letter, and poetry and prose, that the book is at pains to theorize throughout. In fact, Jack's first letter to Lorca attempts to establish the very boundaries that Spicer felt Dickinson's letters challenged:[10]

> These letters are to be as temporary as our poetry is to be permanent. They will establish the bulk, the wastage that my sour-stomached contemporaries demand to help them swallow and digest the pure word. We will use up our rhetoric here so that it will not appear in our poems. Let it be consumed paragraph by paragraph, day by day, until nothing of it is left in our poetry and nothing of our poetry is left in it. It is precisely because these letters are unnecessary that they must be written. (*CP*, 110)

Spicer will go on in this letter to further distinguish a valorized poetry from a debased prose, but in a manner which might seem surprising – he associates "invention ... the enemy of poetry" (*CP*, 111) with prose, while asserting that on the contrary "poetry discloses" (*CP*, 111). Even before examining its subsequent revisions, we need to read this initial program with some caution. First of all, if Spicer here evokes the "pure word" in contradistinction to prose we should hesitate to read that as an endorsement of "pure poetry." As he famously wrote in 1949 in the University of California's *Occident Magazine*, at the height of the Berkeley Renaissance, "The truth is that pure poetry bores everybody. It is even a bore to the poet. The only real contribution of the New Critics is that they have demonstrated this so well" (*H*, 230). Indeed, such "purity" is what Spicer there opposes to his favored model of Orpheus the singer, who is not interested in poems being "beautiful in and of themselves," as we have already seen, but in the capacity to move "impossible audiences" (*H*, 230). It is possible to suggest that

After Lorca represents a modification of such a position, but already certain elements hint that this is not entirely the case. For example, even in this letter, the very term Spicer applies to poetry, "disclosure," itself implies an opening onto otherness, a breaking of boundaries, which is incompatible with "purity" as habitually conceived. This is a point the subsequent letters to Lorca will take up, along with a related question Spicer has put in play from the outset: how could a "pure" poem result from an impure, collaborative authorship? "Lorca" stresses this in his preface when he writes of Spicer's modified, composite "untranslations": "Even the most faithful student of my work will be hard put to decide what is and what is not García Lorca as, indeed, he would if he were to look into my present resting place. The analogy is impolite, but I fear the impoliteness is deserved" (*CP*, 107).[11]

The second letter to Lorca takes up another of the crucial distinctions of the first – permanence as opposed to impermanence – and complicates it. Here, Spicer explicitly addresses the question of "transfer" in two contexts: that of meaning between an "original" text and its translation, and that between the poet's interiority and the poem into which he expresses it. Already, the joint emphasis on "transfer" conflates translation and "original" composition in highly significant ways, but it also signals a different conception of temporality. Spicer writes that while the poet wants to "transfer the immediate object, the immediate emotion to the poem" (*CP*, 122), this will always come encumbered with "hundreds of its own words clinging to it, short-lived and tenacious as barnacles" (*CP*, 122). Yet these impermanent impurities are precisely what the poet must preserve: "And it is wrong to scrape them off and substitute others. A poet is a time mechanic not an embalmer. The words around the immediate shrivel and decay like flesh around the body . . . Objects, words must be led across time not preserved against it" (*CP*, 122). It might seem that the barnacle-words can be retained precisely because they will decay on their own, leaving the object intact. Yet the letter closes on a different note: "Words are what sticks to the real. We use them to push the real, to drag the real into the poem. They are what we hold on with, nothing else. They are as valuable in themselves as rope with nothing to be tied to" (*CP*, 123). Words, then, are only useful in their service to the real, yet that very real is what they cannot make appear, if they are indeed like "rope with nothing to be tied to." The "permanence" which the first letter pointed to is not abandoned, but is reconsidered as something other than a *preservation against time*, here signified by the ghoulish "embalmer" (a position already rejected in other figural guises in the "Elegies," as the previous chapter has argued): it is now seen as being achieved by a "mechanic" working within and through time. If it is a presumably Eliotic and New Critical "mummy-sheet of tradition" (*CP*, 122) that would seek to embalm, the "time-machine" can only function through correspondence.

This is examined in the third letter, the pivotal text which Spicer selected as his "statement on poetics" for the *New American Poetry* anthology, in which he posits "correspondence" as the solution to the problems of "transfer."[12] Here, Spicer famously proclaims his desire for a poetry of the real:

> I would like to make poems out of real objects. The lemon to be a lemon that the reader could cut or squeeze or taste – a real lemon like a newspaper in a collage is a real newspaper. I would like the moon in my poems to be a real moon, one which could be suddenly covered with a cloud that has nothing to do with the poem – a moon utterly independent of images. The imagination pictures the real. I would like to point to the real, disclose it, to make a poem that has no sound in it but the pointing of a finger. (*CP*, 133)

If this passage helpfully elucidates Jack's earlier comments on poetry as disclosure rather than invention, note that the adhesive "barnacles" of the previous letter are here not only tolerated but even called for: a poem whose moon allows for a "cloud that has nothing to do with the poem" is a poem entirely open to the "accidental." More than this: it is a poem which refuses its own borders, actively dis-closes itself, opening out onto that which has "nothing to do with it." Here the poem is part of and penetrated by the "real"; no purity is possible. The letter, though wary of regimes of representation, is more than just the familiar mourning of the failure of words to "be" what they represent, as the "real" itself is not immediately available, being as much subject to the law of "correspondence" as language. Poetry is therefore conjuring – "phantasia non imaginari" (*CP*, 133)[13] – a formulation which also leads to the phantasm, the ghost, "Lorca." But this rejection of representation as opposed to disclosure – the call to "make things visible rather than to make pictures of them" (*CP*, 133) – is at the same time largely a poetics of mediation, rejecting proximity as indicated by "connection" in favor of a relationship constituted by difference and absence: "Things do not connect; they correspond" (*CP*, 133).[14] And correspondence is the means to bring "real objects . . . across language as easily as . . . across time" (*CP*, 133):

> That tree you saw in Spain is a tree I could never have seen in California, that lemon has a different smell and a different taste, BUT the answer is this – every place and every time has a real object to *correspond* with your real object – that lemon may become this lemon, or it may even become this piece

of seaweed, or this particular color of gray in this ocean. One does not need to imagine that lemon; one needs to discover it.

Even these letters. They *correspond* with something (I don't know what) that you have written . . . and, in turn, some future poet will write something which *corresponds* to them. That is how we dead men write to each other. (*CP*, 133–4)

The theory of co-respondence obviously accounts for what might seem like mistaken translation choices in some of Spicer's renderings, but more than this, it figures all translation as dialogue, and conversely, all poetic dialogues as translation, in a vast network of co-respondence which is the only "tradition" Spicer wishes to countenance: "Tradition . . . means generations of different poets in different countries patiently telling the same story, writing the same poem, gaining and losing something with each transformation – but, of course, never really losing anything" (*CP*, 110–11). Tradition is Lorca writing on Whitman in Spanish to be rendered by Spicer in a version which dialogues with the practice of Steve Jonas and calls out to him by name. But it is also, as this letter makes clear, an exchange between "dead men," and this is crucial: Spicer does not gesture here to the immortality of the great poet. Rather, for Spicer one is only a poet to the extent one is "dead."

This is made clear in the fifth letter, one which also quite clearly looks forward to the letter to Robin Blaser in *Admonitions*. Here, Jack begins by returning to the question of "pure poetry," and offers an account which in its broad contours might initially seem in line with classic Kantian "disinterestedness" and Eliotic impersonality: "Loneliness is necessary for pure poetry. When someone intrudes into the poet's life (and any sudden personal contact, whether in the bed or in the heart, is an intrusion) he loses his balance for a moment, slips into being who he is, uses his poetry as one would use money or sympathy . . . The poet, for that instant, ceases to be a dead man" (*CP*, 150). In such an instant, Jack goes on, "even the objects change," becoming "counters" to be "traded for a smile or the sound of conversation": "Nothing matters except the big lie of the personal – the lie in which these objects do not believe" (*CP*, 150). The close of this letter, one of the most important passages in Spicer's work, must be quoted at length:

That instant, I said. It may last for a minute, a night, or a month, but, this I promise you, García Lorca, the loneliness returns. The poet encysts the intruder. The objects come back to their own places, silent and unsmiling . . . And this immediate thing, this personal adventure, will not have been transferred into the poem like the waves and the birds were, will, at best, show in the lovely pattern of cracks in some poem where autobiography shattered but did not quite destroy the surface. And the encysted emotion will itself become an object, to be transferred at last into poetry like the waves and the birds.

And I will again become your special comrade.

Love,
Jack (*CP*, 150)

Jack's objection to the "big lie of the personal" seems clear enough, and he will return to it in his last letter to Lorca, when he wonders if the whole project wasn't just a "game made out of . . . a need for a poetry that would be more than the expression of my hatreds and desires" (*CP*, 153). But more difficult to understand is the "truth" which Jack implicitly opposes to this lie, for it certainly does not correspond to a disinterested "impersonality." On the contrary, what Jack contrasts to the "intrusion" of the other in the heart or the bed is a moment when he can once again become Lorca's "special comrade," and comrade, of course, is Whitman's preferred term for gay lovers.[15] Going beyond the "big lie of the personal," then, does not imply an "objective" poetry in the simple sense, or the transcendence of desire, erotic correspondence, and exchange; Spicer's poetry is one of affect from beginning to end. Rather, what seems required is for emotion and desire to occur within the space which Spicer calls loneliness and death. That is, if poetry admits of or even demands the mutuality of "co-respondence," Jack would seem to imply that it shuns "connection" and "contact." In fact, it is that very contact which has to be severed for the "loneliness" to return, and this happens when the alterity of company is both negated and preserved. The intrusion which rouses the poet "into being who he is" (*CP*, 150) is brought fully *within* but allowed to remain alien, is incorporated but not assimilated, as the term "encysting" makes clear. It is only from the position of this internalized difference that the "emotion" can be objectified and made fit for the poetic. Through encysting, the poet is breached and divided from himself, yet crucially alone, and it is from that condition that the "dead men write to each other." Although Spicer's references to it are surprisingly sparse, this passage also seems to be a reworking of some of Lorca's thoughts on the *duende*. In his famous essay on the subject, Lorca specifies "the duende does not come at all unless he sees that death is possible . . . the duende wounds. In the healing of that wound, which never closes, lie the strange, invented qualities of a man's work" (*In Search*, 67). Certainly, "encysting" sounds like the way to heal an unclosed wound, and the *duende*'s relationship to death would correspond to Spicer's dead men writing to each other. And here emerges one of the centrally important motifs of the letter for Spicer: it is a medium predicated on absence and the possibility of death, a medium indifferent to the life or death, presence or absence, of the interlocutors. Nowhere is this more so than in Dickinson's letters, whose double-play has been brilliantly analyzed by William Merrill Decker. On the one hand, Dickinson constantly insists on the manner in which her letters, down to their very handwriting, extend and transport her own body and touch to their receiver – an aspect Dickinson emphasized by her frequent habit of sending pressed flowers, bread, or other gifts betokening physical presence (Decker, 41). At the same time, her epistolary rhetoric forcefully insists on the properly "spectral" power of such gifts and the letters that accompany them, as they assert the "presence" of someone very emphatically elsewhere, whose being these tokens can only mediate, and not convey. As Decker has put it, "Absence as death is the fundamental trope of her epistolary writing" (160). But equally important is the corollary: that epistolary writing is in many ways the fundamental trope of her poetry, exemplifying the mediating, haunting distance she finds constitutive of all forms of presence.[16] Late in her life, Dickinson famously often preferred exchanging letters to conversation, and preferred conversation through a door ajar over face-to-face meetings. Spicer's poem-letters – like Dickinson's, very often erotically charged – also write the "death" that is necessary to poetry into love and sex. The dynamics of address in Spicer are then very much the symmetrical inverse of Frank O'Hara's "personism," of which "one of its minimal aspects is to address itself to one person. . . thus evoking overtones of love without destroying love's life-giving vulgarity" (O'Hara, 499). O'Hara continues: "It puts the poem squarely between the poet and the person, Lucky Pierre style, and the poem is correspondingly gratified. The poem is at last between two persons instead of two pages" (499).[17] The last sentence very beautifully describes much of Spicer's poetics; however, for Spicer, Pierre is out of luck, not enjoying the connection of the poet and his lover but materializing their estrangement. Or as Jack writes in the *Letters to James Alexander*: "The letters will continue. The letters will continue after both of us are dead. The letters would continue even if we were in the same room together, even though our faces were so close that we could hardly speak – or so distant that our hearts could not touch" (*CP*, 213).

But for Spicer are letters ultimately opposed to poems or, as for Dickinson in his reading of her, in a continuum with them? If *After Lorca* begins by drawing a line between them, it is not certain that this book which Spicer thought should be read "like a novel" finishes with the same position.[18] To start with, the fact itself that the book intersperses Jack's letters among the poetry rather than cordoning them off would seem to argue for giving the former equal status, as does an implicit irony: it is only in the "prose" of the letters that poetry's superiority to prose can be disclosed. That is, the prose letters accomplish what they define as poetry's task.[19] But there is another, more fundamental issue at stake: the theory of "co-respondence" establishes the letter as the privileged model of poetic practice, one which, while predicated on direct address and the emotive circuitry established between a sender and a receiver, is nevertheless beyond the "big lie of the personal." By the late 1950s, Spicer is clear that the point is not to abandon the "personal" but rather to refuse to allow it to separate itself from that to which it is habitually opposed. It is certainly not coincidental that the first place he explicitly theorizes this is within a letter, and one which takes letter-writing as a potential model for such a poetics. In July 1955 he writes to Allen Joyce: "By the way, I hope you show other people these letters I write you. They are personal letters for you and they are also public letters. I measure their success by how well I can succeed in being deeply personal and deeply public at the same time. Like my poems" (143).[20] By 1958 and the *Letters to James Alexander* Spicer is deliberately bringing to crisis the "problem" he had noted in Dickinson two years earlier, gleefully writing:

> I read them all (your letters and mine) to the poets assembled for the occasion last Wednesday. Ebbe was annoyed since he thought that letters should remain letters (unless they were essays) and poems poems (a black butterfly just flew past my leg) and that the universe of the personal and the impersonal should be kept in order. George Stanley thought that I was robbing Jim to pay James. They sounded beautiful all of them. (*CP*, 210)

As Vincent Kaufmann has stressed, the difference between the letter and the poem, or the personal and the impersonal, ultimately corresponds to another, which grounds literary studies to this day: that between the "life" and the "work," that is, the boundaries of the aesthetic itself. As Kaufmann puts it, a writer's letters are traditionally seen as a sort of "empty lot" which would be "hidden between the life and the work; an enigmatic zone connecting what he [the writer] is to what he writes, where life sometimes seeps into the work, and vice versa" (8).[21] It is just this sort of "seepage" that Spicer is interested in fostering in his letter-poems, and in this regard, Spicer's gesture of using the same text as both letter and poem creates consequences which are no less pragmatic than they are theoretical: until the most recent edition of Spicer's poetry, these letters to Alexander had been classed with his correspondence, and the decision to publish them among his "works" has not gone unopposed.[22] If such objections are ultimately unconvincing for the reasons examined above, they are not entirely beside the point. The "disordering" of the divide between the "personal" and the "impersonal" that Spicer stresses here is only meaningful if the letters lie uneasily among a collection of poems, which they do, just as they had previously been difficult to leave beyond the margins of the poetic corpus.[23] In this way, the *Letters to James Alexander* are not simply a formal experiment in writing but an act. And as such, they achieve Spicer's goal of being personal and public at once: they effect the collapsing of the grounds for such a distinction, rather than simply discussing it. Rather than "exchanging" an emotion for poetry, the epistolary model allows the life of that emotion as lived to be the poetry itself.[24] Therefore, on the most intimate level of the heart and the bed, Spicer follows the perlocutionary agenda of his poetry which Michael Davidson has helpfully examined, noting that for Spicer "the function of poetry . . . was often to perform and engage social alliances, not represent them separate from the poem" (*Guys*, 17–18). This is certainly true of a book like *Admonitions*, and it is true of the *Letters to James Alexander*, which perform the disclosure they call for. But this also brings to the fore another underlying model for *After Lorca* and the poetics of co-respondence and address generally, which Spicer further elaborates in *Admonitions*: the letter as seduction.

Interestingly enough, if the "big lie of the personal" is equated very precisely with using the poems as a means for seduction within the poet's life – that space in which poetry can be traded for a "smile" or "conversation" – at the same time seduction is the model Spicer uses to discuss how a poem can make itself available (or not) to a reader. In the fourth letter to Lorca, Jack writes that "some poems are easily laid. They will give themselves to anybody and anybody physically capable can receive them . . . I swear that if one of them were hidden beneath my carpet, it would shout out and seduce somebody. The quiet poems are what I worry about – the ones that must be seduced. They could travel about with me for years and no one would notice them. And yet, properly wed, they are more beautiful than their whorish cousins" (*CP*, 138). Subsequently, Jack suggests that the problem of audience is alleviated when the poet is in love, because the beloved, through sheer narcissism, will automatically be interested in the poem: "The person you love is always interested because he knows that the poems are always about him. If only because each poem will someday be said to belong to the Miss X or Mr. Y period of the poet's life. I may not be a better poet when I am in love, but I am a far less frustrated one. My poems have an audience" (*CP*, 139). After a brief consideration of the possibility of an audience composed of the two "friends" capable of reading his work (undoubtedly Blaser and Duncan), Jack concludes: "All this is to explain why I dedicate each of our poems to someone" (*CP*, 139). Obviously, some of the concerns here are implicitly addressed in the subsequent

letter on the "big lie of the personal," but what is equally notewor-
thy is that this letter announces the program of Spicer's next book,
Admonitions, in which not only does every poem have a dedicatee, as in
After Lorca, but that dedication is in fact the title of every piece. In other
words, if every poem in *After Lorca* is *addressed* to someone, every
poem in *Admonitions* is an address to someone: the interpellation is the
poem, and the "personal," in the form of the dedicatee, is what determines the poem itself, rather than being appended onto it. *Admonitions*,
then, represents very much a return to the "personal" that the final two
letters of *After Lorca* seem to recuse.[25] Yet this book, incorporating
Spicer's single most important statement on poetics in the very form
of a letter, seems to be addressed to a version of the "personal" which
wouldn't be a "big lie." In fact, the emphases of *Admonitions* need to
be read as a response to problems left open in *After Lorca*. In this way,
the two books are quite precisely in co-respondence with each other in
Spicer's sense, establishing a correspondence between "books" which
only extends the concept of seriality which Spicer expounds in the letter
to Robin from *Admonitions*. That is to say, just as seriality breaches the
boundaries of the lyric, thrusting the "single poem" into the sequential
"book," Spicer's larger networks of correspondence break the boundaries of the "book," bringing them into uncertain exchanges with each
other. This is something Spicer implicitly theorizes in an important
unpublished letter to Blaser, from 1958:

> Dear Robin,
>
> I can't help thinking that you have been reading all of my poetry from the
> presuppositions that my poetry previously had. As I so long read Duncan's
> judging everything from the aesthetic that belonged to Medieval Scenes
> alone. Each of my books (starting with The Elegies) contradicts the last,
> builds a world and an aesthetic of its own. Each is not written by the same
> poet as the last, is not a progress but a transformation. (*B*)

If such a statement does assert the autonomy of the "book," each with
an "aesthetic of its own," nevertheless the emphasis on contradiction
and "transformation" only makes sense within the broader network of
correspondences in which these relationships operate, even if these correspondences are ultimately those of the various "Jacks" writing to each
other. And *After Lorca* and *Admonitions*, read as a kind of diptych,
display both the correspondence and the transformation beautifully:
the correspondence through the epistolary model which joins them, the
contradiction through the poetics of the lyrics in the two books. In this
exchange, Whitman, and Lorca's *Ode* to him, are crucial.

In terms of the "untranslations" of *After Lorca*, the most notable stylistic feature of most of them is Spicer's flat voice of constatation, proffering classically surrealist verse built very largely upon the foundation of unlikely images and comparisons: "He walks / Upon a soundless carpet made / Of pigeon feathers" (*CP*, 109) the first poem tells us; "But the sky is an elephant / And the jasmines are water without blood" we find in the second (*CP*, 110). Almost at the end of the book, "The Moon and Lady Death" begins like this: "The moon has marble teeth / How old and sad she looks!" (*CP*, 151). In this respect, Spicer's use of Lorca is broadly consonant with the latter's reception within the American "deep image" movement of the 1960s and 1970s, which Jonathan Mayhew has helpfully sketched in his book on Lorca and American poetry.[26] However, as Mayhew notes, the centerpiece of *After Lorca* is in some ways also off-center with regard to the rest of Spicer's book: "'Ode for Walt Whitman' is somewhat anomalous within the text of *After Lorca*: it clashes stylistically with the more lyrical side of Lorca that Spicer prefers, as well as with his own apocryphal Lorquiana" (120). This is because the *Ode* is above all a poem of direct address, interpellation, and invective, culminating with Lorca's remarkable list of regional derogatory terms for gay men, which Spicer as translator could only produce verbatim: "Fairies of North America, / Pajaros of Havana, / Jotos of Mexico, / Sarasas of Cadiz, / Apios of Seville, / Cancos of Madrid, / Adelaidas of Portugal, / Cocksuckers of all the world, assassins of doves" (*CP*, 130).[27] This outrageous mode of direct address, sometimes combined with obscene and insulting invective, is one Spicer adopts to varying degrees throughout *Admonitions*. Poetry here, in contrast with the speculations on translation from *After Lorca*, is not primarily concerned with transfer and expression – of either the self, or the "world," or of the foreign text to which a translator must be accountable. Rather, poetry takes on a primary role of *gesture*, directed explicitly from one person to another: every poem in *Admonitions* is concerned with establishing a discursive relationship between a particular sender – Jack – and a particular receiver. Given the hurt, rage, virulence and obscenity of many of the poems, the dedications often create the effect of an unwilling complicity and violated intimacy, even when no invective is actually directed at the dedicatee, as in the opening lines of the notorious "For Joe": "People who don't like the smell of faggot vomit / Will never understand why men don't like women" (*CP*, 164). "Joe" is Joe Dunn, Spicer's friend and publisher, but curiously, in a letter *to* Joe which opens *Admonitions* and prefigures the subsequent letter to Robin (while extending the correspondence with Lorca from the previous book), Jack is at pains to dismiss this obscenity which the book largely foregrounds.

This opening salvo to some extent echoes the first epistle of *After Lorca* in its devalorization of letters and prose in favor of poetry. After explaining that in the past he would have found that "writing notes on particular poems" was a "confession" of either their inadequacy or a greater interest "in the terrestrial mechanics of criticism than the celestial mechanics of poetry," Jack admits:

> Muses do exist, but now I know that they are not afraid to dirty their hands with explication – that they are patient with truth and commentary as long as it doesn't get into the poem, that they whisper (if you let yourself really hear them), "Talk all you want, baby, but *then* let's go to bed." (*CP*, 157)

Yet as in *After Lorca* such a statement is problematized by its larger context, and to a considerable degree, the book as a whole can be seen as asking where the bedroom is, as the entirely metapoetical commentary of the letter to Robin is explicitly counted as one of the "admonitions" which give the book its name: "This is true of my *Admonitions* which I will send you when complete. (I have eight of them already and there will probably be fourteen including, of course, this letter)" (*CP*, 163).[28] Once again, the book's "mechanics" seem to move against its stated program, and something similar is at work in the Joe Dunn letter's account of obscenity: "In these poems the obscene (in word and concept) is not used, as is common, for the sake of intensity, but rather as a kind of rhythm as the tip-tap of the branches throughout the dream of *Finnegans Wake* . . . It is precisely because the obscenity is unnecessary that I use it, as I could have used any disturbance, as I could have used anything (remember the beat in jazz) which is regular and beside the point" (*CP*, 157). Thus, the "obscene" here parallels the "letters" of the first letter to Lorca: "It is precisely because these letters are unnecessary that they must be written" (*CP*, 110). But at the same time, the rhetoric looks forward to comments from the Vancouver lectures, which have the effect of linking the entire question of the obscene to that of the personal. Discussing the "Tonys" of *The Holy Grail*, Spicer comments: "The proper names in the thing are simply a kind of disturbance which I often use. I guess it's 'I' rather than the poems because it's sort of the insistence of the absolutely immediate which has nothing to do with anything, and you put that in and then you get all of the immediate out of the poem and you can go back to the poem. I've always found it's a very good thing to put in these immediate things which are in your mind and then just ignore them. It's like the 'tap tap tap' the branches make in *Finnegans Wake*" (*H*, 58). What Spicer implies here is that these seemingly most "personal" aspects of his writing are in fact what are the least so, being simply structuring elements which allow another "message" – more "universal," less "intense" – to be elaborated. That would certainly be the sense of the "rhythm" or "beat," to use his jazz metaphor. Yet it should be noted that the word "disturbance" is not entirely in line with this metaphorical chain, for a "disturbance" does not *structure* a "communication" but rather disrupts or obscures it, like noise or static; it is less the steady beat of jazz than a violent syncopation, or a skipped beat – a break or a rupture. It is less the architectonic than the exorbitant and excessive – the "unnecessary" as Spicer says – yet necessarily unnecessary,[29] just as prose is a "disturbance" to poetry, the "book" a disturbance of lyric self-containment, the letter a disturbance to the aesthetic cordoning off of the work from "life." "Disturbance," a word which links personal disorder with affront to the public, traces for Spicer the path which links obscenity to address, voyeurism to introspection, and provocation to lack throughout his work.[30] Spicer's interest in the accidental and contingent which we examined in the previous chapter implies that disturbances – what is "beside the point," or the cloud that can cover the moon inside the poem – are (un)necessarily always part of the point. Indeed, the "disturbances" represented by the personal are at the very heart of *Admonitions*, at least as the letter to Joe explains it:

> The point. But what, you will be too polite to ask me, is the point? Are not these poems all things to all men, like Rorschach ink blots or whores? Are they anything better than a kind of mirror?
>
> In themselves, no. Each one of them is a mirror, dedicated to the person that I particularly want to look into it. But mirrors can be arranged. The frightening hall of mirrors in a fun house is universal beyond each particular reflection.
>
> This letter is *to* you because you are my publisher and because the poem I wrote *for* you gives the most distorted reflection in the whole promenade. Mirror makers know the secret – one does not make a mirror to resemble a person, one brings a person to the mirror. (*CP*, 157)

If the poems are mirrors, then, they are neither "reflections" of the poet nor of the addressee that gives the poem its name. The poems are at once universal, yet also *aimed* at a particular individual, and the role of the poet is to create effects through the matching of subject and mirror. This pointing works quite concretely in *Admonitions*, as we have seen in "For Joe" or, for example, in "For Dick," which begins, "Innocence is a drug to be protected against strangers / Not to be sold to police agents or rather / Not to be sold" (*CP*, 161). Here, what could be read as a general statement is transformed into a veiled accusation, by virtue of its inclusion in a book titled "Admonitions" – a word meaning a reproof, warning, or call to reform – and the use of the proper name. But one of the finest poems in the book occurs when Jack leads himself before his own distorting mirror:

FOR JACK

Tell everyone to have guts
Do it yourself
Have guts until the guts
Come through the margins
Clear and pure
Like love is.
The word changes
Grows obscure
Like someone
In the coldness of the scarey night air
Says –
Dad
     I want your voice.

(CP, 166)

This poem is a meta-admonition – not only because Jack addresses himself, but also because he admonishes himself to remember to admonish: "Tell everyone to have guts." But the guts – traditional sign of masculine resolve and male physical strength – here seep through onto the margins of a body thin as paper, of a violated text, itself permeable like a physical body. In fact, the poem seems to force one colloquial expression to seep into another. "To have guts" is of course often a euphemism for "to have balls," and thus the guts one has and should have are a displaced synecdoche of masculinity. On the other hand, the image of guts pouring into the margins evokes the expression "to spill one's guts," which means, on the other hand, to speak or express what one shouldn't, to be indiscreet, to allow what should remain inside and intimate to become public and exposed, itself a parallel to the public dissemination of a private message or letter. The proximity of the two expressions makes clear that this form of exorbitant self-exposure is often figured as essentially unmasculine, feminizing, castrated. But having guts, Spicer seems to imply, means inevitably spilling them – out, over, through the borders of the page and the body. Thus the word guts – related etymologically to the Old English *géotan*, meaning "to pour" – pours out into two meanings: "The word changes / grows obscure." This "obscurity" of the word contrasts with "love," defined as "clear," and introduces the grammatical and syntactical obscurities of the poem's last lines, which center around the question of the subject of enunciation. That is, does the phrase "I want your voice" belong to the "someone" who calls out "Dad," or to the speaker of the poem? In the first instance, we have an evocation of an unspecified childish victim of night-terrors invoking the comfort of the patriarchal voice, the voice which would re-establish, one imagines, the proper position of the "guts," the line of the margin. In the second instance, we might read the poet as desiring to speak with, to write poetry with, the voice of the child who calls for his or her father in the night. The poem gives us no means for deciding between these two readings, but note that each attributes a different valency to the term "voice." In one instance, we have a voice with which to speak, with which to express, but in another, we have a voice that we hear, the voice of the other, the voice that arrives from the outside, speaking to us, entering by the ear and reaching down straight to the guts. This uneasy balance between sending and receiving is appropriate in a poem of self-address, a poem of auto-admonishment which is also one of injury and lack – a poem which begins by warning against the lack of guts, and then hints that an abundance of guts can lead to the same dangerous distancing of them. Even more, the double instability regarding both the possession of guts and the location of voice indicates the dialectic of imprecation and aggrievement which Spicer's poetry unfurls and refolds: that is, the dialectic that joins a positioning of injury and lack to a positioning of the pleading and insulting voice. Spicer's foregrounding of allocution displays invective, along with other forms of address, as a ritualized construction not only of the abjected receiver, but also of the sender who inevitably partakes of the abjection his language conjures – who spills and displays his own guts when pointing to, or "mirroring" his addressee. One of Spicer's literary and, it appears, biographical modes was to forge a complicitous group identity through a shared opprobrium for an abjected, external scapegoat.[31] Yet Spicer at his best also explodes these very gestures. This can be seen in his wildly aggressive and notorious admonition, "For Joe":

> People who don't like the smell of faggot vomit
> Will never understand why men don't like women
> Won't see why those never to be forgotten thighs
> Of Helen (say) will move us into screams of laughter.
> Parody (what we don't want) is the whole thing.
> Don't deliver us any mail today, mailman.
> Send us no letters. The female genital organ is hideous. We
> Do not want to be moved.
> Forgive us. Give us
> A single example of the fact that nature is imperfect.
> Men ought to love men
> (And do)
> As the man said

It's
Rosemary for remembrance.

(CP, 164)

Spicer's biographers and Michael Davidson have examined at length the scandal that came to surround this poem in Spicer's circle: Spicer read it at a large gathering organized by Robert Duncan in honor of the visiting Denise Levertov, and thereby managed to insult the guest and mortify her host in a single hostile, divisive gesture. Levertov was to respond a few years later with her poem "Hypocrite Women"; at the time, she clearly felt targeted by a specifically male homosexual form of misogyny.[32] Yet as Davidson points out, despite its misogyny the poem is "hardly a celebration of homosexuality" (*San Francisco*, 173). Indeed, if the gesture of its public reading implies the exclusion of Levertov as a woman from a group of poets defined as gay and male, an initial problem – obliquely acknowledged in the letter to Joe Dunn – is that Joe himself wasn't gay, and apparently had no objections to the "female genital organ." Already, the object of the poet's rage is revealed as more complex than it might seem, for the poem does not only exclude Denise Levertov from the company of poets, but also clearly marks what separates Jack from Joe; rather than establishing a group identity it exposes the fissures within the group it gestures at constructing. This is emphasized in the hyperbolic category of "People who don't like the smell of faggot vomit" – a group which would presumably include many if not most gay males too. Davidson suggests that this line posits "the most extreme version of sexual preference: either 'faggot vomit' or the 'hideous' vagina" (*San Francisco*, 173), but the logic of the poem seems rather to imply that only by acquiring the taste for faggot vomit can one learn that the vagina is "hideous." Spicer equates a dislike of women with a particular, abject gay subject position, one which revels in the filth and stench of a fluid interiority always liable to ooze its way out – qualities which much traditional heterosexual misogynist discourse ascribes to women. "We / Do not want to be moved," the poem continues, apparently echoing a disdain for the hetero-normative exaltation of romantic love which can be traced right back to the phallic avant-garde modernism of the early twentieth century, as seen in figures like Marinetti and Wyndham Lewis. Meanwhile, in the context of both the poem and Spicer's practice generally, "deliver" and "mail" ask to be read as puns – it is after all the "female genital organ" (and not "sexual organ"), here invoked as the object to shun, whence men are "delivered." And it is possible to see the implicit male-man's "male" as the representative of a new category, against which both "women" and the lovers of "faggot vomit" are opposed. If "Forgive us" seems to imply the "crime" of homosexuality in the large sense – not wanting to be moved, not loving the female genital organ – a great deal turns on how one reads: "Give us / A single example of the fact that nature is imperfect." Does one hear this as a defiant challenge, implying nature is always "perfect" even in what others see as abnormalities, such as homosexuality? Or as a plea, asking that "imperfections" of nature, such as homosexuality, be acknowledged? Ought men to love men because nature is imperfect, or because women are imperfect, or because men are imperfect? Interestingly, in the letter to Robin which immediately precedes "For Joe," imperfection is associated with serial poetry. In a rhetoric echoed by "For Joe" on two levels, Jack states that his early work never evolved into "books" because "I thought, like all abortionists, that what is not perfect had no real right to live" (*CP*, 164).[33] But if it is from imperfection that men ought to love men, then following the abject logic of the poem, by the same token they should love women too. The poem ends, surprisingly and emphatically, with the normative category "man" and his authoritative if gnomic declaration: "As the man / said / It's / Rosemary for remembrance." This is particularly striking as the poem began with a pointedly non-gender specific category, "people," even as its later development suggests that a gender-specific term for men would have fit better. The "man" emerges to close the poem with another odor, one less objectionable than that of "faggot vomit" but which testifies to memory, loss, absence, and death, as rosemary is associated with burial rites. Indeed, if "rosemary for remembrance" is a conventional expression, it is most famously uttered not by any "man." Rather, Ophelia mentions it in *Hamlet*, in a context which might have interested Spicer for a variety of reasons: it comes in the same scene as her "good night sweet ladies" (196) which Eliot used in *The Waste Land*, it is followed by her singing "For bonny Sweet Robin is all my joy" (189), where "Robin" is conjectured to be slang for the male sexual organ, but above all, it is followed by an invocation of other vegetation, with other implications: "There's rosemary, that's for remembrance – pray you, love, remember – and there is pansies, that's for thoughts" (189). Another notable instance of the topos that Spicer would almost certainly have known is again the work of a woman, Emily Dickinson:

Essential Oils – are wrung –
The Attar from the Rose
Be not expressed by Suns – alone –
It is the gift of Screws –

The General Rose – decay –
But this – in Lady's Drawer –
Make Summer – When the Lady lie
In Ceaseless Rosemary –

(345)

Here again, nature is in some ways "imperfect," its solar majesty explicitly requiring the supplemental violence of the "screws" for attar – an essential oil derived from rose petals – to be "expressed." This latter term encourages the extracting of essential oils to be read as an allegory of poetic production, with Dickinson implying that poetic "expression" is anything but harmonious, natural blossoming. In *Admonitions* Spicer also stages a rupture with dominant organicist poetics of his time, as derived from Olson's projective verse. In "For Harvey," Spicer rejects any sense of a "new / Measure" or alignment of the poetic line with how you "breathe" (*CP*, 160).[34] Rather, poetry is about cutting and division, in a poem which enacts what it describes with great virtuosity:

Break
Your poem
Like you would cut a grapefruit
Make
It go to sleep for you
And each line (There is no Pacific Ocean) And make each line
Cut itself. Like seaweed thrown
Against the pier.

(*CP*, 160)

In Dickinson's poem, the "Rosemary" would seem to be a cover for the decay of the Lady who, unlike, the dried herb, is in no way "Ceaseless." Opposed to this is the attar which has preserved its summer freshness, but at the expense of the destruction of the rose. Dickinson's poem opposes three forms of decomposition and transmutation: that of the body, that of the dried herb, and that of the expressed attar.[35] What "Rosemary" reminds us is that the preservation of and in the human is effected through memory by way of a turn of the poetic screw – that the absence of the body, the summer, the rose, is the origin of the poem. Spicer begins "For Harvey": "When you break a line nothing / Becomes better" – a phrase which speaks against a fetishization of line breaks and the line as unit, while also showing how the line may create effects by "cutting itself." That is, by breaking the line after "nothing" Spicer encourages a reading of that word not only as an article of negation but also as a noun, implying that line breaks, or lines that cut themselves off and open, improve on the "nothing" without negating it.[36] Again, against a naturalized Whitmanian-cum-Olsonian poetics of the body, presence, and totality, Spicer's "broken" lines join Dickinson's jagged and enjambed quatrains in a poetics of absence, void, negation, and trace, in which expression is not liberation or expansion but violence and destruction. This is a poetics of letters, not voices and songs. Spicer formulates it this way in his "series of true propositions" (*CP*, 206) in the second letter to James Alexander:

> THAT POETRY ALONE CAN LOVE POETRY
> THAT POEMS CRY OUT TO EACH OTHER FROM A GREAT DISTANCE
> THAT POETS, BEING BASTARD FATHERS, LOVE EACH OTHER LIKE BASTARD
> FATHERS WHEN THEY SEE THEIR CHILDREN PLAYING TOGETHER
> THAT POEMS PLAY TOGETHER FROM A GREAT DISTANCE (*CP*, 206)

In the *Letters*, this love, these cries, and their play are coordinated through a space of exchange Spicer calls the "postoffice": "I don't know if there is room in the world for a postoffice but you come across 'em often enough, if you don't make the mistake of pretending that they're in a fixed place (like the moon) and if you don't let their continual changes bewilder you" (*CP*, 207):

> The letters, poems, kisses (since the original game of postoffice is stuck in the mysterious regions of childhood) are directed by a fantastically inefficient system up to the place where poetry comes from and then back down again to the person whose poetry, or letters, or love was meant to receive it. It is a lot different from Air Mail.
> And it is almost impossible to list the random places from which they will deliver their letters. A box of shredded wheat, a drunken comment, a big piece of paper, a shadow meaningless except as a threat or a communication, a throat. (*CP*, 207)

In a subsequent letter, Jack refers to the house Robert Duncan and Jess Collins shared at Stinson Beach as a "postoffice" and concludes, "This I promise – that if you come back to California I will show you where they send letters – all of them, the poems and the ocean" (*CP*, 208). These passages stress the poet or lover as *receiver* of "letters" and messages, wildly and unpredictably dispatched from sites as likely as a lover's throat or as random as a cereal box. However, the fifth letter proves a decisive moment in the history of Spicer's poetics, as his consideration of the place of the poet within this system of relays leads the postoffice motif to morph into the metaphorics of radios, haunting, and dictation via Cocteau's *Orpheus*, which will dominate Spicer's late poetics:

> We proclaim a silent revolution. The poems above our heads, without tongues, are tired of talking to each other over the gabble of our beliefs, our

literary personalities, our attempts to project their silent conversation to an audience. When we give tongue we amplify. We are telephone switchboards deluded into becoming hi-fi sets. The terrible speakers must be allowed silence. They are not speaking to us.

How is it then our business to talk of revolution . . . ? It is because we as their victims, as their mouthpiece, must learn to become complete victims, complete pieces of their mouth. We must learn that our lips are not our own. (*CP*, 209)

Again, this seems a call for a sort of "impersonality" that would surpass and transcend the strictly personal epistolary relationship of James and Jack, yet predictably, the letter will end by reversing course at its culminating point: "We do not write for each other. We are irritable radio sets (but the image of the talking head of a horse on the wall in Cocteau's first Orpheus was a truer image) but our poems write for each other, being full of their own purposes, no doubt more mysterious in their universe than ours in ours. And our lips are not our lips. But are the lips of heads of poets. And should shout revolution" (*CP*, 209). Yet these "heads of poets" are precisely what the "poems above our heads" are defined *against* when the letter opens: ". . . the poems beyond nature that call to each other above the poets' heads. The heads of poets being a part of nature" (*CP*, 209). The silent revolution is now shouted, as the poets' disowned lips are allowed to voice themselves as such yet in their victimhood, within a "nature" now presumably inhabited by an alien and alienating voice. This receptivity is crucial: the poet is deluded when in the role of amplifier, rather than that of the wholly relational switch-board. The trope of the switchboard recalls Ezra Pound's famous defini-tion of "luminous details," the historical facts which "give one a sudden insight into circumjacent conditions, into their causes, their effects, into sequence, and law" (22). Pound writes: "These facts are hard to find. They are swift and easy of transmission. They govern knowledge as the switchboard governs an electric circuit" (23). This seems very much analogous to Spicer's view of the poet as stated above: a node through which other voices, vectors, and networks of exchange become audible, organizing and revealing the correspondence of the poems writing for each other, with their own purposes. Interestingly, if the trope of the switchboard and amplifier imply voice, the penultimate letter stresses the assault on voice operated by James Alexander's graphic play in his book, "Sun Dance": "How can they be read by voice? But why in hell should we have to use our mouths to hear messages? And the letters of the alphabet (as Thoth and Rimbaud both told me) are more than mere sounds. But I want to hear the words from your mouth – that's what one unsurprised part of me demands" (*CP*, 215). Here, the words in their sounds are eroticized metonymies of James Alexander's mouth and in this respect desirable, but Jack stresses messages which, if "heard," bypass the vocal. The post office of these *Letters* finishes with poetry as letter in the most literal fashion: an unsayable poetry beyond the mouth, but not devoid of address. The last letter, in fact, focuses on the postage stamp.

At the same time, the *Letters to James Alexander* become themselves a kind of postoffice, coordinating a dense network of Spicer works which are all in clear intertextual correspondence with each other: *Fifteen False Propositions Against God, Apollo Sends Seven Nursery Rhymes to James Alexander, A Birthday Poem for Jim (And James) Alexander,* and less obviously, *The Heads of the Town Up to the Aether.* But even more than this, the *Letters* become a post office enabling another series of exchanges, at the heart of Spicer's interests: those between "life" and "work," or "poem" and "act," or "event" and "representation." In this respect, the *Letters to James Alexander,* in their refusal even wholly to assert themselves as a work, are the purest expression of Spicer's sought-after impurities.

Notes

1. See *P*, Chapters 2 and 3, for a detailed account of these years.
2. Ellingham and Killian cite a December 19, 1957 letter from Duncan to Blaser in which, in reference to Spicer's latest work, he suggests "Boston seems a good sprouting if not a good sporting ground" (*P*, 106).
3. Spicer's own term, used in the "Letters to Robin Blaser" which in their entirety provide the best window onto Spicer's thoughts about this project.
4. For a recent example of this which takes *After Lorca* as an explicit model, see Christian Hawkey's fascinating *Ventrakl*. Daniel Tiffany's *Radio Corpse* brilliantly demonstrates how interwoven tropes of translation, haunting, and radio were for Pound, who in this respect seems to provide an implicit template for Spicer's later poetics.
5. Yao's work on the translation projects of Pound and H.D. make clear how forcefully Spicer dialogues with their "tradition," a word he uses both within *After Lorca* and when describing his project in a letter to Blaser: "What I am trying to do is to establish a *tradition*. When I'm through (although I'm sure no one will ever publish them) I'd like someone as good as I am to translate these translations into French (or Pushtu) adding more. Do you understand? No. Nobody does" ("Letters to Blaser," 48).
6. Among the indispensable early work on *After Lorca* is Clayton Eshelman's "The Lorca Working," which very helpfully isolates the Lorca elements of the book from Spicer's transformations and additions, Burton Hatlen's "Crawling into Bed With Sorrow," and above all, Lori Chamberlain's "Ghostwriting the Text." More recently, important articles have been

written by Eric Keenaghan, whose focus is above all queer poetics, and Ross Clarkson, and there is also an interesting chapter in Jonathan Mayhew's *Apocryphal Lorca*; I dedicated a chapter to *After Lorca* in *American Modernism's Expatriate Scene*.

7. *Admonitions* was not published in Spicer's lifetime, although it was completed and in circulation among Spicer's friends by late December 1957.

8. The article is reprinted in *The House that Jack Built*, and all references will be to that edition.

9. As Michael Snediker has pointed out, Spicer in some ways anticipates the work of Susan Howe, in his sense that Dickinson is liable to produce a series of variants without a single, definitive version, and in his attention to the materiality of her manuscripts (*Queer*, 136–7).

10. Norman Finkelstein cites the same passage from the Dickinson review, as evidence for his contention that the "question of prose and verse" is "fundamental to Spicer's project" (174, n. 11). I heartily concur.

11. This sense of the composite is furthered in the preface by Lorca's characterization of the typical "untranslation" which mixes Lorca with Spicer as an "unwilling centaur" (107) – a figure which Thomas Parkinson suggested Yeats privileged in a similar sense, as we saw in the last chapter. Thanks to Peter Gizzi for reminding me of its occurrence here. The sense of poetry as collaborative undertaking in the Spicer-Duncan-Blaser circle should be considered in light of David Herd's excellent work on collaboration in the New York School (see above all pp. 52–6). In this regard, Herd argues for the importance of Paul Goodman's writings on community and occasion for the New York poets; as *Poet Be Like God* points out, Spicer knew these texts well, as well as Goodman himself, who spent a year teaching in Berkeley in 1949–50, and became erotically involved with Duncan's circle in complex ways. Spicer's own references to "occasion" are fascinating, and it is certainly by way of Goodman that a long overdue examination of the relationship of Spicer's poetics to those of O'Hara – surprisingly enough, in many ways the contemporary with whose work his own corresponds most powerfully – could begin.

12. Spicer wanted to graphically mark his quibble on "correspondence" as a multi-directional exchange of messages. In the *New American Poetry*, the verb is italicized and hyphenated in three occurrences: "*co-respond*" (414). Blaser's *Collected Books* drops the hyphen, and italicizes all letters but the second and third: "*correspond*" (34), thereby isolating an "or." *CP* simply italicizes the entire word, without hyphens (133–4). The problem mattered to Spicer, who queried Don Allen about possible typographic solutions in two unpublished letters (*B*). It appears he wanted above all to set apart the first two letters of the word, through italicization or underlining – something which none of the editions of his poems has duplicated. In her discussion of this problem, Kelly Holt argues that the White Rabbit Press edition might most reliably reproduce Spicer's desires, underlining the word "correspond" in its entirety with the exception of the first "r" (see Holt, 59–60).

13. Kelly Holt reads this distinction in terms of Aquinas' neo-Aristotelianism (54–5).

14. Such a "correspondence" would seem to be the model of whatever kind of

cohesion the Spicerian "book" may be said to possess. In the letter to Blaser from *Admonitions* the invocation of poems that would "echo and re-echo against each other" (*CP*, 163) is consonant with an epistolary exchange, and in the declaration that "Things fit together ... Two inconsequential things can combine together to form a consequence" (*CP*, 164) this "fitting" takes on a different valency if read as a "correspondence" rather than a "connection."

15. The introductory poem of the "Calamus" section of *Leaves of Grass*, "In Paths Untrodden," closes: "I proceed for all who are or have been young men, / To tell the secret of my nights and days, / To celebrate the need of comrades" (268). Examples of this usage abound throughout Whitman.

16. As Decker puts it regarding Dickinson's conceit that a letter might betoken her, "If the word failed to become flesh, flesh failed too as a medium of full presence" (163).

17. Michael Davidson has also noted the pertinence of the last phrase to Spicer's poetics (*San Francisco*, 154).

18. In an unpublished note Spicer sent to Charles Olson along with a copy of *After Lorca*, he writes, "Here's my book. Please don't skip around in it as it's supposed to be read like a novel" (Poetry Collection of the University Libraries, University at Buffalo, State University of New York).

19. Certainly, the inclusion of the letters here corresponds neatly with what Stephen Fredman has identified as a fundamental drive behind "poet's prose": "the freedom to construct a poetic entity capable of including what poetry has been told to exclude" (10). I agree with Susan Vanderborg that the "generic distinction between poetry and prose" in *After Lorca* "gradually breaks down" (47) over the course of the work.

20. In a helpful recent reading of Spicer's "poetic correspondence," Kelly Holt also concludes that the opposition between poetry and prose (including the letters) and the devalorization of the latter is ultimately undone by the mechanics of *After Lorca*, noting that "In order to correspond with Lorca, Spicer must utilize the very rhetorical mode he dismisses" (56) and "the prose that Spicer suspects ... functions more and more as the poetry it attempts to explain" (58). She also points to the letter to Allen Joyce as an example of how Spicer "combine[s] public and private correspondence" (64). I would only add that not only does he combine them, he forces us to rethink the terms of their separation.

21. My translation. Kaufmann's French term, "terrain vague" is more evocative of undefined space than the corresponding English, "vacant lot."

22. In a review for *The Nation*, Barry Schwabsky objects to the inclusion of the *Letters to James Alexander* in *The Collected Poetry*, arguing that Spicer's poetry "was written to no one and for no one." That point is debatable, but even should one concede it, at issue in Spicer is precisely how he substantivizes that negation.

23. Somewhat analogously, in his *Helen: A Revision*, of 1961, Spicer abruptly interrupts a third-person, constative mode with a second-person epistolary address: "Dear Russ, I am writing to you in the middle of a poem about Helen" (*CP*, 243). In other moods, however, Spicer was capable of ruing what he had so brilliantly wrought, standing on the ground he had set out to undermine. Thus, in a 1959 letter to Stan Persky he writes "Letters are a

trap for me as a person and, I suspect, for me as a poet. They're impure. I'd give a great deal (have given a great deal) not to have written the Alexander ones" (*B*).

24. As Michael Davidson points out, this also corresponds to the agenda of *After Lorca*: "A letter, after all, is an actual piece of communication ... The letter is real in the way a 'newspaper in a collage is a real newspaper'" (*San Francisco*, 160).

25. Robin Blaser saw it this way, at least to some extent. In a February 17, 1958 letter to Duncan referring to what must be *Admonitions* he writes: "It interests me that Jack has moved the personal to the dedication. O stratagem" (BANC MSS 79/68).

26. See Chapter 4 of *Apocryphal Lorca* for this (pp. 78–101). See Miriam Nichols, pp. 158–67, and especially p. 164, for interesting thoughts on how Spicer's strategy of surrealist "juxtaposition" differs from Breton's.

27. I have discussed Spicer's translation of the "Ode" and its pejorative terms, along with Lorca's homophobic rhetoric, in *American Modernism's Expatriate Scene* (see above all pp. 132–9). See Eric Keenaghan for an extended examination of Spicer's use of the obscene in this rendering.

28. Including both the letters to Robin and Joe and the "Postscript for Charles Olson," there are eighteen in all.

29. Or as Susan Vanderborg puts it about the parallel passage in *After Lorca*: "these prose passages are vital precisely because they are an unnecessary or imperfect communication" (49).

30. As early as 1977, Jed Rasula identified "disturbance" as an essential Spicerian concept (60–71), perhaps following hints dropped in Blaser's "Practice of Outside" which mentions Spicer's "magic of disturbance" (*The Fire*, 123), but few critics have followed his lead. My suggestions above are indebted to his insights, particularly his far-reaching observation that "there would seem to be a contradiction between the notion of disturbance and the image of the poet as transmitter" (70). Additionally, as the Introduction to this book demonstrates, the term might also be part of an ongoing correspondence between Spicer and Duncan about the former's work.

31. Thus, a large proportion of Spicer's appallingly anti-Semitic texts are found in a passionate exchange with Steve Jonas, in which a white man and a black man forge a bond of shared racist negative attachment, directed against the Jew. See *P*, pp. 71–3, for an excellent account of this.

32. See *P*, pp. 123–7, for a full account, which includes a letter from Levertov about the event.

33. John Vincent also notes that the poem presents the "paradox" of "perfection as hideous" (*Queer*, 150).

34. As Ron Silliman noted years ago, this poem "may be Spicer's sharpest assault on the indulgences of projectivism" (*New Sentence*, 150). Silliman is right to name the tendency rather than the poet who coined the term, as Olson's essay "Projective Verse" and his poetics generally are much more subtle and conflicted than they are often presented as being; in the Vancouver lectures Spicer considers himself fundamentally aligned with Olson, albeit an Olson that many of his followers might not have recognized. It is certain, however, that the primacy of body as substantial

subjective self-presence, and breath as grounding natural rhythm for the line, which many derive from Olson, are both rejected by Spicer.

35. To be contrasted to Whitman, who closes "Song of Myself" with an invocation of his body's dispersion and dissemination throughout the natural world: "I bequeath myself to the dirt to grow from the grass I love, / If you want me again look for me under your boot-soles" (247).

36. Spicer's quibble on "nothing" as substantive should also be read as in dialogue with Wallace Stevens' "The Snowman," a poet with whom Spicer shares a great deal. Throughout the latter part of his life Spicer increasingly used line breaks to pressure syntactic negation generally; Chapter 5 examines this in detail, as well as another quibble on the "nothing" of "The Snowman," this time in the first poem of *Language.*

Chapter 3

The Metasexual City: Politics, Nonsense, Poetry

> "Polis
> is this"
> Charles Olson, "Maximus to Gloucester, Letter 27
> [withheld]" (185)

> "Nonsense is an act of friendship."
> *The Unvert Manifesto* (CP, 75)

As we saw in the previous chapter, at a crucial moment in *After Lorca* "Jack" addresses himself to the Spanish poet as "your special comrade," a term that joins the Whitmanian euphemism for gay lover to the discourse of international communist fellowship which came to the fore so prominently among the American left during the Spanish Civil War – the occasion, of course, of Lorca's death. While Spicer was not a communist, it is hardly by chance that at the heart of the McCarthyite 1950s he chose such a politically charged term of endearment. Nor is it a coincidence that the book which Spicer himself considered his breakthrough in terms of poetics was written under the auspices of an exchange with a gay predecessor, and holds at its heart a reckoning with Whitman, for if the work is concerned throughout with the possibilities of contact, exchange, community, and "correspondence" in general, it is utterly specific in its address to gay poets. As Robert Duncan retrospectively stressed in his 1972 preface to *Caesar's Gate*: "It seemed to us, to Jack Spicer as to me, in our conversations of 1946 and 1947 as young poets seeking the language and lore of our homosexual longings as the matter of a poetry, that Lorca was one of us, that he spoke here [in the "Ode to Walt Whitman"] from his own unanswered and – as he saw it – *unanswerable* need" (xxii). For Spicer, *After Lorca*, with its insistence on "correspondence" and epistolary dialogue, is very much a gesture of response to just such a demanding "need": the dispatch of an answer to the dead and now literally unanswerable Lorca. Although Spicer *also* defines such "death" and the attendant "loneliness" of the demand that can never be met as fundamental to *all* poetry, it is certainly the case that his elaboration of the "book" is inextricable from his reflections on queer poetics, and concomitantly, queer politics and queer community. Such concerns date back at least, as Duncan suggests, to their meeting and remain at the center of Spicer's poetry and poetics throughout his life; indeed, even the most extreme dictates of "dictation" never have the consequence of obscuring the specifically homoerotic affect of what is written "through" Spicer. That said, it is worth noting that Spicer's most extended explicit engagement with queer culture and queer writing was composed during the crucial year in Boston, at around the same moment that *After Lorca* began to take shape. This is the *Unvert Manifesto*, with its accompanying and apparently unfinished "Oliver Charming" papers.[1] Ironic, bitter, deflationary, campy, and funny, the "Charming" papers are a very different work from *After Lorca*, but nonetheless are as earnest an effort to think through possibilities of gay culture, subculture and exchange as the latter text, while making recourse to quite different but recognizable traditions of queer writing – notably, as the name suggests, those deriving from Wilde. As we shall see, the "Charming" papers represent in some ways a culmination of Spicer's thinking on the problems of queer writing, identity, and politics that had been occupying him very greatly ever since the early days at Berkeley. Indeed, if the Berkeley Renaissance can be said to begin with the meeting of Spicer, Blaser, and Duncan, then at its origin lies the placing of just such questions to the forefront, notably by Duncan himself: an entirely extraordinary interlocutor for a very young gay poet to come across in 1946, and quite possibly the pre-eminent exemplum of the imbrication of the sexual, the poetic, and the political for American gay poets of his generation. The example of Duncan is crucial to an understanding of what – perhaps surprisingly – emerges as a consistent and decidedly political focus throughout Spicer's life and thinking, notably from 1946 to 1953.

In 1944, two years before he and Spicer first met, Duncan had published the almost unprecedented essay, "The Homosexual in Society," in Dwight MacDonald's influential journal, *Politics*.[2] The short essay portrays the "homosexual" as forced to skirt two traps: "persecution" by and "excommunication" from society at large (319), and what Duncan saw as the exclusionary and soul-destroying "homosexual cult of superiority" (321) obtaining even among "the most radical, the most enlightened 'queer' circles" (320). According to Duncan, too many gay artists caught in this dilemma ultimately betray the "struggle toward self-recognition" in order "to sell their product, to convert their deepest feelings into marketable oddities and sentimentalities" (319). Tellingly, in *Admonitions* Spicer will write of poetic alienation in a rhetoric which echoes that which Duncan had used to discuss the homosexual variety over a decade before, lamenting his former practice of converting his "angers and frustrations" into poetry "as one would exchange foreign money" (CP, 163). Like "self-recognition" for the gay artist, poetry in its highest sense demands and makes possible a new economic relationship to one's experience, and even to the concept of oneself, as the theory of dictation makes clear. In Duncan's essay, the imperative to this self-recognition remains absolutely paramount – so much so that despite his ambivalence about gay subculture (one which echoes in many ways Lorca's anguished attack on the "maricas" in his "Ode to Walt Whitman"[3]) and his call to "disown *all* the special groups (nations, religions, sexes, races) that would claim allegiance" (322, original italics), Duncan still insists that the gay artist must express himself openly, eschewing coded or oblique references: ". . . in the face of the 'crime' of my own feelings, in the past I publicized those feelings as private and made no stand for their recognition but tried to sell them disguised, for instance, as conflicts rising from mystical sources" (321). Crucially, fidelity to the call of "recognition" also led Duncan to rebuff MacDonald's offer to publish the essay anonymously, insisting to the contrary: *"the whole thing has no meaning if it is not signd [sic]"* (cited in Faas, 150, original italics). Duncan was soon reminded of the stakes of such a courageous stance: after reading the essay, John Crowe Ransom, editor of the leading poetry outlet *The Kenyon Review*, withdrew Duncan's "African Elegy" on the grounds that it seemed to him "an advertisement or a notice of overt homosexuality, and we are not in the market for literature of this type" (cited in Faas, 153), and this despite having happily accepted the "very brilliant" contribution about a year before.[4] *The Kenyon Review* was among the most important academic poetry journals of its day, and Duncan's exclusion from the mainstream and ultimate positioning among the avant-garde, as this story demonstrates, was due at least as much to the sexual identity he caused to be associated with his signature as to the characteristics of his poetry.

If I've dwelled on the immediate aftershocks of Duncan's essay at some length, it is because I believe the episode is foundational for both the Berkeley scene of the late 1940s and for Spicer's subsequent ethical and political positionings to an extent not fully registered in most of the criticism. Throughout the Berkeley Renaissance, Duncan faithfully stood by the principles of "The Homosexual in Society" and the implications of being its signator. The circle of mostly younger, often gay poets gathered around him – most notably Spicer and Robin Blaser – worked energetically and deliberately to create spaces where they could live uncloseted and circulate their work freely, with remarkable success. It is little short of astonishing that in the late 1940s, to all appearances Robert Duncan was able to read lines like these at officially sanctioned, on-campus University of California events: "Yet here seeks the heart solace. / Nature barely provides for it. / Men fuck men by audacity. / Yet here the heart bounds / as if only here, / here it might rest" ("The Venice Poem," *First Decade*, 90). But not surprisingly, such "audacity" did not long go unobserved or unpunished: Duncan, Spicer, Blaser, and their circle had been prime movers in the English Department affiliated "Writer's Conference" student workshops, and the associated publication, *Literary Behavior*. Both were quashed by the Department in 1949, largely from concern over the homosexual cast of so many of the participants and so much of the work.[5] This must have seemed a perfect example of the "persecution" and "excommunication" to which Duncan had alluded in 1944, and both he and Spicer wrote poems commemorating the event. Moreover, another pernicious institutional attack on civil and political rights arrived in 1950, when the Sloan-Levering Act of the state of California imposed a McCarthyite "loyalty oath" on all university employees, a category including graduate teaching assistants. Although too much an anarchist to feel more than limited sympathy for communism, Spicer subscribed to Duncan's insistence on a politics that recognized the power of the signature, and refused to sign on ethical grounds.[6] He was forced to spend nearly two years at the University of Minnesota as a consequence, until changes in regulations allowed him to return to California.

The question of the loyalty oath and of loyalties generally was to return to haunt Spicer in 1953, when he joined the semi-clandestine gay rights organization, the Mattachine Society, becoming a prominent member of its Berkeley and Oakland chapter. While broadly leftwing and progressive in its original inspiration, the Society was rapidly taken over by more conservative assimilationists who, in their zeal to demonstrate the compatibility of homosexuality with "American values," embarked on an anti-communist witch-hunt of their own, demanding public repudiation of communism by the Society, and threatening to ferret out communist sympathizers among their membership. Along with most of the Berkeley and Oakland chapter, Spicer left in disgust in the autumn of 1953, but Kevin Killian's recent archival research into the detailed minutes of Mattachine meetings has revealed Spicer as one of the most active members of his chapter during his time with the organization, particularly within the discussion groups devoted to questions such as the aetiology of homosexuality, minority culture and assimila-tion, and the presentation of gay life histories and experiences.[7] To facilitate these groups, Spicer developed a questionnaire which, Killian convincingly argues, is a direct precursor to the famous questionnaire of the "Poetry as Magic" workshop (*CP*, 99–104): a crucial example of the constant link in Spicer between pedagogy, poetry, and eros. More generally, it would seem from Killian's account that true to form, Spicer very frequently took up positions received as contrarian, or delibera-tively provocative, such as that gay men with bisexual feelings should cultivate them as long as possible (26), or that Irish Americans in the nineteenth century offered a good case study of how a "scorned" minor-ity group came to enjoy social acceptance; he also questioned whether integration into the mainstream was even a desirable goal (29). Indeed, it appears that Spicer's most interesting interventions were on the ques-tion of minority culture generally and gay culture in particular, as in this fascinating speech from a statewide meeting held in Los Angeles, May 23–24, 1953:

> In the beginning I objected to the word 'culture' on these grounds: when asked whether I am homosexual, I answered by asking 'When?' Then it was pointed out to me that I am homosexual not only when I am indulging in a sexual expression, I am homosexual many other times. Perhaps there is something inherent in homosexuality that gives me a different response to the world that I live in. Or perhaps there is something inherent to my adjust-ment to homosexuality in contemporary society that determines my method of expression. But at any rate, I am homosexual a good deal of the time and I draw from, I exist in, and I hope I may contribute to an area of expression and activity which may be defined by the name 'culture.'
>
> We think of many men who are prompted because of their homosexuality to do certain things . . . So I like the word 'culture' now because I see it has a meaning, a meaning of activity, thought, or expression. However, we are not an isolated group. We belong to humanity. (27)[8]

Spicer's concluding affirmation that the potentially "isolated group" must never lose its place among "humanity" at large strikingly echoes the position Duncan had outlined in "The Homosexual in Society," where he worried about the exclusionary tendencies of queer subcul-tures. However, Spicer adds a third dimension to the equation, in the form of an anarchist insistence on individual liberty and responsibility; his breaks with the University of California and Mattachine arose not from communist conviction but in support of the principle of "personal and intellectual freedom" (*CP*, xxv) as he put it in his draft protest to the University of California at Berkeley. For Spicer, the problem is not only the danger of suffocating narcissistic parochialism inherent in any subcultural identification, but that group identification in almost any form is seen by him as a threat to the individual in and of itself. In this context, the Mattachine experience seems to have left Spicer seriously in doubt as to whether gay cultural and political organization and activism were a means towards greater "freedom," or another element that would quash it. To a significant extent, Spicer lapses into truism in insisting that they are both, and there is no question that a form of naïve individualism can often lead Spicer's politics into the banal. What gives the politics the depth they have, however, is that in some moods Spicer's suspicion of identification, rather than remaining a defense mechanism to protect an imperiled self, extends even to the identification with that very self as such, as concepts such as "dictation," "the big lie of the personal" or, as we shall see, "nonsense" imply. Ultimately, for Spicer the individual is just as tyrannical a structure as the group, for one's very individuality. And thus, if Spicer is wary of communal constructs and their pressures, at the same time it is community itself and all its "correspondences" which offer the only escape from an individuality that is, for Spicer, fundamentally unfree, a "prison," as he so often deems the body to be. Thus, if Spicer's politics are vexed, incoherent, violent, and at times inspiring, it is precisely because they refuse to divvy up the question of the relations to self, other, and others along the traditional lines of public and private, ethics and desire. In certain ways, his politics resist the political and its domain in ways analogous to how his poetry resists the poem. At the same time, both the abstract question of the polis and more concrete ones concerning gay experience, culture, and activism are recurrent throughout his work, and seem to have been brought to the boil by his immersion in Mattachine. All these ambivalences come together in the diary of Oliver Charming, which in several complex and coded manners revisits much of Spicer's life of the previous few years, including his political activism and commitments, and his musings on queer identity and culture.

The diary, preceded by the *Unvert Manifesto*, begins with an entry in which Charming decides to "unvent" a young man named man Graham Macarel (*CP*, 75), an operation that is "more successful than I [Charming] expected" (*CP*, 76): Charming meets his creation in the flesh, along with his teacher S. (*CP*, 76), a transparent parody of Spicer at his most truculent, surly, misogynistic, and anti-Semitic. Meanwhile, Graham Macarel, as Spicer's drafts confirm, figures Spicer's former student, close friend, and future publisher, Graham Mackintosh.[9] The diary entries, dated from October 31, 1953 (a likely day for raising ghosts or "unventing" a young man) through April 4, 1954, detail Charming's idle thoughts and speculations in addition to encounters with such figures as Macarel, S., Charming's psychiatrist, Robert Berg,[10] and another important "unvention," Emily Dickinson's dour Yankee editor, Thomas Wentworth Higginson, now returned as a cloying, campy, fey "angel." The dates Spicer chose are important: he probably worked on the piece between late 1955 and the autumn of 1956 (when he returned to California), yet he places the diary two years earlier, having it begin very shortly after he left the Mattachine. Additionally, almost exactly a year *after* the fictional date commencing the diary – that is, early October 1954 – he began his intense, affectionate, and erotic correspondence with Graham Mackintosh, which, like the diary entries, is at its highest volume between the months of October and January.[11] In other words, at the very moment that Spicer is thinking through Dickinson's letters and feeling his way toward the epistolary model of *After Lorca*, he reworks a relationship he lived as epistolary into a fictional form which is in many ways the dialectical obverse of the letter: the diary, in which the outward dispatch circles back to the sender, in a closed economy of accumulation and hoarding. For these reasons, the "Charming" papers are a fascinating chart of *how* Spicer moves from the Mattachine to *After Lorca*, while testing an ultimately rejected model of writing that would control the epistolary energies he would soon let loose as a properly poetic mode. The project begins, however, with a pastiche of another hallowed modernist form, one notable for collapsing the distinctions between artistic and political discourse: the manifesto.

The first tenet of the *Unvert Manifesto* is: "An unvert is neither an invert or an outvert, a pervert or a convert, an introvert or a retrovert. An unvert chooses to have no place to turn" (*CP*, 74). If such a statement defines the "unvert" as someone stuck within a sexual impasse that he or she has willingly created, it is also worth noting that given the etymological play which is a constant of Spicer's work, "unvert" can be glossed as "straight." Indeed, an important suggestion throughout the "Charming" project is that homosexuality per se is not particularly interesting or, at the very least, epiphenomenal to the broader question of sexuality. The Manifesto's sixth point reads: "An unvert must not be homosexual, heterosexual, bisexual, or autosexual. He must be metasexual. He must enjoy going to bed with his own tears" (*CP*, 74). Similarly, in his diary Charming will express his amazement that ". . . even the people who struggle most against the limits of art are content to have sex in ordinary academic ways, as if they and their bed-partners were nineteenth-century paintings" (*CP*, 77–8), including Cocteau among the culprits, before classifying Kinsey as the Zola of sex, who is hopefully "preparing the way for the new Lautréamont" (*CP*, 78). As a remedy, the Manifesto proclaims: "Unversion is the attempt to make the sexual act as rare as a rosepetal. It consists of linking the sexual with the greatest cosmic force in the universe – Nonsense, or as we prefer to call it, MERTZ" (*CP*, 74). It goes on to specify that "Sex should be a frightening experience like a dirty joke or an angel" (*CP*, 74), which should also be frightening themselves. Mertz, then, is very much a project of the dedomestication of sexuality, countering a peril to which homosexuality is just as prone as any other form of sexual life.[12]

An important episode in the diaries reinforces this impression. If Charming begins by suspecting that S. "is secretly an unvert" (*CP*, 76), he is not long in deciding that S. "does not understand unversion" (*CP*, 79), following a discussion at the Black Cat, a famous San Francisco gay bar.[13]

> We began discussing homosexuality. I, by bringing in subtle pieces of unvert propaganda, and he, embarrassed and overintellectual as if he thought, or rather hoped, that I was trying to seduce him:
> "We homosexuals are the only minority group that completely lacks any vestige of a separate cultural heritage. We have no songs, no folklore, even our customs are borrowed from our upper-middle-class mothers," he said.
> "What about camping?" I asked. "Isn't that a cultural pattern worthy at least of Ruth Benedict's cunt?"
> "What about camping?" he asked rhetorically. "A perpetual Jewish vaudeville joke – or, at the very best, a minstrel show impeccably played by Negros in blackface."
> The trouble with S. is that he doesn't understand Martian. I must tell him about the time . . . (*CP*, 79)

While S. echoes aspects of Spicer's Mattachine speech on the question of gay culture, note that here its attributes are found to be only negative and derivative, objects of shame and disappointment. Even more, the diary as a whole implies that S.'s obsession with gay cultural definition and identification leads inevitably to an identity politics of aggressive anathematization of other "competing" minority formations, in what Maria Damon has pithily called: "a jockeying for one-down on the hierarchy of the oppressed, a rivalry that comes out in bitterness and resentment" (*Dark*, 165). As Damon rightly stresses, this often racist and misogynist "more-oppressed-than-thou *ressentiment*" (165) can be found in many places in Spicer's work, but the fact that a good many of its most extreme expressions are proffered by S. indicates that Spicer exercised at least some critical perspective on this type of rant.[14] Thus, S. angrily demands of Charming "Why don't you tell us a story that doesn't depend on the Jews? . . . Why don't you tell a story with an Aryan hero in it?" (*CP*, 86), and later sneers "Women are the enemies of the sexual imagination" (*CP*, 89). On the other hand, rather than launch insults, Charming enjoys serious sessions with his psychiatrist, who seems to unvert standard practice (certainly, standard practice in the America of the 1950s) by privileging the manifest dream over its interpretation, and psychic interiority over adaptation to any sort of "reality principle": "It is his theory that psychiatrists should teach people how to dream properly . . . It is his feeling that the world of Mertz is the world of the dreamer" and that the "truly Mertzian act" cannot be forced upon "reality" (*CP*, 81–2). With Berg and in opposition to S., Charming continues his Mertzian devotion to nonsense, suggesting the historical precursors to unversion might be: "The men who almost succeeded in freeing us from the yoke of sexual meaning" (*CP*, 83).

Thus, one of the work's implications is that S.'s angers and frustrations derive from his refusal to embrace the "nonsense" underlying all sexual relations, hiding instead behind the bulwark of an over-invested homosexual identity, of which the positive content escapes him in any event. At the same time, the ironic structure of the entire piece greatly complicates any such neat division: as one of Charming's "unventions," S. can be seen as a self-serving straw man, existing only to give comfort to Charming's own hardly tenable positions. For example, if the concept of "metasexuality" remains tenuous throughout, Damon's definition of it as a "preoccupation with sex not necessarily accompanied by sexual activity" (*Dark*, 164) is reasonable. Moreover, Charming himself is capable of echoing S.'s reliance on racist categories, as in the *Unvert Manifesto*: "Jews and Negros are not allowed to be unverts. The Jew will never understand unversion and the Negro understands it too well" (*CP*, 75). This passage, conjugated with S.'s dismissal of camping, aligns Blacks and Jews with homosexuals as groups opposed to or incapable of unversion, and in an unhappy proximity to one another as minorities. What seemed to be the liberating potential of affiliating homosexuals with other minority groups in the Mattachine meetings is turned upside down. Meanwhile, "unversion," despite its devotion to nonsense, reveals its essential likeness to so many other post-Enlightenment universalist (or better, perhaps, "unversalist") projects: its nonsense is transcendental, and cannot accommodate the specificity of historically determined, marginalized cultural positions, and the particular forms of nonsense they entail. Spicer's double-bind again revisits the opposition between oppressive mainstream society and constricting gay subcultural identity that Duncan had sketched in "The Homosexual in Society." An attempt to build a gay cultural identity leads only to paranoid and hollow defensive gestures of differentiation, while the desire to transcend "sexual meaning" ultimately annihilates differences that are in fact meaningful.

Charming himself seems to respond to Duncan's dilemma in one short, fragmentary entry: "To appear as human among homosexuals and to appear as divine among heterosexuals . . ." (*CP*, 77). This evocation of the "divine" ties into the concept of "angelism" that increasingly dominates Charming's reflections and distinguishes the unvert position, in language which again recasts some of Spicer's Mattachine speculations: "The negro's aim is integration. The Jew's and the homosexual's aim is segregation. The unvert's aim is a grand degradation between men and angels" (*CP*, 83). If "angelism" is never defined, its non-definition revolves, like Mertz, around the question of the existence of meaning itself: "'Angelism is merely a symptom of wanting forbidden meanings,' Mac said . . . 'Angelism is merely a symptom of wanting there to be forbidden meanings,' Kathy says sweetly . . ." (*CP*, 90). The "papers" end with the partial transcript of an Alice in Wonderland-like trial where Charming, accused of "contagious angelism" (*CP*, 91) is defended by the television series lawyer, Perry Mason, on the following grounds: "Your honor, I have evidence to prove that my client does not exist" (*CP*, 93). That evidence is disallowed, yet the trial ends with S. being sworn, and the prosecutor asking the tantalizing question: "Are you acquainted with the defendant?" (*CP*, 94) – a final gesture that effectively reverses Charming's "unvention" of S., suggesting a mise-en-abyme in which S. himself is responsible for the entire story of his own imaginary genesis.[15] This also implies that if Charming's non-existence is in fact a legitimate ground of defense, then S. will have to answer for Charming's crimes. The ending of "Charming" is inconclusive to say the least, but his ultimate trial for spreading a contagious and corrupting philosophical doctrine with clear sexual implications leads beyond Wilde to another crucial gay predecessor and another S., indeed, one of the most important thinkers of all on the relationship between homoerotic affect, community, and thought. This would be Socrates, whom Charming had previously dubbed the "first and greatest of Dada poets who was able to unseduce Alcibiades as if he were a piece of rough trade" (*CP*, 83).[16]

Indeed, in the late 1950s Spicer revisited that first trial, in a short lyric titled "Socrates": "Because they accused me of poems / That did not disturb the young / They gave me a pair of glasses / Filled with tincture of hemlock" (*CP*, 179), it begins, reversing the crime of the historical Socrates. Here, he is guilty of *failing* to rouse the young, rather than the contrary. As punishment, the pun on "pair of glasses" implies not only a poisoning of his body but a poisoning of his vision, leading perhaps to a more "disturbing" stance. However, in Spicer's version, the "young" also accuse Socrates "Of piles, horseradish, and bad dreams" and he is given "three days / To burn down the city." The poem ends with this regret: "What dialogues / (If they had let me) / Could I have held with both of my enemies" (*CP*, 179). The burning of the "city" is not an idle detail: this poem is entirely consonant with Michael Davidson's still unsurpassed, paradigm-forging work on community and the trope of the "city" in Spicer, the latter term naming the place where "poetry is created in dialogue and argumentation . . . If that dialogue is contentious . . . so much the better" (*San Francisco*, 154). Davidson focuses above all on *The Heads of the Town up to the Aether*, in which "the city that we create in our bartalk or in our fuss and fury about each other" (*CP*, 306) becomes the ideal space of the dialogic sociality of argument and exchange which enables poetry.[17] I would only like to add that Spicer's city seems very much that of Socrates also.

As Leo Bersani has recently specified, at the outset of *Phaedrus* – a text to which Spicer explicitly refers in *The Heads of the Town up to the Aether* – Socrates pointedly expresses his displeasure at being outside the city, despite the beauty of the countryside. It is the city and its people with their questions which provide the proper space for thinking and philosophy, as in Spicer's city of bartalk that Davidson examines. But even more, as Bersani stresses, for complex, ostensibly philosophical reasons that *Phaedrus* explores at length, Socrates "needs to be in the company of beautiful boys" in order to think properly, and "the city's meeting places are the sites of a metaphysical sociability sympathetic to the beneficent madness of love" (81). For Spicer too, Eros, dialogue, and pedagogy go together, with poetry taking the place of philosophy, and all of them finding their locus in a city which seems to owe much to that of Socrates, as one can hear in this letter to Robert Duncan from 1960, lamenting the failure of what might be thought of as a Spicerian Lyceum: the alternative White Rabbit College, which he and Duncan had hoped to launch:

> The word is responsibility. It seems to me that poets have a bond of responsibility to each other even more sacred than that of lover to lover. It was not to influence Rimbaud or to be influenced by Rimbaud that I wanted this college, but so that we both (he and I) could begin to learn a map of this city we walk in so seldom. The responsibility between lovers is, after all, an act of love. All the rest is traffic noise.
>
> Why should I tell you this? You were the first person to show me that the city was there.
>
> > Love
> > Jack
>
> (Poetry Collection of the University Libraries, University at Buffalo, State University of New York)

Typically, the Spicerian "city" is one in which the beautiful boy is also both a great poet and a ghost, and the cityspace itself anything but a tangible reality to be mapped terrestrially. But if such a city feels quintessentially Spicerian, he was, as we have seen, entirely right to credit Duncan with showing him that a city of poetry, a gay city, and a city of gay poetry, if only virtual, might be somewhere. The Oliver Charming project was an initial attempt to sketch such a place, in its fantastic melange of the Boston Public Library's rare book room and well known San Francisco cafes and bars, like The Place and the Black Cat. But this project is continued and extended five years later in *The Heads of the Town up to the Aether*, with its unspecific "city," an overdetermined term able to condense the City of God, Dante's Florence, and Socrates' Athens, for a start. Via the "city," Spicer explores the political through its etymon, using a word which both translates the Greek *polis* and also references the shorthand by which San Francisco is known in the greater Bay Area. And for Spicer, the political is still also the pedagogic, the poetical, and the sexual, which explains why "A Textbook of Poetry" reworks Charming material in the heart of a dense discussion of poetics: "And this is a system of metasexual metaphor. Being faithful to the nonsense of it: The warp and woof. A system of dreaming fake dreams" (*CP*, 304).

At the same time, the model of Socrates also serves to emphasize the importance not only of community but of dissidence and isolation in Spicer's politics. If constructing communities is a constant concern for him, no less so is fracturing consensus, through outrageous, provocative speech, or acts of principled, ostentatious defiance that take on their meaning from the price they exact: death for Socrates, exile for Dante and also Spicer, when he refused to sign the loyalty oath. Such oppositional positions are valuable not only because they chastise or "admonish" a complacent community in need of reform, but also, as we have seen, because the anarchist Spicer remains deeply suspicious of the community as form, and therefore divisiveness is often posited as a value in itself.[18] Indeed, in *Three Marxist Essays* Spicer values homosexuality precisely because of a possibility for isolation he attributes to it:

> Homosexuality is essentially being alone. Which is a fight against the capitalist bosses who do not want us to be alone. Alone we are dangerous.
> Our dissatisfaction could ruin America. Our love could ruin the universe if we let it. (*CP*, 328)[19]

All important discussions of Spicer's politics have emphasized his tendency to paranoid fantasies of victimization and projected aggression. In an incisive recent reading, Christopher Nealon has argued that for

Spicer poetry "works as a kind of counterenclosure to the encroach-
ments of mass culture, the culture of business, and the enlarged scale
of violence after the world wars" (110) but he also points to the occasional "paranoid" aspects of this position, such as their manifestation
as anti-Semitism (120) or the personal quarrels Spicer himself tended to
provoke. Nealon quite aptly summarizes the pressures felt by Spicer's
own coterie in these terms: ". . . the poets around Spicer felt a constant
tension between the world-making possibilities of the poem, as Spicer
expounded on it, and the world-enclosing strategies meant to protect
'poetry'" (114).[20] Such tensions, I would argue, both give rise to and are
dictated by Spicer's properly oxymoronic conceptualization of communal political agency, itself the outgrowth of Spicer's take on the position
of the homosexual in society: "Alone we are dangerous." *The Heads of
the Town up to the Aether* is very much concerned with how the first
two words of that proclamation can be placed beside each other, how
one can remain a first person plural, yet alone. This is what makes it a
love poem. It is also a political poem in its interest in a social economy
in which the satisfactions of solipsistic separateness and those of communal belonging, rather than being reconciled, each serve to shatter the
other.

   The Heads of the Town up to the Aether is the longest and most
complexly structured of all Spicer's books, and in many ways, the most
ambitious. It is composed of three separate subsections which, while
brought together within the larger structure, can still to some extent
be read as separate "books"; in his first Vancouver lecture, Spicer only
reads the last section, *A Textbook of Poetry*.[21] According to Spicer,
the work's three sections – *Homage to Creeley*, *A Fake Novel about
the Life of Arthur Rimbaud*, and finally, *A Textbook* – correspond
to the tripartite structure of Dante's *Commedia*, and move from Hell
through Purgatory and on to Paradise. Spicer specifies that despite these
distinctions, all three sections "connect in very important ways" (*H*,
18), explaining, "Throughout the whole book runs the business of the
pathway down into Hell and the methods of communication – the radio,
the dead letter office, and the fake novel. And finally, this 'Textbook'
which is printed as if it were prose and has to be read more or less as if
it were prose" (*H*, 19). Spicer's comments here have a few interesting
implications. First of all, as the entire work is concerned with pathways
and "methods of communication," Spicer's three eternal realms don't
entirely stay in their places, but are constantly displacing themselves
within the larger structure, and finding new ways to forge links to and
spaces within each other. Second of all, the emphasis on the prose of the
Textbook is important. *Homage to Creeley* refers to the poet it names

most clearly in its use of the line; throughout the book, Spicer experiments with the sharp, chiseled, angular lines of Creeley's brilliant early lyrics more than anywhere else in his corpus. By the *Textbook*, on the contrary, the line has lost all structuring power whatsoever, giving way not only to the sentence, whose importance for Spicer Ron Silliman has so crucially noted, but even more to an even less likely unit: the paragraph. *The Heads of the Town* needs very much to be thought of as a curious journey to prose.[22] Finally, while Dante's realms famously allegorize the Hell of History, the Purgatory of human striving for perfection in Poetry, and the Paradise of Theology, Spicer's alignments are different: now it's obviously poetics – and pedagogy – that correspond to the paradise of the *Textbook*, while Spicer himself stipulates that the purgatorial *Fake Novel* is concerned above all with history.[23]

It's more difficult to gauge where *Homage to Creeley* fits in. This book is itself, like the larger structure within which it sits, divided into three, each section corresponding to a major figure from Jean Cocteau's film, *Orphée*. Thus part one is for Cegeste, the young poet who dies at the film's outset and broadcasts messages from Hell through Orpheus' car radio; part two is for the Princess, a representative of death and the underworld Cocteau adds to the original myth; part three goes to Heurtebise, the Princess' chauffeur and a Hermes-like figure, who moves between the earth and the underworld by way of mirrors. At the same time, as many commentators note, the poem creates its own underworld through the addition of the "explanatory notes" found beneath a dividing line drawn near the bottom of each page. This effect, a nod to *Kora in Hell*, makes the poem also a homage to William Carlos Williams, himself a massively important precedent for Creeley's own approach to line and idiom. Which leads to an interesting note: if the entire poem is conducted under the aegis of Cocteau, who for both Spicer and Duncan practices a specifically queer aesthetic, *Homage* is also the Hell of straight poets, along with being, as the first poem makes clear, the Hell of carnal love:

SEVERAL YEARS' LOVE

Two loves I had. One rang a bell
Connected on both sides with hell

The other'd written me a letter
In which he said I've written better

They pushed their cocks in many places
And I'm not certain of their faces
Or which I kissed or which I didn't
Or which of both of them I hadn't.

(CP, 250)

This poem sets up a series of pathways or communications only to thwart or redirect them: the bell is no intercom between the above and below but only connects hell to itself. As opposed to this enclosed circuit of infernal signals, the other love makes use of the post office, but to effect an exchange which is only about that exchange itself, perhaps a version of the "metasexuality" that *Heads of the Town* and Charming both debate. Crucially, the "notes" stipulate "the letter, naturally . . . was written to somebody else" (*CP*, 250), implying additional triangulation, displacement, and misdirection. Meanwhile, the lovers' faces fade against the pressure of their pushy cocks, leaving the poet "uncertain" not as to what he had, but what he "hadn't" – an entirely Dicksonian evocation of an unmistakable loss which, in its precise contours, is itself precisely what is lost to the poem.[24] The second lyric, "Car Song," raises the question of language and poetry in relation to the infernal crossings that are never quite accomplished in "Several Years' Love": "We pin our puns to our backs and cross in a car / The intersections where lovers are. / The wheel and the road turn into a stair / The pun at our backs is a yellow star" (*CP*, 251). The notes add: "'Intersections' is a pun. 'Yellow stars' are what the Jews wore. The stair is what extends back and forth for Heurtebise and Cegeste and the Princess always to march on" (*CP*, 251). As a pun, "intersections" might refer to the subsections of the larger poem, *Heads of the Town*, or more bawdily, to the interior sections of the body, where lovers meet. Meanwhile, as the road morphs into a staircase to hell reminiscent of the one from "Birdland, California," the pun becomes a stigma, as the poem finishes: "We pin our puns on the windshield like / We crossed each crossing in hell's despite" (*CP*, 251). The demotic "like" is interesting, perhaps implying that the crossings were *not* in fact in "hell's despite," that the defiant blazoning of the poetic badge of oppression in fact defies nothing.[25] But equally important, with its emphasis on crossings and intersections the poem thematizes for the first time in the book the two dialectally opposed principal poetic means of parsing relationships which are debated throughout *The Heads of the Town*: metaphor and pun. The former, as Spicer will gloss it, literally means "bearing across," which would make it in many ways the ideal figure for a poem concerned with "pathways" and methods of communication. At the same time, as *Textbook* will explore, the meaning of "bearing across" can be opened by a pun into "bearing a cross": if the pun is the yellow star of the Jews, the metaphor is Jesus on the road to Calvary. But more than this, if a metaphor is a way of joining the disparate, of taking separate things and bringing them together, note that the energies of the pun work in the opposite direction, taking a single word or acoustic signifier and dividing and dispersing it among various meanings. Metaphor and pun in their tension and collaboration try to write through the "alone, we" at the heart of Spicer's politics, erotics, and poetics.[26]

The next poem is almost entirely structured around the interplay between metaphor and pun: "Your joke / Is like a lake / That lies there without any thought" it begins, with a classical metaphorical comparison, before continuing to pun: "And sees / Dead seas" (CP, 252). Additionally, the poem's title, "Concord Hymn" (stolen from Emerson of course) is glossed in the notes as "Conquered Him" (CP, 252). As Part One continues, the sense of the obstacle, the disparate, and the circular is only intensified, as movement, transmission, and communications of all sorts fail to get anyone into or out of hell. "Wrong Turn" is the title of one poem (CP, 253); another, which begins with a second-person address, ends by saying "the poem does not know / Who you refers to," and adds the note: "In hell it is difficult to tell people from other people" (CP, 255). Meanwhile, Spicer's rhetorical strategies of echo and reflection are seen more as entrapping mazes than forms of symbolic joinings: "Cocteau invented mirrors as things to move through. I invent mirrors as obstacles" (CP, 258).[27] Chief among these obstacles, it might be argued, is the centrifugal and dispersive force of language, as evidenced by the pun: "What I mean is words / Turn mysteriously against those who use them / Hello says the apple / Both of us were object" (CP, 257). However, let us not forget that such a "turning against" by the words also describes for Spicer the essence of a dictated poetics, one which in some ways "objectifies" the poet. Which might be why Cegeste, the poet, needs to stay in Hell. Orpheus, on the contrary, is told in the last poem of Part One: "You big poet / We soldiers from hell's country / Here / Safe as you are / You write poetry / For dead persons." The note explains: "This is definitely a warning to Orpheus which he does not understand – being an asshole. This is too bad because there would have been just as much poetry if he had understood it" (CP, 259). Once again, the mistake is to associate poetry with not being a dead man.

Part Two is for the Princess, described as follows in the opening note: "The Princess has a special form to function as a Representative of The Dead. She is almost a Congresswoman for them" (CP, 260). This section, less kinetic than the previous, is less interested in crossings, passages, and communications (though these motifs are still present), and more in images, memories, afterlives, and preservations. "Ghosts drip / And then they leap" (CP, 263) in this more spectral section, haunted, as is the entirety of *Heads of the Town*, by Jim Alexander: "The figure of Jim begins to emerge in the poem. The Poet uses all his resistance to us to try to create the figure of a person at once lost and unlikely. The unlikelyness [*sic*] is also the first hint of metaphor" (*CP*, 262). This section on the "Representative of The Dead" is less about going to visit them, than on how they visit us, as in the beautiful "Partington Ridge," a poem whose title, while naming a cliff above the Big Sur coast, also punningly evokes departure, the edge the ghost rides between presence and absence:

> A white rabbit absolutely outlined in whiteness upon a black background
> A ghost
> The most
> We can say or think about it is it stays.
>
> . . .
>
> It stays
> In a closet we wear like a ring on our fingers
> The rabbit
> Ghost of them
> Most of what we knew.
>
> (*CP*, 268)

The note specifies, "Rabbits do not know what they are. Ghosts are very similar. They are frightened and do not know what they are, but they can go where the rabbits cannot go. All the way to the heart" (*CP*, 268). At the same time, the heart where the ghosts live is discussed in a resonantly queer rhetoric – as a closet which is nevertheless displayed, in the very place where a straight person might mark her or his erotic bond to another.[28] The final poem in the section, "Coda," is a word-for-word repetition of the first, "Awkward Bridge." Thus the section is bracketed by a declaration of love's helplessness before both the demands of its objects and its own grasping selfishness:

> Love isn't proud enough to hate
> The stranger at its gate
> That says and does
>
> Or strong enough to return
> Or strong enough to return (and back and back and back again)
> What was.
>
> (*CP*, 270)

Part Three, for Heurtebise the go-between, opens by suggesting that connections might now begin to be established, giving us a bell which this time seems more functional: "The bell went 'rrrrr' / And we both went 'rrrrr,'" followed by the note: "The bell is the connection – which is more than junky-talk" (*CP*, 271). The entire section begins to point to the *Fake Novel*, which with its motif of the post office is about nothing other than connections, and as the presence of Rimbaud himself reminds us, especially with James Alexander, who also makes a spectral appearance here through the title of the second lyric in the section, "Fort Wayne." That poem also promises "The messages come through at last" (*CP*, 272) and if the remainder of the poem tends to emphasize their obscurity it also makes as definitive a statement as will be found in *Homage*: "For there are poems and Christmas pies / And loves like ours while you blink your eyes / And love rises up like a butterfly" (*CP*, 272). Indeed it is the modalities of interpersonal connections, especially erotic ones, which concern most of the lyrics in the section. We read "Sheer hell / Is where your apartness is your apartness" (*CP*, 276) in a line eschewing both metaphor and pun in favor of tautological definition through repetition, and which seems also a gloss on the Orpheus story, given its title: "It Is Forbidden to Look."[29] At the same time, automobiles return as possible vehicles outside of Hell's boundaries. "Dash" ends with "Everything is in the street / Then they meet / It with their automobiles," followed by a note that tells us that Cegeste "lacks knowledge of the driver's seat as did . . . Creeley, and all of us . . . He [Cegeste's "personal fate"] will wreck their cars if he can have to [*sic*]" (*CP*, 278). Earlier, "The Man in the Wall" tells of a similar sort of wreck; the poem consists almost entirely of a message to Orpheus and Heurtebise that "The bus crashed / . . . / The whole bus crashed with all the bus team" (*CP*, 275).

Part Three is largely inconclusive, even more than the two preceding sections. But interestingly, it is perhaps even more haunted than they by echoes of earlier poets and poems. The "notes" mention Lewis Carroll (*CP*, 271), Poe (*CP*, 273), and Creeley himself (*CP*, 278). Meanwhile, the title "Prayer for My Daughter" (*CP*, 274) is stolen from Yeats, and various passages resound with echo and pastiche. For example, in its rhythm as well as its concerns, the opening line of "It is Forbidden to Look" is positively Dickinsonian, prior to its immediate deflation. "I couldn't get my feeling loose" evokes many Dickinson openings (for example, "I felt a Cleaving in my Mind" (379) or "I felt a Funeral, in my Brain" (153)), but given Spicer's rhymes and vocabulary and the immediate follow-up: "Like a goose I traveled" (*CP*, 276), the most obvious Dickinsonian backdrop might be the poem beginning: "I saw no Way – The Heavens were stitched – / I felt the Columns close – / The Earth reversed her Hemispheres – / I touched the Universe –" (284). Additionally, in "Dillinger" the vocabulary and rhymes of three juxtaposed lines seem an inescapable reference to Frost's "Stopping by Woods on a Snowy Evening": "The human voices put the angels / Pretty far away. The sleigh-bells / In the distance go / As if we had never seen snow" (*CP*, 277).[30] These considerations should inform a reading of the otherwise rather baffling final poem of *Homage to Creeley*, "Blood":

The jokes
Are ghosts
The joke
Is a ghost
How can you love that mortal creature
Everytime he speaks
He makes
Mistakes
Two for one
Three of us vital

(CP, 280)

The poem is followed by a note consisting only of a short citation from one of Blake's prophetic books, and a typically Spicerian negating addendum: the short phrase, enclosed in quotation marks, "O.K." (CP, 280). But the poem above seems to have different sources of allusion. "Blood" certainly refers to the blood fed to the shades in the Odyssey, during Odysseus's famous visit to Tiresias in Book Nine: the episode which inaugurates Pound's Cantos, as Spicer knew, and a motif to which Spicer returns in the Fake Novel and Textbook. But more importantly, the poem itself seems to condense a few lines from another, equally reso-nant source: W. H. Auden's "Lay your sleeping head, my love," which is one of the most famous gay love poems of Spicer's time, and a notable example of Auden's refusal to specify gender in his love lyrics, a gesture whose implications were obvious to gay readers throughout the most closeted years of the twentieth century. There Auden wrote, "But in my arms till break of day / Let the living creature lie, / Mortal, guilty, but to me / The entirely beautiful" (50). Against the vision of "supernatural sympathy" which Auden's Venus sends his lovers (50), Spicer seems to deride the "mortal creature" who makes the mistake of positing oneness when even in love there must be two, or even more than two: "Three of us vital" speaks of what haunts every couple beyond them both, the living ghost in the blood, the stranger at love's gate.

If A Fake Novel About the Life of Arthur Rimbaud is about "history," it is history of a somewhat Mertzian order, featuring large amounts of nonsense and non sequitur, while riffing very loosely on Rimbaud's poetry and biography. In addition to the postal motif generally, the book is traversed more specifically by reflections on the "dead-letter office" as well as manifold but generally random and unexplained references to President Buchanan. This is history as simultaneity, a post-Dada parody of Pound's historical frameworks of the ideogrammic method, the luminous detail, and the "Paideuma." This means that these strands are brought together initially simply by the fact that Rimbaud was born in 1854, Buchanan was President from 1857 to 1860, and Melville's

"Bartleby the Scrivener" – presumably the impetus behind the dead-letter office – was first published in book form in *The Piazza Tales*, in 1856.[31] At the same time, another logic seems to be at work: one imagines that Buchanan is present because the only bachelor President of the United States was rumored to be gay even in his own lifetime, and Spicer was entirely cognizant of the homoeroticism in Melville; indeed, if the *Heads* as a whole is about the relationship between eros, poetry, and community, this is certainly the most explicitly queer section. On yet another level, Bartleby himself (though never mentioned in the text) could be read as a figure for Rimbaud, the former's "I would prefer not to" a parallel to Rimbaud's shocking abandonment of poetry in his early twenties, despite the hardly believable level of achievement he had already attained. What must be remembered is that all of the above is left entirely to the reader to infer; the rhetorical mode of the text is not metaphorical assertion but wholly implicit "correspondences" which the reader must attempt to establish. And this is entirely appropriate for a work which returns to the "postoffice" of the *Letters to James Alexander*, and considers throughout how messages come to be exchanged.

Indeed, the *Novel*'s first chapter is titled "The Dead Letter Office," and begins by positing the post office as the privileged site of poetry: "Rimbaud was born in the Charlieville postoffice" (*CP*, 281), or subsequently, "He [Rimbaud] wrote poetry at the base of the postoffice" (*CP*, 283).[32] This space, it would seem, is opposed by the Dead Letter Office: "The Dead-Letter-Office was in another part of the building. They put it there deliberately knowing that Rimbaud would not be born in it" (*CP*, 283). But as we might suspect, Spicer shall not be content to contrast the "living poetry" of Rimbaud with a "dead" writing associated with undelivered letters and lost messages, even if it seems so at the outset. By Chapter VII of Book One, we find, "The dead are not alive. That is what this unattractive prose wants to stamp out. Once you see an end to it, you believe that the dead are alive" (*CP*, 284). This transformation of the dead out of their death is increasingly what Rimbaud and poetry are seen as being about: "Rimbaud will turn sixteen, invent what my shrewdness (our shrewdnesses) will not remember, come to a more usable concept of sex and poetry – a machine to catch ghosts" (*CP*, 290). These ghosts are defined in the midst of a series of Sphinx-like riddles: "What is seen in the distance when the murmurings of some defeated ideas, or lives, or even dreams are suddenly manifest? A ghost" (*CP*, 292). Ultimately, the ghost figures a form of being beyond the opposition of the quick and the dead, where both can correspond. The *Novel* closes on this very note: "I mean that the reader of this novel is a ghost. Involved. Involved in the lives of Rimbaud" (*CP*, 298).

This being the case, the question of the death of the "dead letters" and their "officer" is complex. Early in the poem, "The Dead Letter Officer" is the title of Chapter II of Book One and emerges as a figure for the bureaucratic, technocratic state, identified with history over and against poetry: "He [the Dead Letter Officer] had enrolled in the French government when he was very young and liked the thought of being there while history was happening. He took a census of Rimbaud" (*CP*, 281–2). Chapter VI of Book Three, however, bears the very same title, but produces a very different text:

> Inside every Rimbaud was a ready-made dead-letter officer. Who really mailed the letter? Who stole the signs?
>
> The signs of his youth and his poetry. The way he looked at things as if they were the last things to be alive.
>
> The robes of his office are vague and noble. He has a hat that he wears on his head. His arms are attached to his shoulders.
>
> Our contempt for him is general and is echoed even in the house of the dead. Blood would not appease his ghost which stays in us even after we are in the house of the dead. He is in every corpse, in every human life.
>
> He writes poems, pitches baseballs, fails us whenever we have a nerve to need him. Button-molder too, he grows in us like the river of years. (*CP*, 295–6)

A virus infecting both life and death (in every corpse and every life), this Officer is also an imposter (writing poems and mailing letters which might not be his), a thief, and a cheat – "stealing signs" is a classic form of cheating in baseball, a connotation the poem's reference to the sport supports. He bitches our death, the ghostliness Spicer demands of a reader or a poet, as much as our life. And indeed: what would it mean for the house of the dead to be haunted, when haunting is nothing other than the intrusion of death into life? In some ways, the Dead Letter Officer corresponds to "the English Department of the spirit – that great quagmire that lurks at the bottom of all of us" (*CP*, 163), but it is also tempting to align him with Thoth, the Hermes-like Egyptian god of writing, who arrives in the penultimate letter to James Alexander to link the letters of the alphabet to Rimbaud's "vowels," and both of the above to James Alexander's unvoiceable poetry and the epistolary letter as form (*CP*, 215).[33] And of course, all of these concerns reappear massively in the *Novel*, which throws in a consideration of numbers, important to Rimbaud but also because Thoth is god of number and calculation as well as writing. In counting out his own legacy, Spicer seems at times to allude to Thoth's domain: "There is left a universe of letters and numbers and what I have told you. For Jim" (*CP*, 291). Additionally, Thoth, through his association with Hermes, is also often figured as a god of mediation and transmission generally, the central concerns of *The Heads of the Town*. Most of all, the association is strengthened by Spicer's explicit reference to the Platonic dialogue *Phaedrus*; as readers of Jacques Derrida will remember, the myth of Thoth makes a dramatic entrance towards the end of that text to allow Socrates to demonstrate the superiority of speech to writing, and the danger of the latter for memory (and the motif of memory is recurrent throughout *The Heads of the Town*). This is not to suggest that eight years before its first publication in French – a language Spicer's ghost would not have been able to read particularly well – Spicer dictated or dispatched Derrida's epochal "Plato's Pharmacy" via *The Heads of the Town*, perhaps by way of his chapter title, "Plato's Marmalade" (*CP*, 294). Still, in that section Spicer does seem concerned with the problems at the core of Derrida's reading of Plato: the relationship of words or writing as *signs* to the meaning or breath that animates them – that, as the etymology of "animate" indicates, fills them with the life of the soul. Spicer writes: "After the breath stops, the words listen. To each other? To the song of each idea (whatever that means) that they are bound to? To something's heart?" (*CP*, 294). If in the Platonic vocabulary, the "idea" to which words would be bound is "eidos," Spicer's thinking here also clearly implies "logos," a term which is central, of course, to Derrida's reading of Plato and which designates meaning and reason as well as specifically spoken discourse as opposed to writing. As we shall see, Spicer considers this term at some length in the *Textbook*, while later in the same chapter from the *Novel* he plays on the properly grammatological potential of Rimbaud's vowels, again in a manner consonant with Derrida's interests.

Beyond and in parallel to such local concerns, the *Fake Novel* generally, to borrow from Robert Smithson, is what might be called "alogonistic," steadfastly refusing to resolve itself into a meaning or a reading that would account for its elisions and contradictions.[34] Within this greater problem, the various portraits of Rimbaud tend to show him as combining Bartleby-like negativity with proto-Dada attacks on sense and value, wrapped in the package of the perpetually adolescent beautiful boy. The *Novel* contains only two lyrics, and these are explicitly devoted to circumscribing him between the ages of fifteen and nineteen or twenty. The first takes as its title the date of Rimbaud's fifteenth birthday, and is a surprisingly effective autobiographical projection of his poetic trajectory:

> I do not proclaim a new age.
> That I am fifteen God only knows.
> I keep the numbers in my head

When I am dead
I will fall into a rage
And bite off all my toes.

When I am twenty I will see
Eternity
And all those old numbers
And be their anger
When I am dead
I will leave the stage
And bite off all my toes.

(CP, 285)[35]

Here, Spicer plays on Rimbaud's "Roman," with its opening line, "On n'est pas sérieux quand on a dix-sept ans" (29), and reduces the fateful age by two years.[36] "I will fall into a rage / And bite off all my toes" condenses the fury of Rimbaud's violent turn against his own talent and the gangrene that led to the amputation of his leg as he lay dying at the age of thirty-seven. Finally, the first two lines of the second stanza not only evoke the vocabulary of the poems Rimbaud was writing at about the age they mention, but also mimic the stylistic shift of that period, as Rimbaud moved from dense, clotted imagery and vocabulary to thin, ethereal lines with elegant end rhymes: "Elle est retrouvée. / Quoi? – L'Éternité (79). Meanwhile, the second poem of the pair, "Rimbaud," hints at his early burn-out in no uncertain terms, linking it with erotic exhaustion: "They said he was nineteen; he had been kissed / So many times his face was frozen closed" (*CP*, 288). What's interesting, given this poem and the concerns of the work as a whole, is that the *Fake Novel* leaves out entirely what one would imagine to be the central fact for an investigation of queer poetics which this work so clearly is: the love affair with Verlaine. The only hint of this I can detect is in a chapter titled "What the Dead Letters Said," featuring minimal fragments of an exchange between "X" and "Y":

"Dear X,
　I love you more than anyone could ever do.
　　signed
　　Y" (*CP*, 282)

This generic love note could refer not only to the fact that the vast majority of Rimbaud's writings that have come down to us are comprised of his correspondence, but also that among the letters those most to be prized – his correspondence with Verlaine – are irrevocably lost, destroyed by the latter's widow. In fact, the rest of Spicer's short chapter is riddled with omission and ellipsis dots, mimicking the way in which what's left of the Rimbaud–Verlaine correspondence is often printed – as isolated fragments (copied by others) joined by ellipses. The Dead Letter Officer then might also be everything that prevents gay lovers from living peaceably as such, everything that destroys their correspondence, in all the senses Spicer gives to that word. Such an idea might surround the otherwise contradictory statement: "A dead letter is exactly as if someone received it" (*CP*, 293).

Meanwhile the *Fake Novel* itself in some ways takes the place of that other legendary piece of lost Rimbaldiana, *La Chasse Spirituelle*, which Verlaine himself deemed Rimbaud's greatest work. In the late 1940s, this manuscript "appeared" to much fanfare, before very quickly being revealed as a forgery and a hoax, an event known to Spicer – in the *Letters to James Alexander*, he had written, "They [Spicer and James] forged a lost manuscript of Rimbaud's La Chasse Spirituelle for their own purposes. It was mysteriously discovered to have been written in English" (*CP*, 206). But rather than actually proceed with that plan, instead Spicer chose to "fake" a novel and a biography, a text which is in turn likened to a letter in being, in terms of its legibility, folded in upon itself, or "sealed." That at least would be the implication of Spicer's penultimate chapter, "Certain Seals Are Broken." The first such seal is President Buchanan: "He is there because he is there unashamed in his role of building the postoffice" (*CP*, 297), which would further indicate his role as a figure for underground gay exchange. The second seal is "love" and the third is "boredom" which "is called history or politics depending on the context" (*CP*, 297). Then, we have:

> The fourth seal is Jim. A private image. A poet demanding privacy in his poem is like a river and a bank unable to move against each other.
>
> The fifth seal is the eternal privacy words offer. Making them human. (*CP*, 298)

The breaking of the seal portrays the entire poem as being like a private letter now exposed to a massive readership of third parties placed in the position of voyeurs, violators of a personal exchange, which was also true of the *Letters to Jim Alexander*. Except that in the case of the *Letters*, that only told half the story, for they were also essentially public documents, themselves appropriated and placed within the frame of interpersonal exchange. Of course, these disturbances in the valencies of public and private, the migrations of address which make the second-person position unstable ("the poem does not know / Who you refers to" (*CP*, 255)), and therefore, that of the first-person too, whether singular or plural, also disturb the distinctions around which the "political" and the "communal" are structured. Finally, the last "seal" can be read two ways: is it affirming the "eternal privacy" of words, or, as the title suggests, displaying the breaking of the seal of that privacy?

This question of the public, of the identity of the ultimate addressee, opens the *Textbook of Poetry*: "Surrealism . . . was the first appearance of the Logos that said, 'The public be damned'. . . that really he did not have a word to say to them. This was surrealism" (*CP*, 299). The book closes by suggesting that it exists above all for a private addressee, whose "seal" is once again broken towards the poem's end: "Now the things that are for Jim are coming to an end, I see nothing beyond it. Like a false nose where a real nose is lacking. Faceless people," and the final lines are these: "To be alive. Like the noises alive people wear. Like the word Jim, es-specially [*sic*] – more than the words" (*CP*, 313). "To be alive" seems like a straightforward affirmation, yet throughout the book, as in the two previous, the living are often subordinated to ghosts, within a text continually concerned with remnants, relics, and afterlives, and perhaps above all, with the "afterlife of the poem" (*CP*, 301). Such an emphasis is political in the broadest sense, in stressing the future enclosed within our "present" as a horizon inseparable from our "now": "Hold to the future. With firm hands. The future of each afterlife, of each ghost, of each word that is about to be mentioned" (*CP*, 309). But at the same time, the Spicerian "afterlife" also continually recalls the extent to which our "present" is itself *already* composed of, haunted by, the other afterlives among which it transpires, takes its place. This is why the poem is also at times "An argument between the dead and the living" (*CP*, 301) or "An argument with the dead" (*CP*, 304).[37]

This positing of an argument – a largely inconclusive one – is again essential. The *Textbook*, despite and because of its real commitment to pedagogy ("Or why this will be a textbook concerning poetry for 20,999 years" (*CP*, 311)) is even more resistant to logical resolution and coherent exposition than the rest of *The Heads of the Town*, while composed to an extraordinary degree of proclamation, constatation, and explanation: "A textbook of poetry is created to explain" (*CP*, 313). Thus, despite its structure of twenty-nine demarcated parts replete with repetitions hinting at development and elaboration, its energies are very largely epigrammatic, and defeat any real sense of the forward motion of a developing thesis or dialectic. Yet at the same time, none of the epigrams entirely resonate outside of their relationship to the other statements and treatments upon which they comment and which they resemble, albeit with no ultimate resolution or conclusion to be drawn. The entire work, then, is very much like an interminable argument, like the city of "chittering human beings" (*CP*, 307) the poem evokes, exploding the dialectic meant to guide the conversation in traditional Socratic dialogue. The poem seems to comment on its own resistance to coherence in a metatextual section which is itself uncharacteristically consistent:

> It does not have to fit together. Like the pieces of a totally unfinished jigsaw puzzle my grandmother left in the bedroom when she died in the living room. The pieces of the poetry or of this love.
>
> Surrealism is a poem more than this. The intention that things do not fit together. As if my grandmother had chewed on her jigsaw puzzle before she died.
>
> Not as a gesture of contempt for the scattered nature of reality. Not because the pieces would not fit in time. But because this would be the only way to cause an alliance between the dead and the living. To magic the whole thing toward what they called God.
>
> To mess around. To totally destroy the pieces. To build around them. (*CP*, 306)

Despite the relative clarity, this section still leaves many questions open. Is the *Textbook* a poem which, like so much else in the world, doesn't really fit together, and which therefore in some way reflects the world, is mimetic? This would mean that it and the world in some way "fit" or "correspond" – an anti-Mertzian position. Or is it rather, like "surrealism," a deliberate sundering of and attack on things that otherwise might very well fit together, as pieces of a jigsaw puzzle do, if they haven't been chewed on? And in either case, why would the destruction of the pieces, the breaking of what fits, "cause an alliance between the dead and the living"? Presumably, this would be brought about through what might be thought of as reverse "magic": by destroying what should fit together, we can inversely bring together what should not: the living and the dead. But that is no better than inference, and note that the statements, which seem quite categorical as they begin to unfurl, end up much more hypothetical by the end of the section, as we move from the declarative mood in the definition of surrealism, to the conditional "would" which governs the third paragraph and also quite plausibly the fragments that comprise the fourth. Verbal mood is one of the central poetic devices of this poem, which moves very deviously between assertions and their qualifications, or the hypothetical. Be that as it may, a fundamental hypothesis put forward in this section is that the destruction of the "pieces" suggested here is ultimately constructive, creating a grounds "to build around." But once again, within this complex passage it's easy to lose track of an equivalence at its heart: "The pieces of the poetry or of this love"; this poem also asks to be taken as a Textbook of Eros.

However, the "beloved" emerges as no less tricky than the poem that could house him. He is: "Sounded ahead by the trumpets of unreason. Barely accounted for by the senses. He is what he is because he is never where he is" (*CP*, 302). But this is not because he is an image, a representation, or a memory: "his body is more abstract than all the messages my body sends my brain of him. And he is human" (*CP*, 302). It is this essential, corporeal abstraction that puts him beyond his potential "names": "Eros, Amor, feely love, Starlight" (*CP*, 302). The erotic transpires and is transferred in a space not beyond the presence or absence of the beloved, but immaterial to it. The "metasexuality" of "Charming" returns, veering absurdly (in the strict sense) close to the Platonic paradigm of the sublimation of the carnal, by virtue of its emphasis on what is beyond sex:[38] "And this is a system of metasexual metaphor. Being faithful to the nonsense of it: The warp and woof. A system of dreaming fake dreams" (*CP*, 304). We should remember the insistence in "Charming" on the importance of nonsense for sex: "Sex without love is better than love without sex. Sex without Mertz is never better than Mertz without sex. Nonsense is an act of friendship" (*CP*, 75). Behind the solemnity of the *Textbook* (quite probably Spicer's least funny major poem) lies a similar commitment to nonsense, the nonsense of love and friendship, the nonsensical logic of mourning: "Being faithful to it. All the ache of remembering the past, what the body doesn't know – the ache that isn't really there" (*CP*, 304). Mertz means fidelity not only to the ache of absence, but to the ache that's absent.

As the poem reaches towards its close, it gestures to Yeats, Section 26 beginning "And yet they two bake hearts. Immortal mockers of man's enterprise" (*CP*, 312). This of course echoes the phrase from "Among Schoolchildren," "And yet they too break hearts" (*Poems*, 263), in which the antecedent to the pronoun is "images." That is why Spicer's next paragraph mentions "photographs." But more importantly, the entirety of Stanza VII of "Among Schoolchildren" is concerned with those images of perfection or plenitude – whether temporal or eternal – compared to which human life in its actuality is inevitably disappointing. Earlier, Yeats asks if any mother, seeing her son with "sixty or more winters on its head," would feel his life to be a "compensation for the pang of his birth, / Or the uncertainty of his setting forth" (262). At this point in the poem, however, he also discounts as a valid solution the nun's renunciation of the temporal in favor of eternal recompense:

> Both nuns and mothers worship images,
> But those the candles light are not as those
> That animate a mother's reveries,
> But keep a marble or a bronze repose.
> And yet they too break hearts – O Presences
> That passion, piety or affection knows,
> And that all heavenly glory symbolise –
> O self-born mockers of man's enterprise;

(263)

Interestingly, an important earlier section of the *Textbook* is explicitly devoted to comparing the value of a "human love object" to a "divine love object" – the precise matter of these passages from "Among Schoolchildren." Indeed, when Spicer ends his grumpy dialogue on the subject with the invitation to "Imagine this as lyric poetry" (*CP*, 307), "Among Schoolchildren" might be the poem he has in mind. Yet section 26 of *Textbook*, rather than being "a poem to prevent idealism – i.e. the study of images" (*CP*, 254) as "Among Schoolchildren" might be read as being, cautions not against the image but rather the heartbreaking flesh:

> And yet they too break hearts. These humans – uncoded, uncyphered, their sheer presences. Beyond the word "Beauty."
>
> They are the makers of man's enterprise. Beyond the word "blowtorch," the two of them, holding a blowtorch at all beauty. (*CP*, 312)

"Presences" is revelatory here. In a first instance, it indicates the sheer thereness of "these humans" – a simple fact whose import is beyond any question of the aesthetic. Yet at the same time, the use of the plural "presences" pressures the word into its Yeatsian register, where it is one of the preferred terms for ghosts. Throughout Yeats' poetics, and certainly within *A Vision*, a text which was central to Spicer, nothing is ever more "present" than a ghost, nothing so ghostly as a "presence." And the next section of Spicer's poem will depict the converse of what the reference to Yeats sketches, moving not from ghostly image into flesh, but the other way around:

> What I am, I want, asks everything of everyone, is by degrees a ghost. Steps down to the first metaphor they invented in the underworld (pure and clear like a river) the in-sight. As a place to step further. (*CP*, 312)

Spicer here seems to be referring to the trope of katabasis, the descent to the underworld of death, memory, and the past as a figure of the search for understanding, or as in Dante's mobilization of the trope, more specifically understanding of self, "in-sight," figured as steps along a path.[39] Closer to Spicer, William Carlos Williams had used this trope too, writing just a few years prior to *Heads of the Town*, "The descent beckons / as the ascent beckoned" ("The Descent," *Pictures*, 73). This massively modernist motif, even more central to Pound, Joyce, Beckett, and Eliot than to Williams, very largely organizes *The Heads of the Town* throughout, where it is, as in Beckett, pushed to the place of its own exhaustion. However, the essentially solitary and transitory journey of katabasis is counterbalanced in Spicer by the trope of the city – a motif stressing locale, and community. Spicer's city is itself, of course, largely ghostly. Miriam Nichols, for example, titles her excellent recent reading of the *Textbook*, "The City as Ghost Town." However, once again the relationship between the dead and the quick is none too obvious. Spicer writes, "Every city that is formed collects its ghosts" (*CP*, 305), and much in the *Textbook* tempts us to think that his ideal community would be precisely that of "the dead and the living, the ghosts and the angels," with all their "differences" (*CP*, 306). But such an ideal is not accepted, as the following passages make clear:

> But the city in that sense is as far from me (and the things that speak through me) as Dante was from Florence. Farther. For it is a city that I do not remember.
>
> But the city that we create in our bartalk or in our fuss and fury about each other is in an utterly mixed and mirrored way an image of the city. A return from exile. (*CP*, 306)

Oddly enough, then, the true Heimat to which one can return is only a city from which the "ghosts" are excluded, in which the ghostly city can only be mirrored. And this city can never be an entirely satisfactory mirror of that other beyond memory: "When the gas exploded the ghosts disappeared. There was merely a city of chittering human beings . . . This was supposed also to be the story of the creation of the universe. The pieces of the explosion coming afterwards together breathless . . . When the heart explodes, there is a tremendous loss. But when the gas explodes the ghosts disappear. There is merely a city of chittering human beings" (*CP*, 307–8). The etymology of "gas" links it to chaos, the originary chaos from which the universe should have been created, but Spicer's big bang succeeds only in dispersing the ghosts. Spicer's ghost town is oddly ghostless, and that might be why "We are all alone and we do not need poetry to tell us how alone we are" (*CP*, 311).

Again, note Spicer's use of the plural, the paradoxical aloneness which dominates the shimmering mirrors of community. Spicer's poetry is less concerned with how alone "I" might be than how alone "we" always are, bound together by a separateness which divides, and without the kind of "company" that Beckett too investigates. As Henry James could have told Spicer, it is of the essence of haunting for it not entirely to happen. In the end, as the penultimate words of the *Textbook* remind us, the death of the dead only has meaning to the extent that their ghosts are *not* identical to the living, as the past perfect tense of this passage indicates: "The real sound of the dead. A blowing of trumpets proclaiming that they had been there and been alive" (*CP*, 313). But this means the return from exile, "utterly mixed and mirrored," is also an exile, an incarnation of an ideal virtuality one can only die into.[40] Spicer's city is elegaically Mertzian, a place that is driven by eros and nonsense and always ready to be dissolved by them and what they produce: "Magic, which is trying to hold onto people with your own hands, is funny while surrealism is not funny. There is a place where we can talk and we cannot talk" (*CP*, 309).

However, throughout Spicer's work hovers the possibility of another space of potential comradeship, beyond the City – San Francisco, Socrates' Athens, Rimbaud's "villes" – and over and against the infolded loneliness of katabetic descending and ascending. This is the world of gay companionship Whitman sketches in his "Calamus," or even more, in his non-katabetic, non-teleological "Open Road" of encounter and sympathy.[41] While consistently ranking Whitman among the greatest of all poets, Spicer excoriates this vision in his "Some Notes on Whitman for Allen Joyce," and interestingly, one of his first moves is to refigure the Whitmanian road into something that seems much more akin to the Spicerian staircase negotiating the passage to the underworld: "In his world roads go somewhere and you walk with someone whose hand you can hold. I remember. In my world roads only go up and down and you are lucky if you can hold on to the road or even know that it is there" (*CP*, 55). But what ultimately separates Spicer from this "Rimbaud without wings" (*CP*, 55), is the latter's inability to understand betrayal, deception, perfidy, or "cruelty": "Calamus cannot exist in the presence of cruelty. Not merely human cruelty, but the cruelty of shadows, the cruelty of spirits. Calamus is like Oz . . . And there one is, at the other side of the desert . . . And one needs no Virgil, but an Alice, a Dorothy, a Washington horsecar conductor, to lead one across that cuntlike mirror, that cruelty" (*CP*, 55). This willful, false, forced innocence makes Calamus somewhat less than a children's tale:

> So when I dreamed of Calamus, as I often did when I touched you or put my hand upon your hand, it was not as of a possible world, but as a lost paradise. A land my father Adam drove me out of with the whip of shadow. In the last sense of the word – a fairy story. That is what I think about Calamus. That is what I think about your damned Calamus. (*CP*, 56)

Spicer doesn't simply reject Calamus as a "possible world" (*CP*, 56), he also repositions it as a "lost paradise" (*CP*, 56) in a topographical relationship to an actual Hell on the wrong side of cruelty. Spicer violently rewrites what Whitman leaves open into a map, with fixed positions.[42] The possibility of transit depends not on the classical wisdom of a Virgil, but the magic of a Dorothy, or even more, the nonsense of an Alice. If Calamus is a "fairy story" in two ways, its only chance would lie in the Mertz that Spicer sees as essential to both kinds of fairy tale. Short of this, or because of it, one has the post office, which does its work without needing its protagonists ever to get anywhere or cross anything, which doesn't think that people must meet, or that their meeting could be enough. Perhaps it is the varying letters of Rimbaud and Dickinson that by disarticulating or imprinting the unspeakable words of love best point the way to the unverted comrade. Meanwhile, the fairy story will take on yet a third sense in Spicer's next major work, *The Holy Grail*.

Notes

1. The deliberately cumbersome full title of the piece is "The Unvert Manifesto and Other Papers Found in the Rare Book Room of the Boston Public Library in the Handwriting of Oliver Charming. By S." See the note in *CP*, pp. 445–6, for the textual history of this work, unpublished in Spicer's lifetime.
2. All references will be to the essay as reprinted in Ekbert Faas, *Young Robert Duncan*.
3. For an excellent analysis of Lorca's convoluted attempts to divide homosexuality into valorized and abjected categories in the "Ode to Walt Whitman," see John K. Walsh, as well as the remainder of Duncan's preface to *Caesar's Gate*.
4. Faas tells the fascinating story in detail, pp. 147–54. Ransom concluded his correspondence with Duncan by asserting that homosexuality was "biologically abnormal" and expressing entire agreement with laws which would prohibit it. When Duncan suggested that their entire exchange be published he demurred (154).
5. See Faas, pp. 274–8, and *P*, pp. 17–19 and 24–5, for details.
6. In this he followed one of his most important mentors, the famous Medievalist Ernst Kantorowicz who, though frankly anti-communist and arch-conservative, chose Princeton over compliance with demands that he found all too reminiscent of the Nazism he had previously fled. In Spicer's archives is a pencil-written draft of a petition against the Oath, which Peter Gizzi and Kevin Killian have published in *CP*, pp. xxiv–xxv.
7. For an excellent history of the organization, see John D'Emilio, *Making Trouble*, Chapter 3. For Spicer's involvement, see *P*, pp. 46–9, and above all, Kevin Killian's "Spicer and the Mattachine," pp. 16–35.

8. Although this intervention was anonymous, Killian argues very persuasively that the speaker was Spicer.

9. See the editors' note, *CP*, pp. 445–6, for this and other details about the cast of characters.

10. The real Robert Berg, who was not a psychiatrist, was at the center of a "somewhat louche" (*P*, 45) gay social circle in San Francisco, which Spicer frequented. Charming's reference to Berg's collecting "photographs of nude horses" (*CP*, 85) must allude to his penchant for picking up sailors and marines to photograph naked (*P*, 45–6).

11. Peter Gizzi has stressed the importance of the Mackintosh correspondence in "Jack Spicer and the Practice of Reading" (*H*, 208–10), and Jed Rasula finds within it the first "seeds of composition by book" (66), while germs of the "Charming" project are quite visible too. Mackintosh had been Spicer's student at the California College of Fine Arts, but his military service at Ford Ord, California, occasioned his absence from San Francisco and Spicer's letters to him. Halloween night has further links to Mackintosh in that Spicer wrote a poem for him titled "A Prayer for PVT. Graham Mackintosh on Halloween," which Spicer apparently refers to in a letter to Mackintosh dated October 31, 1954: "My poem for you is up on the wall" (presumably of the 6 Gallery, which, the letter specified, opened that day; "Letters to Graham Mackintosh," 93). Intriguingly, the same letter states: "You keep seeming realer to me the longer you're away and that's a bad sign. Maybe Graham Macintosh [*sic*] is only all the poems I'm going to write" (93).

12. My entire reading of "Charming" is greatly indebted to Maria Damon's indispensable early work on the text, and this particular argument to her thoughts on Spicer's imperative that poetry and sex *both* defamiliarize in a frightening yet liberating way. See *Dark*, pp. 163–7, especially p. 166. Meanwhile, Spicer's terminology clearly derives from Kurt Schwitters' "Merz." In notes to the *Collected Books*, where fragments of "Charming" were first published, Robin Blaser stresses that during their time in Boston he and Spicer were immersed in Robert Motherwell's *Dada Painters and Poets* anthology (351), which contained Schwitters' text of that name. Schwitters' piece begins with a long critique of realist painting, and celebrates the importance of nonsense to art.

13. See D'Emilio, *Making Trouble*, pp. 82–3 for more on the Black Cat, apparently Allen Ginsberg's favorite gay bar.

14. That Spicer indulges but also critiques this position within the "Diary" opens the possibility that a poem like "To Joe," which we examined in the last chapter, represents to some extent a self-parodic, deliberately exaggerated and abjected stance. Certainly, the gratuitous reference to Ruth Benedict's "cunt" echoes the style of misogyny seen in "To Joe." However, Catherine Imbroglio intriguingly suggests that hostility to Benedict might be motivated by the latter's account of homosexuality in *Patterns of Culture* according to "inversion theory" with its corollary that "homosexuality feminizes men" (111). As Imbriglio stresses, these are not positions to which Spicer was sympathetic. A flirtation with resentment-fueled anti-Semitism can be found in Spicer's "An Answer to Jaime de Angulo" (*CP*, 13), which exists in an alternate version, "An Answer to a Jew." Here too, however, the poem is more complex than it might seem.

15. As Damon points out, S. seems to have the last word (*Dark*, 167), but I would add that in the act of so doing he steps out of the narrative frame in such a manner as to entirely rebracket and meta-ironize his previous discourse.

16. Socrates was also of course crucial for Wilde himself. The Wildean underpinning of Charming is variable, but much of the text is given over to a familiar urbane wit and penchant for paradox, and passages like the following are of unmistakable descent: "A crime against nature must also be a crime against art. A crime against art must also be a crime against nature. All beauty is at continuous war with God" (*CP*, 77).

17. Davidson's chapter on Spicer from *The San Francisco Renaissance*, "The City Redefined" (pp. 150–71) is one of the most important and influential pieces ever written on the poet. For this argument, see above all pp. 153–9.

18. Robin Blaser has stressed ". . . the importance of community in Spicer, and his *negativity* within that community: the use of *black magic*, so to speak: misogyny, anti-semitic remarks, blasphemy, the Magic Workshop . . . All to charge the community up . . . these negations are all admissions of the fact that the small, specialized community [for poetry] . . . was not what he wanted" (*The Fire*, 259; original italics).

19. Or as Maria Damon elegantly glosses this passage: "Spicer deconstructs traditional Marxism's emphasis on solidarity rather than solitude, emphasizing instead (like Genet) the revolutionary potential of the discomfort of isolation" (*Dark*, 164). It's the relation of this deconstruction to destruction outright that I hope to explore in the following. This sentiment hearkens back to "Charming" in other ways too: John Vincent has suggested that "loneliness" is the unvert's "greatest trait" ("Pinnacle," 91).

20. In *The San Francisco Renaissance*, Davidson points to something very similar: "Unfortunately, Spicer's cultivation of group affiliations and cult loyalties tended to exacerbate the poet's own xenophobia, misogyny, and anti-Semitism . . . Spicer chose the . . . route of cadre and cell with their attendant restrictions and prejudices" (159). Or as John Emil Vincent has wittily put it, "His nurturing a circle could sometimes . . . become nothing more than a circling of wagons – more paranoid than productive" (*After Spicer*, 2).

21. Because *A Textbook* was the focus of the first Vancouver lecture, we have far more direct commentary from Spicer on it than for any of his other works, save for *The Holy Grail* and the *Book of Magazine Verse*, the subjects of his next two lectures.

22. Silliman's "Spicer's Language," where Spicer is presented as a poet of the "sentence" rather than the "line," is one of the most important pieces ever written on Spicer's poetics, and also to a large extent the main theoretical underpinning of the book in which it appears, Silliman's *The New Sentence*. We will return to this in Chapter 5. On *Heads of the Town*'s formal variations, Susan Vanderborg notes "the progress toward paradise involves more and more space devoted to paratextual prose" (52).

23. See *H*, p. 29, where Spicer also surprisingly aligns history to Dante's *Purgatorio*, in contrast to the traditional parsing.

24. For example, in the poem beginning "A loss of something ever felt I – / The first that I could recollect / Bereft I was – of what I knew not" (436).

25. Maria Damon brilliantly shows how this poem also engages with William Blake's discussion of the annihilating destructiveness of love in "The Clod and the Pebble," which Spicer's last line echoes (*Dark*, 161–2). More recently, she has expanded this analysis to show how by appropriating Blake, Spicer here also challenges Ginsberg ("Ghost Forms," 145–7).

26. It must be said that I'm departing here from Spicer's own account of puns in the Vancouver lectures, where he reads them as a form of metaphor, yielding "interconnections between things" and deriving from "our recognition that things are like other things and words can sound alike and it can be something which brings you closer to the nature of reality as well as being quite funny" (*H*, 31). Spicer's explanation notwithstanding, the puns he actually uses seem to work differently, causing humor, surprise, or anxiety, because the identity or equivalence metaphor can create is shattered by the instability of a word or a term as revealed by the pun. The Spicerian pun is entirely in line with what Ron Silliman has under the name "overdetermination" defined as the "essential Spicerian effect": "No logos . . . can exist which does not contain contradiction, negation or some effacing otherness within itself" (*New Sentence*, 149).

27. Peter Gizzi cites this passage in an extended look at the duplicity of the mirror motif found throughout Spicer's work. See *H*, pp. 218–23, especially p. 220. In a very early poem titled "Homosexuality," Spicer depicts the subject of his title as a kind of endless narcissistic mirroring producing a deathly replication, the eternal return of the same: "Roses that wear roses / Enjoy mirrors / . . . Roses that wear roses are dying / With a mirror behind them" (*CP*, 6). This classically homophobic reading of homosexuality as the refusal of difference is not prevalent in Spicer.

28. Susan Vanderborg glosses this figure as "a mixed trope in which the shared history of a gay poets' circle becomes a symbolic marriage pledge among participants to conceal that past" (55).

29. The technical term for such a device is ploce. Jean-Michel Rabaté has brilliantly studied its prevalence in Pound, where emphatic repetition is mobilized against the menace of catachresis (173–82) but also to some extent, metaphor: "A new economy of the sign should bypass conventional rhetorics by replacing metaphors, either too formal or too worn out, by ploces" (181). This is a position that Spicer's poetics mimes in places.

30. It's possible that references to Dickinson and Frost are nods to Creeley as very much a New England poet in Spicer' eyes, in this way fundamentally distanced from his California scene.

31. This sort of simultaneity was the basis of how Spicer taught history at the California School of Fine Arts, and his biographers also link that practice with the basic set-up of *A Fake Life* (*P*, 52).

32. Spicer refers to Rimbaud's hometown of Charleville as "Charlieville" throughout the poem. Rimbaud did something similar himself in a letter to a friend, dubbing the city "Charlestown" within the body of his French text (267–8).

33. See Chapter 2 of the present study for more on this.

34. Smithson titled one of his early sculptures *Alogon*, a title which "comes from the Greek word which refers to the unnameable, and irrational number" (292). In an interview with Dennis Wheeler – one of the audience

members of Spicer's Vancouver lectures – Smithson associates the *Alogon* with a "surd area" which would be "a region where logic is suspended" and "there's no commensurable relation . . . So you're into a kind of irrational area" (199). "Surd" is the Latin translation of *alogon*, the root of our common "absurd." Spicer's Dada poetics dialogue with the origins of metaphysics as dialogue, in Plato.

35. One wonders to what extent the lyric is a conscious or unconscious reworking of the translation of a Paul Eluard poem which appeared in the Motherwell anthology, opening with lines like these: "I am fifteen years old, I take myself by the hand . . . / I am not fifteen years old. From the past is born an incomparable silence" (228).

36. Rimbaud's penchant for playing on numbers and ages is also seen in his title, "Les poètes de sept ans." Meanwhile, Rimbaud's attribution of the title "novel" ("roman") to a lyric poem might be behind Spicer's fake "novel" about his life.

37. Ross Clarkson unfolds the implications of this with great subtlety in "Jack Spicer's Ghosts and the Immemorial Community," an article which has informed my thinking here.

38. "Beyond" being one potential meaning of the Greek prefix "meta" in English.

39. See John Freccero, p. 107, for more on this.

40. In her forceful reading of *Textbook*, Susan Vanderborg also stresses Spicer's emphasis on the city as a space of exile, while insisting that such a shared calamity does not eliminate conflicts within the "community" brought together in such a manner (59).

41. It is also implicitly the world of the couple, as opposed to both community and the individual.

42. See John Vincent for acute analysis of Spicer's relationship to Whitman, and this poem in particular, in *Queer*, pp. 168–76.

Chapter 4

From Mythopoetics to Pragmatics: *The Holy Grail* and *A Red Wheelbarrow*

One of the most obvious elements of Spicer's poetry is its frequent and at times near obsessive recourse to myth and legend. Here, Orpheus is the outstanding figure by some distance, but references to Greek mythology and Ovidian tales are found in many places, as well as Arthurian romance and popular mythology and Americana, as in his major books *The Holy Grail* and *Billy the Kid*. Two other more recently published late books, *Helen: A Revision* and to a lesser extent, *Golem*, underscore this aspect of Spicer's practice, which has far-reaching implications for his poetics as a whole, but also for his positioning among his peers and predecessors. In many ways, the air of familiarity but also of belatedness, unoriginality, and incompletion which Spicer's allusions foster is at the heart of his entire project, encapsulated in the concept of "tradition" as elaborated in *After Lorca*: "generations of different poets in different countries patiently telling the same story, writing the same poem, gaining and losing something with each transformation – but, of course, never really losing anything" (*CP*, 110–11). But such a justification notwithstanding, it needs to be stressed that the plethora of learned allusion and very largely Eurocentric high classicism sets Spicer apart from many contemporaries – such as Creeley, O'Hara, and Ginsberg, or going farther afield, John Berryman – whom he otherwise resembles in his preference for a relaxed colloquial American idiom and a decidedly contemporary set of authorial postures, references, and situations.[1] Of course, nearer to home, this emphasis on myth and legend is entirely consonant with that of Robert Duncan, a poet to whom Spicer was personally much closer, but whose tendency to mysticism and mystification was a constant source of friction from the outset of their relationship, at times distinguishing their two different Kantorowicz-inflected medievalisms.[2] Duncan himself stressed the importance of his own work of the 1940s, particularly "Heavenly City, Earthly City," for what he called Spicer's "vocabulary" of myth and legend; meanwhile, on several occasions Spicer singled out for praise Duncan's roughly contemporaneous series "Medieval Scenes." Interestingly, Duncan inscribed this latter suite of poems within a larger, dualistic structure, which echoes the dichotomy between the divine and the temporal to which the title "Heavenly City, Earthly City" also points. Thus, while featuring poems such as "The Kingdom of Jerusalem," "The Adoration of the Virgin," and "The Albigenses," the series "Medieval Scenes" is joined to the companion suite "Domestic Scenes," with poems of starkly contrasting titles like "Real Estate," "Bus Fare," and "Mail Boxes"; notably, it is this latter series that bears the dedication "for Jack Spicer" (*First Decade*, 44).[3] In many respects, such examples are hardly surprising; indeed, the poetic collation of the mythic and the contemporary is one of the central stories of twentieth-century American poetics. That said, from the late 1940s to the mid-1960s – the period of Spicer's writing life – the stakes of such a project generally, and more specifically for Spicer, were particularly fraught. On the one hand, nothing at this time was more "academic" than the "mythical method" as defined by T. S. Eliot, whose critical prestige within American English departments was then quite possibly at its height. On the other, a parallel concern with myth, archetype and magic, this time filtered through the analytic psychology of C. G. Jung, was prevalent among the avant-garde, and notably so within Spicer's own segment of it, especially the circles surrounding Duncan and Charles Olson. One reason Spicer's poetry so frequently puts into play the question of the value of myth is that such a move allows him to critically engage the poetics of both the academy and his own coterie with a single gesture. Not surprisingly, Spicer tends to steal and take his distance from both camps, in some ways playing them off against each other, but constantly signaling his dialogue with both. This is particularly in evidence in *The Holy Grail*, which in its very title confronts Eliotic material head on.

As is well known, it was in his enormously influential essay of 1922, "*Ulysses*, Order, and Myth," that T. S. Eliot first proposed the concept of the "mythical method," which he defined as "simply a way of controlling, of ordering, of giving a shape and a significance to the immense panorama of futility and anarchy which is contemporary history" (*Selected Prose*, 177). This Joyce had done in *Ulysses*, Eliot argued, by juxtaposing Leopold Bloom's aimless wanderings with those of the Greek hero. With regard to his own work, of course, Eliot implied that this method was also his own in *The Waste Land*, published the same year, where the foundational myths were not Homeric tales but Arthurian legend, particularly as read by Jessie Weston in *From Ritual to Romance*, the book Eliot famously designated as the key to the puzzles of his poem.[4] Such a context would have been unmissable to any reader of poetry in 1962, when *The Holy Grail* was published, and Spicer's work would have been read, reasonably, as an assault on some of the most precious tenets of English Department orthodoxy: predictably, Spicer never bequeaths on legend the authority to ground contemporary experience in transcendent meaning, and his approach is deflationary and demystifying throughout. To some extent, he simply reverses Eliot's hierarchies, and throws Arthurian legend fully within the contemporary "futility" and "anarchy" Eliot hoped it could counter. But at the same time, it would be hasty to claim that Spicer's venture in *The Holy Grail* is only an attack or parody. However violently he treats the material, for Spicer the Grail legends clearly remain generative, and Eliot was a poet whom Spicer always took seriously. Moreover, if Spicer himself notably discounts Weston in his Vancouver lecture on *The Holy Grail*,[5] his dismissal needs to be tempered, first because his poem evinces a fairly solid knowledge of her book, but also because in one instance Spicer unequivocally offers her faint praise: precisely in the interest of damning Jung, the leading exponent of myth for so many of his own contemporaries. In a list of comments he sent to Duncan about a section of the latter's *H. D. Book*, Spicer marks one passage as "the second place I was tempted to stop reading . . . Jung is not even as good or as true as Jessie Weston" (*B*).[6] Rather than counter Eliot's "mythical method" and Jessie Weston with Jungian archetypal mythopoetics, he seems to put them more or less in the same bag, with a slight preference for the former. Yet if Spicer recuses almost all of Eliot's assumptions, his work also eschews the simple contemporaneity of, say, Duncan's "Domestic Scenes" or the untrammeled modernity of O'Hara's "lunch poems," along with the primary grounding in everyday American life which both imply.

In fact, a critical engagement with just such an emergent poetics of the immediate, the demotic, and the American, as inspired above all by the work of William Carlos Williams, was very much on Spicer's mind at this time. Only a few months before embarking on *The Holy Grail*, Spicer wrote a book whose title, *A Red Wheelbarrow*, announced its engagement with Williams – a poet Spicer respected immensely – as loudly as his subsequent book proclaimed its sparring with Eliot. This biographical detail can help give context to what at first seems an oddity of *A Red Wheelbarrow*: the massive prevalence within it of Ovidian reference and allusion, creating a context seemingly more in keeping with no one more than Eliot, Williams' arch-rival. In some ways, Spicer's maneuver here seems a counterbalance to the converse procedure of *The Holy Grail*, smeared throughout with the stain of American ephemera. In other words, *A Red Wheelbarrow* and *The Holy Grail* ask to be read as companion pieces – Spicer's own diptych of Medieval and Domestic scenes – in which he confronts the two American poets of the previous generation who were probably most important to him, and in some way bangs them against each other, subjecting Arthurian legend to the demotic and mass culture, bathing Williams' objectivism in classical allusion. Indeed, if Spicer's serial poetics of the "book" coalesced in the mid-1950s through a critical engagement with Lorca, Whitman, Dickinson, and a Poundian ideogram of translating, haunting, and radio broadcast, then the turns which the poetics take in the early 1960s emerge by way of a reparsing of the legacies of Williams, Eliot, and H. D. – a project which also allowed him to stake out his position with regard to Duncan and Olson. In particular, Duncan's work on H. D. seems a crucial instigation to Spicer in his own investigation of the relationship between poetics and myth, and the theories of the psyche such a relationship must imply. Witness this intriguing suggestion in a letter to Duncan, roughly contemporaneous to the comments on *The H. D. Book* cited above: "Heard from Robin [Blaser] about the HD book. Wonderful . . . Isn't the key to her poetry that her belief in mythology was Freudian rather than Jungian – ie. pragmatic rather than mythopoetic?" (27).[7]

What might Spicer mean by this unelaborated opposition? On the one hand, a mythopoetic Jungianism seems reasonably easy to grasp. This would be a mobilization of myth in accordance with the universal and transhistorical symbolizations of the collective unconscious, allowing poet and reader to transcend the contingencies of their historical situations and random, symptomatically riven egos, in order to achieve a deeper "self" and more authentic relationship to the human collectivity. While this in some ways rhymes with Spicer's distrust of the "big lie of the personal," it posits a transcendentally coherent impersonality and ultimate human concord of meaning which is very much at odds with Spicer's poetics of disturbance, fissure, argument, and accident. Indeed, as a principle of order, as Spicer's remarks to Duncan hinted, Jungian mythopoetics veer closer to Eliot's mythical method than many of Jung's partisans might like.[8] Less easy to fathom, however, is a relationship to mythology that would be "Freudian" and "pragmatic" instead. Obviously, one important aspect here is that H. D. herself was analyzed by Freud, and Spicer almost certainly read her account of this in *Tribute to Freud*, published in 1956. In one sense, "pragmatic" would simply imply the practical dimension of the working-through, the brass-tacks process of the cure, which in H. D.'s case involved an extremely large quantity of mythological topoi. At the same time, however, I think we also need to read Spicer here as the trained linguist he liked to remind his interlocutors he was, for whom "pragmatics" refers to a particular area of linguistic study: the ways that meanings are produced through context, social exchange, and cultural connotation and weighting, rather than through strict semantic definition or syntactical organization.[9] As an initial and preliminary definition, one might suggest that a poetry of pragmatics is a poetry that would be concerned less with what words mean than with how they work in different discursive situations; with how they "stick" to the real of human exchange, to use Spicer's rhetoric. Indeed, Spicer's own fascination with the power of obscenity and injurious, derogatory language falls fully within the field of "pragmatics," as would his sense of Orpheus as above all the poet who creates affect in his audience.[10] Now, among the major American poets of the generation preceding Spicer's own, it is almost certainly William Carlos Williams whose work would most neatly fit with a "pragmatic" emphasis, as one of the most important effects of the oral or demotic in Williams is precisely to haul pragmatics inside the poetic, thereby historicizing and localizing the latter in ways very much against the grain of Jungian mythopoetics or Eliot's "mythical method."[11] For the effect of the demotic in Williams is less to give an impression of immediacy than to forge a poetic idiom out of a language bearing all the marks of the specific social scenes in which it emerges – an aspect of his practice which will prove as crucial for Creeley and O'Hara as for Spicer. And while we should be wary of bestowing undue importance on a stray speculation found in a letter, nevertheless, Spicer's comments offer a fruitful perspective as to why and how Spicer confronts the poetics of Eliot and Williams in these two works: taken together, they might represent Spicer's own articulation of mythology as pragmatics. In *A Red Wheelbarrow*, for example, Spicer can be seen to mobilize a "pragmatics" of mythology precisely as a means of engaging Williams' poetry of the object, which is also a poetry of language as praxis, of language as social process and fact. To see how this works, we need to follow the book as it moves from an initial emphasis on the object – Williams' "things" – to a very different sort of poetry of allusion and myth.

A Red Wheelbarrow, comprised of nine short and sometimes very short poems, begins by extending the title it lifts from Williams even further into easily recognizable territory:

> Rest and look at this goddamned wheelbarrow. Whatever
> It is. Dogs and crocodiles, sunlamps. Not
> For their significance.

(CP, 325)

Although Williams' characteristically inviting tone here gives way to the no less characteristic Spicerian note of crotchety querulousness, we are nevertheless on familiar ground: "No ideas but in things" these lines seem to say, with their negation of "significance" and their recusal of metaphor, while the imperative to "Rest and look" immediately valorizes the visual, in line with Williams' emphases again.[12] Equally important, if dogs, crocodiles, and sunlamps seem to point away from any single coherent depicted scene, unlike that in the Williams original, they nevertheless echo him by placing the animal or "natural" and the manufactured on the same level in terms of their essential dignity as objects of contemplation; Williams had situated his red wheelbarrow "beside the white / chickens" (*Imaginations*, 138). Spicer thus pointedly emphasizes that Williams refuses a mystification of nature or the natural in "A Red Wheelbarrow" – the poem centers on a manufactured object – while problematizing Williams' proximity to a nostalgically totalizing sense of cultural tradition, here troped as rural. As Spicer reminds us, from some perspectives a wheelbarrow is more closely related to a manufactured sunlamp than to a white chicken. Finally, as he grumpily points out, if the imperative is to gaze on and acknowledge the object as object, in its absolute otherness from the gazing subject, then the precise nature of the object in question, whatever it may be, by definition has no bearing on the poetical imperative as such. When Spicer writes "Whatever it is," he is being entirely accurate, not lackadaisical or dismissive. Indeed, in his Vancouver lecture on dictation, Spicer links this essential alterity of Williams' conception of the "thing" to his own concept of the Outside – that transcendental distance from which dictation arrives at the poet. Spicer there suggests that Williams "sees in objects essentially a kind of energy which radiates from them. The fact that this chair has a chairness, a nimbus around it, a kind of an electrical thing which gives energy enough so that it can be transformed almost directly – *it*, the thing that the chair in its chairness radiates – into poetry" (*H*, 10). In this way, Williams joins Yeats (and more surprisingly, the seemingly proprioceptive Olson) as one of the chief exponents of "dictated" poetry, as the "thing" in its very difference from the poet materializes Spicer's Outside. But what must be noted is the modality of such a "transformation" of the thing into poetry, in Williams' terms. As Marjorie Perloff has stressed, in *Spring and All* Williams insists that the medium of poetry – the word – must itself be not a "symbol" of nature but a "part" of it, which implies that the relationship of language to what it represents is to be thought of metonymically rather than metaphorically or symbolically.[13] Williams says something very similar later in the book, claiming, nature "is opposed to art but apposed to it" (*Imaginations*, 121). This sense of opposition conjoined to apposition is a line Spicer follows in many places, almost seeming to comment on Williams' claim when he suggests in *After Lorca*, "Words are what sticks to the real. We use them to push the real, to drag the real into the poem. They are what we hold on with, nothing else. They are as valuable in themselves as rope with nothing to be tied to" (*CP*, 123). This imperative to haul into the poem that which remains Outside it, while paradoxically allowing the outside to nevertheless persist in its exteriority – both opposed and apposed – is at the center of what one might call Spicer's variation on a theme by Williams in the first poem of the book *A Red Wheelbarrow*.

But as is obvious, the rest of Spicer's "book" hardly seems to continue this discussion. We move from the stark gaze at random objects in their enigmatic Otherness to the vagaries of Eros, that is, of nothing other than object-choice, every subsequent lyric bearing the title "Love." Likewise, emphasis shifts from the ostensibly concrete to the blatantly abstract, from the quintessentially Williamsian refusal of figural logics of comparison and equivalence to a simile bearing down upon the reader in line one of poem 2: "Tender as an eagle it [love] swoops down" (*CP*, 325).[14] Most importantly, perhaps, we leave the tactile and visual immediacy of the everyday for an immensely mediated set of mythological figures and tropes, only to arrive at the punning conclusion in the final poem, "Love VIII": "Love ate the red wheelbarrow" (*CP*, 327).

Given the above, one might be tempted to surmise that Spicer simply loses interest in his exchange with Williams, and slides into the subjects and motifs that obsess his poetry throughout: the circulation of desire in its relation to the bounds of the body and the subject; the myth of Orpheus; a frequently coastal landscape of stones, cliffs, and waves. But I would like to suggest that in fact the dialogue with Williams does indeed continue to the end, and that "love eating the red wheelbarrow" is in no way a jokey throwaway, but the summation of the various readings of Williams which Spicer proposes in this book. For example, in the Vancouver lecture cited above Spicer briefly returns to Williams, suggesting that if for the latter objects are the "magickers" or "source of energy," this is especially true "in *Desert Music* [*sic*], where "the objects were taken over by something else" (*H*, 28). And one thing Spicer seems to be doing in this sequence, as lapidary as it is stony, is to trace the career of Williams from his early "objectivism" through to the poetics of affect and memory which dominate the late work. If the journey Spicer proposes ends with love, let us remember that "Journey to Love" is very much in keeping with how Williams at times viewed his own trajectory, this phrase naming his last book of poems. Of course, Spicer's journey to "Love" in the book *A Red Wheelbarrow* differs greatly from that of

Williams in its mediation through Greek and Roman myth,[15] a media-tion which taken as a whole becomes in an intriguing way a journey to stone. Indeed, the extreme heterogeneity of the dogs, crocodiles, and sunlamps of the first poem is replaced in the subsequent lyrics by a field of objects which one might well be tempted to call monolithic, as every one of the following poems except the last features "marble," "rock," or "stone" prominently among a restricted and reduced vocabulary. The implications of this progressive petrification are crucial to the function-ing of myth generally in the book's complex exchange with Williams' poetics.

First of all, the foregrounding of rock and stone can be read as a journey backwards through geological time, taking the wheelbarrow back into the rock from which its iron would have been quarried. This is not so much a return to the natural or to origins, I would argue, as an effort to reinscribe the frozen instant of Williams' short lyric into a tem-poral context of movement, evolution, and change. To use the salient term, we have a sort of metamorphosis, but in reverse. For clearly, the rocks, stones, and cliffs have a more obvious function in this poem, which is to mobilize a complex series of allusions to and rewritings of tales from Ovid's *Metamorphoses* and classical mythology generally. "Love VII" mentions Prometheus, and the figure chained to a rock and subject to the whim of an eagle which we see in "Love" could evoke Prometheus and his punishment:

> Tender as an eagle it swoops down
> Washing all our faces with its rough tongue.
> Chained to a rock and in that rock, naked,
> All of the faces.
>
> (*CP*, 325)

Yet at the same time, one might imagine here Andromeda, also chained to a rock, to be rescued by Perseus, who swoops down, like an eagle and out of love, in winged sandals. Meanwhile, there are clear echoes of Echo in "Love III": "Who pays attention to the music the stone makes / Each of them hearing its voice. / Each of them yells and it is an echo bouncing the stone hard" (*CP*, 326), and in addition to Prometheus, Eros and Ganymede are both named in "Love VII." Indeed, the latter might function here as a pointer to the figure who tells his tale in Ovid: Orpheus, as we know by now, Spicer's favorite mythological character. It is hard to sort out in any definitive way Spicer's conflation of these varying mythological figures, scenes, and what Spicer almost suggests are stage props: "The wax figures of Ganymede, Prometheus, Eros / hanging" (*CP*, 327). But as can be seen, what Spicer does with them here is in no way archetypal or thematic, but rather collage-like and meto-nymic. That is to say, it would seem that the sequence of "Love" poems is working with a *rhetoric* of stone, not a mythopoetics of it.

Thus, rather than plumb the myths for deep structure or archetypal truth, Spicer suggests that Williams, as poet of love, might be made to rhyme with Ovid, who is also, of course, a poet of natural objects. The effect of Spicer's book is to push the objectivist suspicion of metaphor towards an Ovidian poetics of metamorphosis, and it does this through morphologies of citation and pastiche: forms of textual incorporation or encysting, to use another crucial term of Spicer's poetics, which correspond with Love's eventual ingestion of the Red Wheelbarrow. These various forms of borrowing and superimposition create differences and disjunctions rather than essential unities. Thus in "Love," for example, we do not have the revelation of an essential similarity between Andromeda and Prometheus, both chained to the rock; rather we have that bit of Ovidian staging itself riven by the differences between the two myths, just as the eagle swoops down not to peck out Prometheus' liver but to newly wash the lovers' faces. If "There are no holds on the stone," as we read in "Love IV," it is not only to differentiate this cliff from the one Ovid describes when recounting that Perseus, his winged sandals too sodden with dragon's blood to keep him aloft, grabbed onto a rock with his left hand and used the sword in his right to finish off the monster guarding Andromeda. It is also because this stone, circulating between the tales of Perseus, Prometheus, and Echo, will not allow the reader to achieve any symbolic purchase on it. Like the dogs, crocodiles, and sunlamps, it cannot be read for its "significance" in a mythopoetic sense. Therefore, if the reader is inevitably led to try to sort out and sift through the various mobilizations of stone, rock, and marble in the poem, the process yields no totalizing resolution: "Nothing in the rock hears nothing / The stone, empty as a teacup, tries for comfort" (*CP*, 327). The stone is at once deaf and an empty receptacle, liable to be filled with mythological figures rapidly reducing themselves to wax figurines.

The rock which hears nothing, however, also recalls the death of Orpheus, finally stoned to death when a tumult is raised which drowns out his song, whose power was such as to persuade the hurled rocks to fall harmlessly beside him. It is the myth of Orpheus which seems to be evoked in "Love V," however with a reversal of the usual emphasis:

> Never looking him in the eye once. All mythology
> Is contained in this passage. Never to look him in the eye once.
>   His exclusive right to be

Seen. That is the God in the stone
Who barely comes up to expectation.

(CP, 326)

"Never looking him in the eye once" can be seen as telling the story from the perspective of Eurydice's gaze. That is to say, Orpheus' prohibition on looking at Eurydice in no way prevents her from looking at him, but it does prevent him from seeing himself being seen, as he would if she looked him in the eye. In Spicer's telling here, the key privation faced by Orpheus is not his loss of the right to gaze at the beloved object, but his loss of the narcissistic moment when he sees that object turn a privileged, "exclusive" gaze back at him. And when in *Spring and All* Williams writes of "A world detached from the necessity of recording it, sufficient to itself, removed from" the writer (*Imaginations*, 121), he too is writing of a world that does not gaze back, that does not honor the singer's "exclusive right to be seen." Williams' red wheelbarrow never once looks the poet or the reader in the eye, as it were, and its refusal to do so is largely behind the readerly rage greeting Williams' work which he paraphrases in *Spring and All*: "Is this what you call poetry? It is the very antithesis of poetry. It is antipoetry" (88). Spicer's *A Red Wheelbarrow* both highlights and extends the violence to readerly narcissism that Williams meant for his work to provoke. At the same time, the poem recalls that even the most "objectivist" Williams was cognizant of objects as appearing within circuits of affective investment and exchange, and therefore of love. In a quibble on the Latin root, Ganymede, Prometheus, and Eros all "hanging" remind us that a red wheelbarrow is also that upon which so much depends.

The unlikely incipit of *The Holy Grail* is in fact entirely in keeping with such concerns. "Tony / To be casual and have the wish to heal / Gawain, I think, / Had that when he saw the sick king squirming . . ." (*CP*, 331) the poem begins. By now we are familiar with Spicer's poetics of address, but to start a long poem by isolating as a single line a proper name which is not the subject of the work but rather the addressee of a speech act is jarring to say the least. Rather than bearing a dedication or the superscription found in a letter, as in *Admonitions* and *After Lorca*, this poem begins with what reads as an example of phatics, the proper name functioning to establish a line of communication between two people, signaling to the unexplained "Tony" that he is in fact the addressee being spoken to (while the following modifying clause is left floating suspended, its subject, "Gawain," post-positioned). This, of course, is another instance of pragmatics, and the poem insists in various ways on the primacy of its concern to bring this register within its bounds. For example, "The Book of Lancelot" echoes the opening "Book of Gawain" by starting with the line "Tony (another Tony)" (*CP*, 339) and *The Holy Grail* never makes the slightest gesture of explaining who either "Tony" is or what they're doing in the poem. What is important to the text, then, is not the relationship between a specific imagined sender and a particular "Tony" or "Tonies" (in contrast to the structuring importance of the letters in *After Lorca* being addressed to that particular poet) but that the stories that will be told and the lyrics presented be received as forming part of an exchange between the poet and some intended, specific recipient, whoever that may be; that they be read as offerings, gifts, or exclamations. Once again, the mythological hypotext is from the outset proposed as caught up within a network of exchange rather than as grounding or ordering a contemporary futility, as the poems take within themselves and posit as their subject the affective and erotic network in which they circulate.[16] This in turn is echoed by Spicer's sense of the historicity of the circulations and evolutions of the grail stories themselves, as evidenced by the incursion within his book of a radically different tone and mode, which comprises the entirety of poem 3 of "The Book of the Death of Arthur":

> In the episode of le damoissele cacheresse, for example, one stag, one
> brachet, and one fay, all of which properly belong together as the
> essentials for the adventures of a single hero, by a judicious arrangement
> supply three knights with difficult tasks, and the maiden herself wanders
> off with a different lover.
> So here, by means of one hunt and one fairy ship, three heros are
> transported to three different places. When they awake the magic ship
> has vanished and sorry adventures await them all. Not one of them is
> borne by the boat, as we should naturally expect, to the love of a fay
> Plainly we are dealing with materials distorted from their original form.
>
> (*CP*, 356)

This curious poem, as a reader might guess, is mostly found text, being a very slight modification of a passage from the 1903 monograph *Studies in the Fairy Mythology of Arthurian Romance*, by Lucy Allen Paton.[17] I have not been able to determine how much of Paton's book Spicer read – the passage he cites is from the early going – or how seriously he took it, not having found any references to it by Spicer or his entourage. But Paton's book, which antedates Weston's *From Ritual to Romance* by sixteen years, might have interested Spicer for several reasons. Paton's central thesis is extremely simple: that at the heart of Arthurian legend lies the fairy story, and at the heart of the latter, as she claims the etymology testifies, is the fay herself, whose authentic dwelling place is by no means the French romances detailing the "matter of

Britain": "To discover the fay in her true nature we must follow her to her home in Ireland and Wales, where among the earlier traditions of the Celtic people she stands nearer simple myth than in many of the twelfth-century lays and romances of France" (1). This is a position Spicer seems to jokily echo in "The Book of Lancelot," writing "The Irish have only invented three useful things: / Boston, The Holy Grail, and fairies" (*CP*, 341), the last term being an obvious pun, and an allusion to the community of gay poets Spicer found in Boston in 1955–6. But beyond that, Spicer seems to have thought seriously about the broader implications of Paton's somewhat bizarre practice. On the one hand, her privileging of Celtic fairy mythology as the original source of Arthurian legend leads her to scour the latter obsessively for traces of the former, and quickly condemn any deviation from the "original" as corruption or distortion, as in the passage Spicer quotes. At the same time, her zeal to find traces of fairy story in Arthurian romance leads her to break down the former into constitutive patterns and typical episodes in a near structuralist manner. For example, the section which Spicer cites deals with a narrative topos Paton calls the "Fairy Induction" – the part of the fairy story in which the fay draws her beloved knight into fairyland – and the broad effect of her work is to present the fairy story in terms of narrative patterns and topoi, not meanings or essences. Indeed, the general tendency of both *The Holy Grail* and the passage from Paton which Spicer cites indicate that her book resonates less for him in its detection of origins than in its tracing of what Spicer in his next major book, *Language*, will call "transformations," in the eminently structuralist context of both linguistic theory and folk material, here songs:

> "In Scarlet Town where I was born
> There was a fair maid dwelling."
> We make up a different language for poetry
> And for the heart – ungrammatical.
> It is not that the name of the town changes
> (Scarlet becomes Charlotte or even in Gold City I once heard a good
>   Western singer make it Tonapah. We don't have towns here)
> (That sort of thing would please the Jungian astronauts)
> But that the syntax changes. This is older than towns.
>
> (*CP*, 390)

To what extent can the opposition of name to syntax be equated to one between Jungian mythopoetics and a Freudian pragmatics of assemblage, overdetermination, revision, and displacement? A tentative answer can be found in *The Holy Grail* which, like almost all of Spicer's poetry, is concerned with nothing so much as the language fit for poetry and the heart, and the grammar and syntax of the narratives the heart tells. Notably, in its charting of these matters *The Holy Grail* works with a more pendular, binary structure than is usual in Spicer, oscillating between clearly demarcated polarities of plenitude and lack, which dominate the poem. Such a structure could be seen as largely dictated by the very nature of the quest narrative as such. However, Spicer's sense of cultural transformation as adumbrated in the poem cited above affords him a method for folding this dichotomy into itself. Explaining how he sees the grail in his poem, in the Vancouver lectures Spicer evokes "Gawain's big thing [in the poem] about the empty cup and the full cup. You see, the grail was, in Irish mythology, something that you could always eat from. It was always filled up with food. And in the Christian versions it's the thing that Christ bled into, which is the empty thing" (*H*, 65). Spicer's comment here, though undeveloped, is revelatory. To start with, it explicitly rejects one of Weston's major arguments, which was to divide the tradition of the Irish cauldron of plenty from the Christian grail in no uncertain terms, claiming that whatever resemblance they shared was from their common derivation from still more ancient sources, in which the cup forms were "sex symbols of immemorial antiquity and world-wide diffusion" (75), representing "the Female, reproductive energy" (75), in symbiotic and unsurprising conversation with the spear and lance. The point is not only that Spicer rejects an ultimate sexual symbolism, but even more that he presents historical transformation or reappropriation not as a muddle to be sorted out but rather as a possibility for figural overdetermination in a Freudian sense; in a quest which is also figured as the poet's ("but they were looking for a cup or a poem" (*CP*, 332)), the grail both fills and bleeds Spicer's knights, and seems to prevent them from always knowing this difference. Spicer makes this clear early on, in the third poem of "The Book of Gawain":

> The grail is the opposite of poetry
> Fills us up instead of using us as a cup the dead drink from.
> The grail the cup Christ bled into and the cup of plenty in Irish mythology
> The poem. Opposite. Us. Unfullfilled.

> (*CP*, 332)

These lines are startling for a number of reasons. To start with, they equate poetry not with plenitude or fulfillment but with an emptying, a leeching that turns the poetic subject into a vessel in the service of the dead. But the poem is more than a simple reversal of expected values, a bit of the metaphysical wit Spicer learned from Donne. Indeed, if the elements above point to a conceit, its development or resolution is stopped in its tracks by the last line quoted above, which refuses to organize its elements into a grammatical and therefore logical conclusion. The line pointedly does not read, for example, "The poem opposite us, unfulfilled," or "The poem opposite, us unfulfilled." Rather, it throws out the elements of its discussion without conjoining them, in fact violently separating them between full stops. As if to recognize the implicit contrast, the next line reads "These worlds make the friendliness of human to human seem close as cup to lip" (*CP*, 332), "worlds" perhaps a play on or transformation of what the prior line offered: isolated "words." "The Book of Gawain" confuses such essential polarities in other places too, erasing any coherent narrative within the lyrics, leaving the classic Arthurian elements strewn as hollowed out, modular elements. Poem 4, for example, is almost a systematic dismantling of a kernel story the poem refuses to give: that Gawain, wearing armor of an identifiable color, defeated another knight in his pursuit of the grail. Instead we have: "Everyone is impressed with courage and when he fought him he won / Who won? / I'm not sure but one was wearing red armor and one black armor / I'm not sure about the colors . . ." (*CP*, 332). At the end, only a slight suspicion of the presence of ravens remains.

In many ways, these maneuvers in "Gawain" are exemplary of the functioning of the rest of the poem. To a considerable extent this poem profits less from explication than many of Spicer's, precisely because it presents itself as already unfolded: the work can often feel like the exoskeleton of a poem with no internal organs. If *After Lorca* debates and theorizes the poetics of collage, it is *The Holy Grail* which in many ways enacts it, seeming such an accretion of fragments, tags, exclamations, interpellations and epigrams that Spicer's habitual poetics of pseudo-arguments and parodic conceits are almost entirely crowded out. Peter Gizzi has stressed the "wide range of narratives" (*H*, 214) Spicer pastes into his later works, particularly *The Holy Grail*, and noted how Spicer works with these elements through procedures of "assemblage" and "arrangement." As his readings of the *Grail* show, "Instead of being determining superstructures, these narrative fragments form the cultural 'rubble' from which the poem is made" (*H*, 215).[18] This, of course, also points to Spicer's ongoing rewriting of *The Waste Land*, whose famous "fragments . . . shored against my ruins" (*Collected Poems*, 69) find themselves washed up on the beaches of the poem's inland sea. Indeed, *The Waste Land* and its own appropriation of Grail legend has now itself become simply one more among the "narrative fragments" Spicer arranges. Yet in spite of this, the poem is in many ways the most traditionally "coherent" of any of Spicer's books. What gives it the consistency it possesses is its constantly elegiac tone, and its emphasis on loss and the essential endlessness and vacuity of desire, along with the latter's incommensurability with any possible object. Frequently, Spicer engages in a dismantling of the structural role of the "object" itself which underpins any quest narrative.

Thus in "Gawain" Spicer partially eschews his favored source, Malory, to lean substantially on "Gawain and the Green Knight," ending his book by echoing the latter text's emphasis on Gawain's "shame." This shame, however, is depicted as not entirely deserved, despite Gawain's clear failure to find either grail or poem: "Gawain no ghostman, guest who could not gather / Anything" (CP, 331), Spicer writes, in lines that mimic the alliterative structures of "Gawain and the Green Knight." But crucially, it is the origin and dimensions of this failure and Gawain's untranscendent qualities which seem to correspond to the properly poetic quest – one which the poem depicts as the opposite of transcendence, or magic, itself:

> They are still looking for it
> Poetry and magic see the world from opposite ends
> One cock-forward and the other ass-forward
> All over Britain (but what a relief it would be to give all this up and find
>   surcease in somebodyelse's soul and body)

> (CP, 333)

Poetry's cock-forward perspective sees its artistic task as interminable and desire as beyond gratification, in line with Spicerian seriality – a poetics in which the poem can never be entirely "completed" anymore than Spicer's grail can be properly "found." And the last line, with what seems a reference to the last phrase of *A Season in Hell*, might indicate that in his acceptance of this Gawain is importantly different from Rimbaud, who reputedly stopped looking for poetry after completing the work mentioned above.[19]

A similar point is hammered home in "The Book of Galahad," which recounts the tale of the only quester who could be considered successful, albeit not in Spicer's telling, where on the contrary Galahad "Found it [the grail] in such a way that the dead stayed dead, the waste land stayed a waste land" (CP, 351). The last poem of the sequence is illuminating:

> The grail is as common as rats or seaweed
> Not lost but misplaced.
> Someone searching for a letter that he knows is around the house
> And finding it, no better for the letter.
> The grail-country damp now from a heavy rain
> And growing pumpkins or artichokes or cabbage or whatever they used to
>   grow before they started worrying about the weather. Man

Has finally no place to go but upward: Galahad's
Testament.

(*CP*, 354)

The waste land is "restored" to no more than standard northern Californian coastal farmland in this typically anti-climactic conclusion, but the lyric turns mostly on the distinction between lost and misplaced, which once again relativizes the opposition between plenitude and lack, presence and absence. A misplaced object is not only more easily recoverable than one lost; the term also implies that knowledge of its location is in some way encysted in a subjective or collective memory of the agency that laid it aside, turning the quest (in quite time-honored fashion) inward, but also robbing it of any link with divine transcendence.[20] Additionally, note that in Spicer's simile this mislaid object is also an instance of address, a message, whose restoration changes nothing. This could be another dead letter perhaps, harking back to *The Heads of the Town*, but the story of the letter also dramatizes a symptomatic ambivalence about the address from the other, here played out through a hiding which itself hides what the finding of the object makes plain: that the letter had nothing to reveal, that there was no point in misplacing or suppressing it in the first place. The poem's close echoes Malory, who writes of Galahad's end: "And so suddeynly departed hys soule to Jesu Cryste, and a grete multitude of angels bare hit up to hevyn evyn in the syght of hys two felowis" (607). Spicer, however, seems to imply that Galahad's "testament" is essentially nihilist, in the Nietzschean sense: that finally, a quest structure which divides objects into the found or unfound fundamentally erases the world, leaving no place available but an upwards heavenly transcendence, or a death that is very different from the poetic, Orphic deathliness of the underworld which Spicer valorizes.

As the lost letter implies, misplacement is tied to missed connections and miscommunication in this poem, especially in "The Book of Merlin," which is particularly telegraphic, and appropriately so. Of the many variants of the Merlin story, Spicer alludes to those that depict the magician as imprisoned in a tower by the deceitful Viviane, from which he first imparts the quest of the Holy Grail to the knights of the Round Table: "Love, / The Grail, he said" (*CP*, 347).[21] But in Spicer's poem, the tower is also a radio tower, Merlin a transmitter listening to and presumably broadcasting "grail-music all day and all night every day and every night" (*CP*, 347). The poem returns to the theme of telecommunications in its final section: "Heimat. Heimat ohne Ferne / You are called to the phone" (*CP*, 349). The telephone, radio, and magic at once point to the ultimate portability of the homeland and to the abolishment of distance (Ferne), but also to the function of telecommunications as uncanny homing devices in every sense, very much like translation in *After Lorca*. Moreover, "The Book of Merlin" not only thematizes such transmissions, but acts as a transmitter itself, as its "messages" are answered or echoed throughout the poem, and above all in the final sequence, "The Book of the Death of Arthur." Thus, "Merlin" begins with another mass-culture tag, as the magician's imprisonment is announced by a board-game card:

> "Go to jail. Go directly to jail. Do not pass Go. Do not collect $200.00."
> The naked sound of a body sounds like a trumpet through all this horseshit.
> You do not go to jail. You stay there unmoved at what any physical or
>   metaphysical policemen do.
>
> (CP, 346)

This passage can be read as a foreshadowing – or prophecy, to evoke another element of Merlin's magic which Spicer stresses – of the puzzling opening lines of "The Book of the Death of Arthur": "'He who sells what isn't hisn / Must pay it back or go to prison,' / Jay Gould, Cornelius Vanderbilt, or some other imaginary American millionaire / – selling short" (*CP*, 355). What must be remembered is that the board game "Merlin" alludes to is Monopoly, and "Arthur" begins with a roll call of famous American monopolists.[22] Of course, the financial operation of "selling short" – selling stock you don't own in the hopes of acquiring it at a lower price later – is here given an erotic connotation, not least because Merlin's imprisonment is a consequence of his desire for Viviane.[23] But this allusion is also a good example of the historical and political detritus, largely modern, that Spicer strews throughout *The Holy Grail*, especially in the last three books, in a practice which harks back to Pound's *Cantos* as much as to anything in Eliot. For example, "Merlin" juxtaposes Gandhi with "colonial Hengest and Horsa" (*CP*, 346), legendary fifth-century Anglo-Saxon conquerors of Britain; cites in German a resistance song from the Spanish Civil War; mentions Sacco and Vanzetti; and likens the apocalyptic promise of the Grail to the Atom Bomb. All this provides a context which powerfully informs the massively elegiac final book, on the death of Arthur: Merlin again sings out to Arthur by way of the line "The naked sound of a body sounds like a trumpet through all this horseshit" (*CP*, 346) along with the evocation of the "grail-music" on the radio (*CP*, 347). Both are taken up in the final poem of "The Book of the Death of Arthur," which is also the end of *The Holy Grail* itself:

A noise in the head of the prince. A noise that travels a long ways
Past chances, broken pieces of lumber,

. . .

Annoys me
Arthur, king and future king
A noise in the head of the prince. Something in God-language. In spite of all
    this horseshit, this uncomfortable music.

                                                                                (*CP*, 358)

Is Arthur's "horseshit" cut through the way Merlin's was, by the clarion call of a body? Or would such a "trumpet" sound be part of the horseshit, along with "uncomfortable" grail music, that "God-language" manages to transmit across? Such equivalences are the sorts of connections the poem gestures towards but suspends, favoring static, bad reception, and half-echoes, in a thematics and technique which look forward to what will become major elements in *Language*, where Spicer's life-long interest in the pun opens into a full-blown discussion of morphemics. If in the *Grail* Lance's "lance," in all its sexual connotations, is never removed from his name, such effects become even more insistent at the poem's close, as "A noise that travels a long ways" blurs over the distance of the airwaves into "annoys," while music, God-language, and a buzzing in the head refuse to distinguish themselves from one another, as Merlin and Arthur play out a shadowy sketch of transmission and reception, poetics as dictation.

In terms of politics, popular culture, and ultimately the uncanny transmission of prophecy, however, one of the most striking moments of *The Holy Grail* is when it parallels Marilyn Monroe with Gwenivere: "Marilyn Monroe being attacked by a bottle of sleeping pills / Like a bottle of angry hornets / Lance me, she said" (*CP*, 355). One might find this unsurprising, given the popular association of the Kennedy administration with Camelot, and Marilyn Monroe's affair with the President. However, this poem was finished by late August 1962; Marilyn Monroe's death on August 5 wafted into the poem – which Spicer appears to have written sequentially in accordance with the dictates of dictation – very shortly after it happened. Meanwhile, the popular Camelot topos only emerged after Kennedy's assassination more than a year later, apparently on the suggestion of Jacqueline Kennedy – indeed, the untimely death of the young leader and the premature end of his reign were meant to underpin the comparison in the first place, itself bolstered by the late president's affection for the Broadway musical *Camelot*, which probably informed Spicer's work too. There is no way of knowing if Spicer meant for his lines to imply a link between Kennedy and Camelot by way of reference to Monroe, whose flirty birthday serenade to Kennedy in May 1962 had raised eyebrows; certainly, Kennedy's assassination is a major element of *Language*. But leaving that aside, Spicer's poem anticipates or prophecies what was to become an extremely important popular mythology, but also a curiously double-edged one, as the Camelot comparison inevitably raises the topic of sexual infidelity, and whether consciously or not, Jacqueline Kennedy's suggested topos seems to have implicitly endorsed the already rampant rumors concerning Kennedy's antics. At the same time, such an equivalence also cross-dresses the tale, casting the unfaithful President as Gwenivere and Marilyn Monroe as Lancelot: a campy retelling Spicer would have liked.

Ultimately, however, Spicer's campy mythical method-like positing of Marilyn as Gwenivere calls attention to the very problematic status of the latter within his poem. "The Book of Gwenivere" is one of the most impressive sections of *The Holy Grail*, and in many ways carves out a separate status for itself: in a poem which relies heavily on deceptive and subtle modulations between first-, third-, and second-person narration, this is the only "Book" told entirely in the first person, and Gwenivere emerges as the most sharply outlined and distinctive of the players in the tale, as well as one of the most sympathetic, thanks to her skepticism regarding the Quest and her affirmation of the primacy of her love for Lancelot over and against it.[24] Yet Spicer is not wrong in repeatedly referring to her as a "bitch" in the Vancouver lectures, though he might have added that the real bitchiness resides with him and where he places her.[25] For Spicer leaves her firmly ensconced in a predictable, stereotypically female position, privileging possessive, private satisfaction and personal pleasure over the male domain of self-sacrifice, public duty, and moral and religious law, as Spicer makes clear when called upon by his auditors to justify his derogatory epithet: "Well, she doesn't want to find the Grail. She'd rather sleep with Lancelot, which is reasonable enough" (*H*, 60). These factors might also explain why Spicer insists that this book is the "easiest" section of the poem (*H*, 59); it is certainly the one that sits most comfortably with familiar tropes and gender clichés.[26] Indeed, here stereotype leads inevitably to the question of archetype, and not only because Spicer typecasts Marilyn Monroe into such a readily available paradigm, but also because his depiction of Gwenivere can seem all too close to this description of the archetypal anima from Jung, cited by none other than Robert Duncan in *The H. D. Book*, manuscripts of which, as we know, Spicer was reading: "the anima is fickle, capricious, moody, uncontrolled, and emotional, sometimes gifted with daemonic intuitions, ruthless, malicious, untruthful, bitchy, double-faced, and mystical."[27]

Such archetypal readings have the function of aligning and controlling diverse stories, to form transhistorical, prescriptive narratives, capable of instantly naturalizing the defamiliarizing brutality of the collage-like juxtaposition of a tabloid queen with the legendary Gwenivere, trivial-izing both rather than demystifying either. With regard to this particular regulatory narrative – the tale of the faithless woman whose infidelity destroys kingdoms and lays waste to heroes – the classical exemplar is less Gwenivere than Helen of Troy, however, whose legacy with regard to normative descriptions of femininity was very much in dispute in the late American modernist poetics of the 1950s. Notably, William Carlos Williams essentializes or perhaps archetypifies the figure of Helen in disturbing fashion in his late poem to his wife, "Asphodel, That Greeny Flower": "All women are not Helen, / I know that, / but have Helen in their hearts. / My sweet, / you have it also, therefore / I love you / and could not love you otherwise" (*Pictures*, 159), in lines less surprising for their sexism than for their appeal to mythic authority.[28] Such a context makes all the more palpable the importance of the starkly contrasting maneuver of Williams' old friend H. D., who in *Helen of Egypt* makes the feminist gesture of radicalizing an ancient counter-tradition, and simply removing Helen from the tale in which she, and by extension womanhood, have been ensconced: "According to the Pallinode [of Stesichorus] Helen was never in Troy. She had been transposed or trans-lated from Greece into Egypt. Helen of Troy was a phantom, substituted for the real Helen, by jealous deities. The Greeks and the Trojans alike fought for an illusion" (1).

In the context of *The H. D. Book*, Robert Duncan engaged in furious reading of and note-taking on *Helen in Egypt* in August and September 1961, and it is not surprising that Spicer entered this overdetermined discussion himself by way of his posthumously published book, *Helen: A Revision*.[29] Fragmentary and uneven like H. D.'s own *Helen in Egypt*, Spicer's *Helen* is a slighter work than *The Holy Grail* by some stretch. Yet the fragmentary variability itself gives it value precisely by leaving the Helen it hints at entirely elusive and uncontained; its first lines tell us:

> Nothing is known about Helen but her voice
> Strange glittering sparks
> Lighting no fires but what is reechoed
> Rechorded, set on the icy sea.

> (*CP*, 237)

The neologism "rechording" seems to preside over the work, which rather than "record" a story or even a voice (like Gwenivere's, which emerges so strikingly from the "uncomfortable music" of *The Holy Grail*) instead "re-chords," offering harmonic counterpoints or perhaps "correspondences" in the form of short lyrics which often have no discernible relation to the tale of Helen at all, while occasionally re-echoing H. D.'s tone and vocabulary in *Helen in Egypt*, as well as her theme: "Now, in Egypt, she who was never there perceives / Two names" (*CP*, 241). But the poem speaks most powerfully when it breaks into an authorial first person in order to express desire for a male love object, as it does twice. We find this mode first in a letter, reminiscent of *After Lorca* and *Letters to James Alexander*: "Dear Russ, / I am writing to you in the middle of a poem about Helen. What there was to her about your body I should have never ceased to wish to know. It is as if there was a dark fleshy space between us labeled, 'I am not myself'" (*CP*, 243). Later, a short lyric explains: "He was beautiful. I am trying to leave him and it at that" (*CP*, 245). That is to say, within a poem thematizing Helen of Troy, Spicer explicitly eschews the time-tested gay poet's device of expressing desire for a man through a female character or persona; quite the contrary, as the letter to Russ explains: "There is utterly no reason for imagining Helen. Whether she was in Troy or Egypt, she would be the same figure of imagination put into being by a vacuum, the same vacuum by which I write poetry or you paint, or, I suppose men fought for her" (*CP*, 243). These lines replace a mythopoetic, archetypal reading of Helen with what almost feels a Nietzschean or perhaps Freudian one, stressing the priority of desire or lack over and against whatever object comes to fill it: man, woman, poem, painting, or grail. Unlike the "easy" *Book of Gwenivere*, this poem concludes: "it is as difficult to get into a poem as into / Helen" (*CP*, 245), leaving Helen here as a figure of resistance to meaning and transcendence, without assimilating this resistance into yet another version of the "feminine mystery" and its unsoundable interiority. Rather, she echoes a "dark fleshy space" of meeting and of separation, where "I am not myself" (*CP*, 243).

On the other hand, the first poem of "The Book of Gwenivere" ends with a very different statement of subjective attribution – "Listen, / I am Gwenivere" (*CP*, 342) – in a love poem where Spicer vamps a woman's voice throughout. The question of the articulation between this I and the body it is and the body it loves – central to Spicer from as early as "We Find the Body Difficult to Speak" – closes "The Book of Gwenivere," as Spicer strews the first-person pronoun of identification and its attributes over his page:

I dreamed last night that your body had become a gigantic adventure. Wild horses
Could not tear it away from itself.
I
Was the whole earth you were traveling over

Rock, sand, and water.
Christ, and this little teacup
Were always between us.
I was a witch, Lance. My body was not the earth, yours not wild horses or
  what wild horses could not tear
Politely, your body woke me up
And I saw the bent morning

(*CP*, 345)

Here, the poem undoes the troping of the female body as landscape which Spicer had already worked with in "Psychoanalysis: An Elegy," while Lancelot's body resists all figures of rending, of not being itself. Still, we should dwell on the specificity of his body as attribute rather than identity in the penultimate line, as the poem ends on the note of a very equivocal politeness ("All your heros are so polite / They would make a cat scream" (*CP*, 345), Gwenivere says earlier). The "bent morning" where the light shines on the lovers' bodies, or maybe doesn't, ends the dream, which is perhaps less interesting than the landscape of day. And in fact, the sense of vision or clarity implicit here contrasts with what follows in "The Book of the Death of Arthur," which insists "The Blackness remains," a "blackness alive with itself / At the sides of our fires," "a simple hole running from one thing to another" (*CP*, 357). *The Holy Grail* will end not with sight, the revelation of the body of the beloved in its splendor,[30] but rather with sound, "A noise in the head of the prince" (*CP*, 358). But earlier in "The Book of the Death of Arthur," in relation not to love but to the Grail, is another image of clarity, but meaningless: "I have forgotten why the grail was important / Why somebody wants to reach it like a window you throw open. Thrown open / What would it mean?" (*CP*, 357). As the shared Latin etymology might indicate, at the heart of the quest is the question.

Notes

1. The difference in cultural weighting and prestige between, say, the tales of Ovid and those of Billy the Kid, along with their commonly received geographic and genealogical implications, means that Spicer's reserve of hypotexts cannot all be lumped together, even if in some ways he might handle the Billy legends much in the same manner as those from classical antiquity. Indeed, this very similarity only becomes meaningful in light of the cultural divide it refuses to recognize, and this becomes even more crucial in Spicer's negotiations with the Eliotic model, as we shall see.
2. Beyond such differences, however, letters in the Spicer Papers at the Bancroft library make clear that among the Berkeley Renaissance poets "irreverent" use of classical topoi was a strong part of coterie identity.

3. Duncan claims that Spicer's interest in the Orpheus figure began "in 1946 with the second part of my poem 'Heavenly City, Earthly City'" (see Duncan's preface to Spicer, *One Night*, xii), while in the Vancouver Lectures, Spicer names "Medieval Scenes" as one of "Duncan's two best poems" (*H*, 52) (the other being "The Opening of the Field").

4. In the notes to the poem, Eliot writes: "Not only the title, but the plan and a good deal of the incidental symbolism of the poem were suggested by Miss Jessie L. Weston's book on the Grail legend . . . Indeed, so deeply am I indebted, Miss Weston's book will elucidate the difficulties of the poem much better than my notes can do" (*Collected Poems*, 70).

5. "I don't know how many of you know anything about the Grail and what the Grail meant. If you've read Tennyson's *Idylls of the King*, it will rather hurt you a bit. If you've read Malory, it will help you. If you don't know what happened in the search for the Grail and all of that, presumably if the poem's good enough, it won't matter. And if you've read Jessie Weston, you might as well leave the room" (*H*, 57).

6. Spicer's comments can often be keyed to Chapter 1 of the section "Nights and Days," which the editors list as having been written by Duncan on March 10, 1961, and revised in 1963. The revisions were substantive, however, as many of Spicer's comments, including the reference to Jung, are impossible to correlate to the text as published in *The H. D. Book*. The manuscript Spicer discusses was in fact a draft of *The Little Day Book*, which Duncan subsequently published in *Origin* 10, in 1963. On the page keyed to Spicer's objections, Duncan writes of "the ground only Art makes for the dream to become communal" before invoking Jung: "The images and utterances that Jung attributes to the Collective Unconscious all occurred in the works of man, are creations of the community of language" (Robert Duncan Collection, Poetry Collection of the University Libraries, University at Buffalo, State University of New York). Many thanks to James Maynard for his brilliant detective work which helped discover this source.

7. As printed in *Acts*, the letter is tentatively dated 1959, but 1960 seems more likely. Lisa Jarnot marks *The H. D. Book* project proper as beginning in the spring of 1960 (193), though Duncan had been intensively reading and writing on her since 1959.

8. For a brilliant account of Olson's relationship to Jung's thought, see Mellors, pp. 90–116. Mellors excels at showing how in these theories the purported submission of ego to the transcendental collectivity of the unconscious in fact ends up as a process of "heroic sublation" (95) which creates an even more authoritarian subject, deriving its grounding from truths seen at once as "collective," "objective" (97), and normative. However he also points out that "the beauty of Olson's method is that, as a principle, it goes far beyond his own prescriptions" (96), a position not dissimilar to Spicer's take on Olson. On Jung's sense that the work of art must transcend the epiphenomenal neuroses of its creator to reach universal archetypes, see, for example, "On the Relation of Analytical Psychology to Poetry."

9. The precise meaning and domain of "pragmatics" in linguistics has been subject to a good deal of evolution and disputation, as outlined by Stephen Levinson (1–35). During the years in which Spicer was active in the field,

"pragmatics" would largely have been taken in the senses suggested by Charles Morris, for whom it is one of the three main branches of semiotic inquiry, along with semantics and syntactics (see Levinson, 1–3).

10. To use the language of the analytic philosophical take on pragmatics, Spicer is interested in Orpheus as a poet of perlocutionary force. Another hint as to how Spicer might have linked Freud to a "pragmatic" sense of mythology is found in another of his comments on Duncan's *Little Day Book*, where he opines "The Freud quote is absolutely right. Now if you can proceed from translation into metaphor . . ." (*B*). The passage in question comes in the midst of Duncan's exposition of Pound's poetics and the place of translation within them: "We may see the deeper significance of the role translation has had for Pound as a poetic task. 'The dream-thoughts,' Freud writes, 'and the dream-content are presented to us like two versions of the same subject matter in two different languages.' As, too, we see the importance of the ideogram for Pound, for it is his route towards – 'as it were a pictographic script' – the *condensare* of the dream" (Robert Duncan Collection, Poetry Collection of the University Libraries, University at Buffalo, State University of New York). The linkage of dream and poetic metaphor to the rebus-like ideogram, along with Duncan's reading of Pound's "Dichtung=condensare" as implying the overdetermination of the Freudian dream-work, leads distinctly *away* from the universal symbology implied by the Jungian archetype. It is interesting to see how insistently Spicer applauds this tendency in Duncan's text, and condemns the other.

11. See Mellors for the very problematic position of the "local," largely derived from Williams, within Olson's mythopoetic structure.

12. Williams' dictum occurs most famously in *Paterson* (" – Say it, no ideas but in things – / nothing but the blank faces of the houses / and cylindrical trees" (6)) but can also be found in the short poem "A Sort of a Song."

13. Williams writes "The word must be put down for itself, not as a symbol of nature but a part, cognizant of the whole" (*Imaginations*, 102) and Perloff comments: "The implication of this distinction is that words will be related metonymically rather than metaphorically" (*Poetics of Indeterminacy*, 114).

14. Attacks on the simile and its implications are an important element in the part of Williams' poetics which is crystallized in "no ideas but in things," as in this passage from *The Descent of Winter*: "poetry should strive for nothing else, this vividness alone, *per se*, for itself. The realization of this has its own internal fire that is 'like' nothing. Therefore the bastardy of the simile. That thing, the vividness which is poetry by itself, makes the poem. There is no need to explain or compare. Make it and it *is* a poem. This is modern, not the saga. There are no sagas – only trees now, animals, engines: There's that" (*Imaginations*, 247–8).

15. It shouldn't be forgotten that the major poem from *Journey to Love*, "Asphodel, That Greeny Flower," is also structured around classical myth: that the roots of the asphodel nourish the dead in the underworld. The poem also displays a fair amount of allusion to Homeric myth, but unlike Spicer here, contains it within a coherent, contemporary poetic voice of reminiscence and reflection.

16. Spicer's own comments on the "Tonys" in his Vancouver lecture somewhat

contradict this reading, as there Spicer claims "The proper names in the thing are simply a kind of disturbance which I often use. I guess it's 'I' rather than the poems because it's sort of the insistence of the absolutely immediate which has nothing to do with anything, and you put that in and then you get all the immediate out of the poem and you can go back to the poem" (*H*, 58). Such statements tend to disparage the "immediate" in favor of what presumably would be the transcendent, but at the same time they insist on the necessity of that very transcendence being "disturbed," implying a logic which is inevitably one of rupture or violation, in which the transcendent as such cannot be posited without a breaching of its borders. For more on Spicer's rhetoric of disturbance, also prominent in *Admonitions*, see Chapter 2 of this study, as well as the introduction. See *P*, pp. 221–3, for information about the Tonys behind these allusions. Meanwhile, the appropriation of Grail myth and symbolism as a strategic element in highly complex and mediated erotic exchanges is the explicit theme of *Armed with Madness* by Mary Butts, a cult novel for the poets of the Berkeley Renaissance.

17. Peter Riley first identified the source over thirty years ago in his excellent article on *The Holy Grail*. He there links Spicer's poem to a passage on p. 233 of Paton's book. In fact, Spicer's text echoes even more closely material found on pp. 18–19 of Paton, which it repeats very nearly verbatim. The Spicer archives at the Bancroft library contain a torn notebook page in Spicer's hand which copies the passage without distortion and enclosed in quotation marks, but with no attribution given. There, "damoisele" is spelled correctly and given the feminine definite article, as in Paton.

18. See *H*, pp. 212–18, for these arguments, as bolstered by incisive close readings of passages from *The Holy Grail*. When Gizzi writes "by the early sixties, Spicer's poems begin to feel more 'assembled'" (*H*, 212), I would add that nowhere is this more the case than with *The Holy Grail*. My argument throughout this paragraph is heavily indebted to Gizzi's insights.

19. Rimbaud's French reads, "et il me sera loisible de *posséder la vérité dans une âme et un corps*" (117, original italics), or in English, "and I shall have leave *to possess the truth in one body and one soul*." Recent scholarship has questioned whether Rimbaud gave up poetry after *A Season in Hell*, but that was the received opinion in Spicer's day.

20. In his unfinished detective novel, Spicer also harps on the losing of objects as parapraxis: "He had a horror of things lost, a certainty . . . that they could never be found, were, in fact, cunningly hidden by the very process of being lost" (*Tower*, 155).

21. This is the version relayed by Thomas Bulfinch, for example, in whose telling Merlin conveys the imperative of the Grail Quest to Gawain.

22. As Jim Goar has pointed out, this proverb is usually attributed to Daniel Drew, an American financier engaged in long-running battles with Vanderbilt and unstable alliances with Gould involving stock-price manipulation.

23. Selling short is also an intrinsically triangular arrangement, in which A borrows stock from B to sell to C, in the hope that a subsequent price drop will allow A to buy back the stock owed to B at a lower price than that

of the sale to C. This echoes the essentially triangular structure of courtly romance, as seen, of course, in the Arthur–Gwenivere–Lancelot affair.

24. The interplay of voices and the difficulty of attributing them securely to specific subjects, despite the names given to the different books, is another element that recalls Eliot's practice in *The Waste Land*.
25. Spicer insists on this epithet over and against repeated objections. See *H*, pp. 57–9.
26. In fact, here Spicer quite closely follows Malory, where Gwenivere bitterly accuses Lancelot of betraying her with another woman when he invokes Christian morality, loyalty, and honor as explanations for a slackening in his attentions to her (611–12).
27. Cited in *The H. D. Book*, p. 489. This text was written in March 1961; there is every chance that Spicer would have seen it.
28. Prior to this, quite classically, Williams identifies "Helen's public fault" (158) as the origin of the disaster of the Trojan War. Predictably, no mention is made of Alexander.
29. *The Collected Poetry* dates the poem to 1960, by which time Duncan was already deep into his study of and correspondence with H. D., and was sharing material with Spicer. This would explain why Spicer's poem seems to echo *Helen in Egypt* in addition to making explicit reference to its theme, although the latter poem, written years earlier, was not published until 1961. It is also conceivable that Spicer's work, dated tentatively, was composed in 1961 itself.
30. An extremely important node in Pound's reading of Troubadour poetry, as Spicer might have known.

Chapter 5

The Poetry of Language and the Language of Poetry: *Language* and the *Book of Magazine Verse*

Spicer's completion of *The Holy Grail* in August 1962 marked the end of a virtually uninterrupted period of creativity which had begun in Boston in 1956 with *Oliver Charming*. Over the next year or so his poetic production dwindled to almost nothing, and probably not coincidentally, his personal and professional life also deteriorated markedly. Sometime over the winter of 1962–3 Spicer was a passenger in an automobile accident of which the resultant physical pain and recurrent anxiety led him to increase his already elevated alcohol intake to even more dangerous levels, which were never to recede. At the same time, his ever more difficult personal behavior during this period alienated many of his closest and oldest friends, such as Robert Duncan, Jim and Fran Herndon – the latter an important artistic collaborator for Spicer as well – and even Robin Blaser.[1] None of these relationships were to be fully repaired before Spicer's death in August 1965. Spicer's professional life, such as it was, also disintegrated over the last months of his life. Since 1957, his main source of income had been as a part-time research assistant on a major linguistics project at the University of California at Berkeley, but Spicer's employment there was terminated in March 1964, when the project was deemed no longer viable (*P*, 286).[2] Although the lead researcher at Berkeley, David Reed, helped Spicer obtain a similar position on a children's literacy project at Stanford, Spicer found the commute to Palo Alto and working hours far less congenial than his Berkeley arrangement, and suffered greatly at this job which he held from May 1964 until February, 1965 (*P*, 290–3). From this point on, Spicer lived in penury until his death.[3] However, this particularly bleak period, even by Spicer's standards, also bore witness to one final extraordinary flowering, resulting in a particularly Spicerian late style in his two last books, *Language* and the *Book of Magazine Verse*, the former arguably his greatest work.

These two books, written from late 1963 or early 1964 up until the last days preceding Spicer's final collapse, represent what are in many ways different projects, and there is a danger in reading them as a "diptych," as Ron Silliman emphasized in a brilliant essay on *Language* in 1985 (*New Sentence*, 148).[4] Yet despite their differences, or even thanks to them, these two books – each very much concerned with correspondence, transmission, and exchange – converse with each other powerfully, and profit from being considered in such a context. Taken together, these last two books respond powerfully to the contradiction in which Spicer felt himself trapped in his final years: it was his very exclusion from official verse culture, as exemplified by magazine poetry, which forced him to labor as a researcher in linguistics, a field related to, but not identical with, his preferred vocation. Indeed, the famous cover of the White Rabbit Press edition of *Language* can be seen as an assertion of this very fact: here one finds faintly reproduced a sepia green photocopy of the cover of the July–September 1952 number of the linguistics journal *Language* (which contained Spicer's one publication as an academic linguist) but messily scrawled across it in a large bold red hand (probably Spicer's own) stands the title "Language" and the name "Jack Spicer." In truth, however, the book represents less poetry asserting its rights to language over and against those of linguistics than a different figure which the cover also suggests: the over-writing or overdetermination of a palimpsest. As we shall see, *Language* as book is not only informed but quite literally formed by the work in linguistics Spicer undertook at Stanford as he was writing it, and stages not so much an opposition of poetry to linguistics, but, as the "Language" poets were quick to realize, their dialectic: the emergence of language *as* poetry, the poetry of language, within a work which makes frequent and explicit recourse to the formal language of linguistic analysis – "morphemics," "phonemics," and "graphemics," for example – in order to emphasize language as system, structure, and code rather than simple expressive medium.[5]

In contrast to this, it could be said that the *Book of Magazine Verse* inverts the previous book's gesture toward a transcendental structuralism, to stress not the poetry of language but the language of poetry – that is, the concrete social and historical mid-century determinations of what had become the accepted mainstream poetic medium – because this later book explicitly took its task as delineating and even courting Spicer's ambivalently constructed exclusion from the world of letters. Indeed, Spicer's very project was none other than to explore the conditions of his own unacceptability, and to force the magazines in question to confront the restrictive nature of their own implicit criteria: the structuring principle of the *Book of Magazine Verse* is "the idea of writing poems for magazines which would not print them" (*H*, 102), and thus the book features sections of poems for *The Nation* and *Poetry, Chicago* as well as less likely venues such as *The St. Louis Sporting News* and the music magazine, *Downbeat*.[6] In this respect, the *Book of Magazine Verse* could seem like a very different sort of proposal from *Language*: while the latter investigates a pure poetry of the American vernacular, which Spicer arrives at through an ultimately dialectical suspension of many of Mallarmé's principles of impersonality, the *Book of Magazine Verse*, acting through provocation, aggression, interpellation, and address, not only returns to the practice of *Admonitions* – now offering a distorting mirror not to an individual dedicatee but to cultural institutions[7] – but also thereby enters into a historical and even political interrogation distant from the more metaphysical preoccupations of *Language*. While there is some truth to this distinction, such a dichotomy is also undercut by various factors. First of all, political and historical references are strewn throughout *Language*, as the "purity" of poetry is seen to derive from the ephemera of popular culture, sporting news, and current events, rather than arise in opposition to them; part of the book's stated task is to situate historical catastrophe in relation to the above, and not in isolation from them. Second, and equally important, is that linguistic code and social act are not seen by Spicer as opposed. On the contrary, for Spicer it is the code itself, and its various "routings" (to use his own term) between phonemes and morphemes, its syntactical transforma-tions, its ambiguities and infelicities (puns, noise, etc.), that position you in relation both to your own desire – to the extent that the possessive is allowed to hold – and to a poetic expression regarding which the possessive, as we have amply seen, is entirely denied by the poetics of dictation. Transmission happens not only "socially" between sender and receiver – the poet with his envelope, the magazine with its rejection slip – but is internal to the production of the semanteme. "The emotional disturbance echoes down the canyons of the heart" (*CP*, 396) before it can echo into the networks of erotic or editorial exchange. Spicer's imperative that community – itself not thinkable except as dissension and difference – be woven into the sounds, signs, and marks of his inter-nal speaking and listening, of his desiring flesh, rather than wait outside to receive him, is the explosive law internal to both his last books, as the unpublishable poet himself becomes the imprint or echo of signs that go unanswered: "If this is dictation, it is driving / Me wild" (*CP*, 423).

*

As a book, *Language* developed very much in public, and within an extremely specific magazine environment. The poems, not yet linked together in any larger structure, began appearing in the journal *Open*

Space from its first issue in January 1964, which featured what would become the first poem of the emergent book; many more were to be published throughout the magazine's year-long run.[8] Given the sequence of the poems as published in *Open Space*, *Language* does seem to have been composed serially, but an important element of the book's final structure was apparently added by Spicer retrospectively once the larger project began to come into focus. That is, the sections "Love Poems," "Intermissions," "Transformations," "Morphemics," and "Phonemics" were all published in *Open Space* under those titles.[9] However, the first poems were only grouped under the crucial title "Thing Language" subsequently, indicating that the thematization of language as such was something that emerged during the serial process, and which Spicer allowed himself to remap onto the earlier production. Indeed, ignoring the first section's title, we can see that if questions of transmission, dictation, and communication are foregrounded early on in poems like "Sporting Life," "Finally the messages penetrate," or "Smoke signals," along with semiotics in number 7 of "Love Poems," the focus on language as such and the explicit linguistic terminology do not come into play until "Transformations," from which point onwards such terminology dominates the volume. Given the dating of *Open Space*, this turn would seem to have occurred in the late summer or early autumn 1964, when Spicer was in the middle of his project at Stanford, which is directly cited in these baffling lines from "Morphemics":

> The loss of innocence, Andy,
> The morpheme -cence is regular as to Rule IIc, IIa and IIb [cents] and
>   [sense] being more regular. The [inn-]
> With its geminated consonant
> Is not the inn in which the Christ Child was born.
>
> (CP, 392)[10]

The "rules" referred to here are mentioned in the copious handwritten notes which survive from Spicer's work on the Stanford project, and their enumerations correspond in part to section headings found therein. While it is difficult to extrapolate from the existing notes exactly what the "rules" in question stipulate, section II of the Stanford notes is devoted to morphology, and specifically the relationships between free and bound morphemes (terms Spicer mentions in the third poem of "Phonemics," *CP*, 394) along with how morphology is marked both phonetically, through intonation, and graphemically, through spelling and punctuation.[11] Spicer considers these questions in light of the special case of children's speech and literacy – a major part of his brief was to identify patterns and principles of "regular" language usage and linguistic development among children – but his overall discussion of morphemes largely follows classic linguistic theory.[12] As Wikipedia explains, a morpheme is "the smallest ... meaningful unit in a language," which means they are meaningful units that can be smaller than words, and of which words are comprised. For example, -ly and -ed are inflectional morphemes, indicating respectively an adverbial construction and either a verb in the preterit or a past participle. They are also "bound morphemes" in that they can never occur alone, but only as part of a larger word, in conjunction with a root and perhaps other bound morphemes. Regarding bound morphemes, part of Spicer's work was charting how children learn to differentiate between phonemes and graphemes that are morphemically significant and those that are not; Spicer's notes distinguish between the -ly in "Sally" and in "fatherly," or the -er in "father" and in "bigger" (*B*).

Free morphemes, on the other hand, are units which can stand alone, and thus of necessity, words, which can themselves be linked together into lexemes, or joined to bound morphemes, as in the case where a root verb takes an inflectional morpheme to indicate tense. The point Spicer is making in the passage above is that phonetic identity and morphemic identity are not the same; that, as he puts it in "Phonemics," the phonemes themselves (which must first be abstracted from sounds) must then be correctly routed "to bound and free morphemes, then to syntactic structures" (*CP*, 394). In other words, while some speakers might say or hear -cence, -cents, and -sense as identical, they remain not only semantically but also morphologically distinct, and that distinction must be effected for any form of "sense" (which, opposed to -cence, is a free morpheme, like cent, whereas -cents features the addition of the bound inflectional morpheme -s to mark the plural) to hold. Similarly, the bound morpheme inn- of innocence, graphemically identical to the place where the "Christ child was born," is not a free morpheme at all, as the latter noun is.

Spicer harps on such questions for several reasons. First of all, morphological analysis provides him with a way of formalizing one of his favorite techniques, the pun. As "Morphemics" demonstrates, puns do more than create semantic confusion, in which one word can be mistaken for another (say, "cents" and "sense"); they also can be mobilized to create a more fundamental structural interference in which the morphological status of a phoneme goes haywire, and basic morphological articulations, such as the distinction between bound and free, are thrown out of kilter as the entire linguistic "routing" system goes awry. Even more in the late poetry than the earlier work, Spicer will cut words across line breaks, very frequently isolating bound morphemes, and thereby forcing them into structural positions the English language refuses to recognize. This leads to another discovery put to work in *Language*. In the Stanford notes, centered as they are on children's reading, Spicer devotes careful attention to the function of graphematic convention on a minute level, considering not only punctuation and capitalization (Spicer remarks that a capital letter alone transforms the common noun "father" into the grammatically distinct proper name, "Father") but also elements such as single- and double-spacing between words and punctuation marks, and the role of blank spaces generally. For example, Spicer notes that for the young reader it is the blank space in the phrase "Let's play house," absent in "It's my playhouse," which indicates the different relationship obtaining between the free morphemes "play" and "house" in each example – the space both differentiates the syntax and calls for a different intonation in each example, should the sequence play/house be spoken aloud. Precisely this recognition of the power of the mark, and particularly the blank mark, allows Spicer to further radicalize his use of line breaks in *Language*, turning them into a fully fledged and independent graphemic element. In these ways, and others which will become apparent, Spicer's structural analysis of language feeds directly into his poetic practice.

At the same time, the Stanford project also informed Spicer's poetic theory, for the crucial idea behind the "computer-assisted instruction" project was of course automation – the breaking down of language into an agentless system which could be managed by a machine. This clearly echoes in many ways the poetics of dictation, and the trope of the poet as a mechanically constructed radio; in some ways, the Stanford project set out to literally create a language machine not wholly unlike Spicer's poet of dictation. That is, the goals of the undertaking seem to have been double: on the one hand, to put early computer technology to peda-gogical use, and on the other, to exploit the data which the pedagogical interface produced to find ways to digitally model and further automate linguistic usage and exchange. Of import to the latter objective, then, was the isolation of the laws which govern the recognition and negotia-tion of signs and structures as such – graphemics, phonemics, and finally morphemics and syntax. Interestingly, however, Spicer's absorption in such details did not in fact lead him to posit an ultimate primacy of the language machine, or language as machine: despite the incredible attunement of *Language* to what might be called semiotics (though as far as I know Spicer never uses this term), the book does not take lin-guistics as the foundational model of the wider semiotics which it every-where considers. On the contrary, *Language* writes language *within* a broader consideration of signs and portents (harking back to "The

Book of Merlin" in *The Holy Grail*), which include earthquakes, smoke signals, assassinations, marginalia and textual cruces, the tremors of the desiring body, and finally love itself as that which demands to be *read*. The question here becomes less who writes and from where – central to the entire problematics of dictation – than who reads, the poet now not only a radio-set tuned into and broadcasting what is heard as dictation but in some way also absorbing the violence of the semiotic onslaught: "The poet / Takes too many messages. The right to the ear that floored him in New Jersey" (*CP*, 373), " . . . the messages penetrate the radio and render it . . . ultimately useless" (*CP*, 376). The poet becomes a reader *of* what Spicer calls "the human crisis" (*CP*, 379), certainly, but qua radio-reader, is now also the *site* of the crisis itself, the crisis where meaning and desire confront the sign in its alterity – every sign already as alien as any radio signal from outer space – and thus the site of the slippage of desire, where affirmation and negation negate each other: "No / One listens to poetry" (*CP*, 373). The poet is the reader of space and time, silence and sounds, words and loves, maneuvering through a universe of smoke signals, baseball scores, and unforeseeable deaths that is larger than the language that describes it, or shouts out to it, while being homologous to that language itself.

The opening section, "Thing Language," is an illustration of many of these points. To start with, the title itself presents an ambiguity which could perhaps be removed through intonation, but not through the graphemes put at our disposal: is "thing language" language *about* things ("thing-language" perhaps; the initial free morpheme in an adjectival slot) or language *as* "thing" (the two free morphemes in paratactic apposition)? The fact that we can't quite tell is precisely what interests Spicer. The very famous first poem works through and develops these very questions. From its outset, in fact, it opposes the deafening yet meaningless roar of "things" – specifically, the ocean – to the comparatively meager sounds of poetry, or human language, which seem to find themselves drowned out:

> This ocean, humiliating in its disguises
> Tougher than anything.
> No one listens to poetry. The ocean
> Does not mean to be listened to. A drop
> Or crash of water. It means
> Nothing.
> It
> Is bread and butter
> Pepper and salt . . .

(*CP*, 373)

This gives us "thing-language" in the first sense: language to talk about a "thing" which in and of itself, unlike language, has no relation to meaning. However, the situation is not so simple given that Spicer's poem makes its own language – perhaps unlike the ocean – constantly lose and accrue meanings, like a wave breaking and receding. For example, when the poem closes, its crucial early declaration is repeated, but with the introduction of a graphematic line break which alone is enough to suggest an entirely different meaning from the first iteration: "No / One listens to poetry" (*CP*, 373). Ron Silliman has pointed out that this radically "semantic" (*New Sentence*, 157) use of the line break is typical of Spicer's practice, and in *Language* it frequently serves to destabilize declarative utterances as they fall across the space of the page. To give another example, the isolation of "Nothing" in line 6 pressures the phrase "it means nothing" into a new connotation: not only that the ocean has no meaning, but that in some way it actively "means" the "Nothing" it represents. In other words, Spicer's Pacific[13] starts to seem like Wallace Stevens' "Snow Man," the object which leads the wintry "listener," who is "nothing himself," to behold "Nothing that is not there and the nothing that is" (8). Just as Stevens substantivizes the "nothing" by way of the definite article, Spicer seems to do something analogous through line break and capitalization, and both poems concern themselves with a "nature" which at once refuses to be anthropomorphized yet comes to "mean" the negativity which such a refusal implies.[14] Going further, the isolation of "Nothing" on a single line also serves to call attention to the word which immediately follows it in the poem, the only other to have a line to itself: "It." This graphematic, structural juxtaposition places "nothing" and "it" in parallel, and Silliman has forcefully demonstrated how in this poem the "it" becomes a paradoxically positive marker of linguistic negativity in its own right, constantly referring to itself as much as to any antecedent: "What 'pounds the shore' is as much It-ness, that which 'means nothing,' as it is any body of water" (159). In other words, as "it" is substantivized in much the same way as "nothing," this poem can quite easily be read as dealing not with the language of things, but with language as "thing," and all the more as the poem so clearly emphasizes graphemic and syntactic elements in a manner which foregrounds language as such.

Similar procedures and questions will recur throughout *Language*, and the opening poem serves as an excellent introduction to the poetic methodology of the entire book. But the poem also leaves first a central and then a subsidiary question open, and seems to beg a response: does one listen to poetry or not? Is "It" the ocean, or only "It"? Certainly, in this massively Stevensian lyric no question is apt to be answered with finality.[15] But one necessary provisional answer is that "It" offers us language as magic, this pronoun by definition always able to be "bread and butter," "pepper and salt," or any other attribute that can be written: if the Pacific Ocean is to some extent Stevens' Snow Man, "It" is Mallarmé's flower that is absent from every bouquet. "Nothing" and "it" are juxtaposed, then, because "thing" language is by definition a form of negativity well encapsulated by the negative capability of "it." This means that the poem gives us at once an instance of "thing-language," of that thing, language, and additionally, the roar of "things" as they relay themselves to us through the conduit of our senses which, as the book emphasizes in many places, are also mediating semiotic networks. And regarding the poetry that one might or might not listen to, and its value which Spicer tirelessly affirms and negates, arises another necessary provisional answer: poetry happens in the space between the alternatives this poem traces, and as the dilemma of those alternatives themselves. Poetry happens between Ocean and It, between listening and insensibility, and finally, between no one and no, one – itself an impossible distinction that, in the form of the ghost, haunts all of Spicer's poetics.

Indeed, if seriality is always for Spicer a reflection on the space of poetry and the conditions of its possibility, even more insistently than Spicer's other books *Language* demands to be read according to two different topographies, as one must at once respect the specificities of each section, often as defined by the title, and also remain attentive to the complex and finely wrought network that moves across the various sections and links them by way of echoes, resonances, and continued discussions. Thus, the sections which take their titles from linguistics tend to explore in detail the elements so indicated. "Transformations I," for example, is built through the possibilities of emptying and filling a syntactic structure with differing pronouns; the poem runs through various permutations of the core structure "'he need (present) enemy (plural)'" (*CP*, 389), while "Transformations II" looks at linguistic transformation historically, and the third poem explores permutations within a formal verse structure.[16] "Morphemics," as we have seen, addresses the topic directly in poem 4 and as well in poem 3, while isolating bound morphemes throughout by way of the line break. "Graphemics," as its title would suggest, is systematically traversed with visual signs, or forms of writing: rabbit tracks in the snow, the play of clouds in the sky, traffic lights, sun dials, hour-glasses, shadows, the written letter "I," and finally postage stamps. There is, of course, one section whose title seems anomalous in this context – "Love Poems." However, one of the major burdens of *Language* is to show that this represents no disjunction; the book tries to think language in terms of love and love in terms of language throughout, and this makes *Language* Spicer's most extended love poem, anything but coincidentally. *Language*, however, is not only about love of language, nor mostly about love as "feeling" or "emotion" to be expressed. Crucially, it posits "love" as act, and particularly, a speech act: love is less something one feels than something one does and says. This relationship between love and language is signaled early on, when "love" figures as the final word of the section "Thing Language," but only when enclosed in quotation marks:

> "If I speak in the tongue of men and angels . . ."
> The sounding brass of my heart says
> "Love."
>
> (*CP*, 381, Spicer's ellipsis)

Meanwhile, as a book of love and language, *Language* also becomes a book of distances. If the concept of distance is implicitly crucial both to seriality and dictation, in *Language* Spicer foregrounds distance as such, seeing it as the major structuring element of poetry, language, and love – indeed, as that which joins them. As we shall see later, *Language* closes on this note, but throughout the book the correspondences between these seemingly disparate elements are stressed. Thus in addition to its ostensible subject, "Love Poems" harps on both "distance" and poetry: poem 3 of "Love Poems" ends, "Going into hell so many times tears it / Which explains poetry" (*CP*, 383) and poem 5 picks up that last phrase as its first line: "Which explains poetry. Distances / Impossible to be measured or walked over" (*CP*, 384). In parallel, "Phonemics" mentions "love" in its very first line, in the context of poems with phrases like "the minds of old men fevered by the distances" (*CP*, 393); "See the sea in the distance. / Die Ferne, water" (*CP*, 393), and above all, "The unstable / Universe has distance but not much else" (*CP*, 393).[17] These relationships are elaborated most fully in a poem from this section, "On the tele-phone," which thus emerges as one of the pivotal lyrics of the entire book.

This poem takes as its starting point the premise of the bridging of distance, or at least the reduction of it through phone technology, only to immediately problematize it: "On the tele-phone (distant sound) you sounded no distant than if you were talking to me in San Francisco on the telephone or in a bar or in a room" (*CP*, 394).[18] Line one, then, starts to tell us that the telephone creates the illusion of proximity, only to emphasize that the "long distance call" is not distance simulating presence, but one form of distance simulating another – one telephone call sounding like another. In fact, this poem which insists on the spacing within the local ends by affirming that distance obtains even at the moment of closest physical contact and intimacy: "The lips / Are never quite as far away as when you kiss" (*CP*, 394). The poem places in parallel the speaking and kissing mouth, but inverts the relationships to distance and proximity we would tend to associate with each, as here speech seems to be a form of intimacy which kissing cannot match.[19] The poem, then, emerges as a highly compacted reflection on language, intimacy, technology, and the body, itself making virtuoso use of the distancing and linking possibilities of the page, the line, syntax, and alphabetic characters. Above all, Spicer employs the line break to distance words from each other, creating a system of "routings" similar to those he discusses, as seen in this passage:

> Long
> Distance calls. They break sound
> Into electrical impulses and put it back again. Like the long telesexual
>   route to the brain or the even longer teleerotic route to the heart. The
>   numbers dialed badly, the connection faint.
> Your voice
>   consisted of sounds that I had
> To route to phonemes, then to bound and free morphemes, then
>   to syntactic structures. Telekinesis
> Would not have been possible even if we were sitting at the
>   same table. Long
> Distance calls your father, your mother, your friend, your
>   lover.
>
>   (*CP*, 394)

Most notable here is how the poem troubles the routing of an identical string of words which is repeated – "Long distance calls" – in a manner analogous to how "No one listens to poetry" was treated in the book's opening poem. Bracketing all context, the string "long distance calls" permits of three syntactic analyses (this is the sort of problem an automated language interpreter, unable to understand context, would need to be programmed to solve): first, there is our habitual understanding, in which "long-distance" is a compound adjective modifying a certain type of telephone call. Equally plausible, however, would be to imagine a compound noun, "distance-calls," modified by the adjective "long." Finally, one could form a compound noun, "long-distance," followed by a conjugated verb in the third-person singular: "calls." The poem is all about how we "route" such information into such structures, and it makes use of the formal elements at its disposal to foreground and complicate such routings. So in the first occurrence, a "semantic" line break inserting distance between "distance" and "long" seems to indicate that the adjective might indeed modify a more general and inevitable phenomenon of something one might dub "distance calls" – cries or gestures against and across distance (the poem's major concern), here proposed in a punning construction of an ad hoc compound noun. However, that particular routing can itself be brought to a stop by the full stop which follows: unless we want to read the previous phrase as a nominal fragment (which contrasts sharply with the elaborated syntax of the poem's opening sentence), we're tempted to re-route the syntax and now read "calls" as a conjugated verb. Should we make that move, however, we immediately stumble over the first word in the next sentence, "They," which necessitates a plural noun for its antecedent and erases our reading of "calls" as a verb. The poem, then, violently leads us through a process which is also that of eros and sex, where connections are perpetually established, re-articulated, and retrospectively erased or recast. Brain, heart, and language are wired together in a circuitry that links sex and eros, but to what? Not to the desired "other," because "language" can't simply correspond to the "voice" of the distant co-respondent, as this voice is never represented as any sort of whole, being merely an assemblage of "sounds that I had / To route to phonemes, then to bound and free morphemes, then to syntactic structures." What comes next can seem rather baffling – one would imagine that "telepathy" would here be more appropriate than "telekinesis," as this would indicate that even in direct mental communication, the "routings" of language would still be necessary.[20] But "telekinesis" seems to refer instead to the physical closeness, invoked two lines further down, for which phonic closeness itself is a traditional substitute: lips are divided here between two communicative functions, speaking and kissing, corresponding in turn to the phonetic and the kinetic. Then comes a crucial turn, where Spicer repeats the syntactic line-draping of "Long / Distance calls," but with a difference. In the first instance we were encouraged to parse the phrase as implying a conjugated verb, only for the next sentence to force us to transform "Long Distance calls" back into a noun, so as to provide the necessary plural antecedent. This time, the phrase works in reverse: with the previous nominal usage in mind, here we are likely to expect "long distance calls" to be the pre-positioned object of a verb will which will follow the listing of a plural subject. But the full-stop forces us to re-route our syntax again, determining "long distance" as the grammatical subject which "calls" to the list of objects which follow. These four central figures of emotional proximity – father, mother, friend, lover – are here marked by distance, of course, yet not only: distance itself is distant to them, "calling" them, drawing them. The "teleerotic" and "telesexual," longer circuits than the phonic, show lips as farther away when kissing than when speaking. If this poem has thrown us into syntax, it has then also thrown us into the "electric system" (*CP*, 394) of love and the routings it implies. Nowhere more than here does Spicer endorse a Dickinsonian model of intimacy as distance – of "meeting apart" – here having telephony supplement dynamics he had previously worked out in terms of letters and letter-writing. This is seen not only in *After Lorca* or the *Letters to James Alexander*, but also in a love letter he wrote to Gary Bottone in the early 1950s anticipating their break-up, and rehearsing the paradoxes of the erotic arrangement detailed in the poem discussed above, when he evokes the lovers' reunion in Berkeley: "But let's have these letters go on, whether it be days, years, or never before I see you. We can still love each other although we cannot see each other. We will be no farther apart when I'm in Berkeley than we were when I was in Minneapolis. And we can continue to love each other, by letter, from alien worlds" (*CP*, 442). "Alien worlds" can't help but evoke the distance from which "Martians" dictate – the networks of poetry, phonemes, sex, and eros in which the poet is a node, receiver, and transmitter – neither personal nor impersonal in a manner adequate to either concept.

This emphasis on transmission and networks inevitably implies delay and deferral, that is, temporality, and of all Spicer's books, *Language* is also the one most fully interested in and open to time, as radical contingency. To some extent, it functions as a calendar, charting an expanse of time which is also pretty much a baseball season – the last complete one Spicer was to know – as we move from the "Baseball Predictions" dated April 1, 1964 (*CP*, 375) to the evocation of Halloween in the final section, "Graphemics" (*CP*, 397).[21] In fact, likened to flora such as "Daffodils" (*CP*, 378) and "buttercups" (*CP*, 382) which the poem harps on as specifically seasonal, the baseball season functions as a sort of indexical time-marker throughout, equated at once with summer (*CP*, 382) and the weary repetition of the seasons marking the rhythm of Spicer's own life, as he entered his fortieth year: "It comes May and the summers renew themselves / (39 of them) Baseball seasons" (*CP*, 378). Baseball is also the vector by which transitory current events enter the book in the form of a newspaper's sports section (*CP*, 379), but the poem responds to the daily news in other ways too. For example, the allusion to Eskimo villages hit by an earthquake in "Thing Language" very probably refers to the Great Alaska Earthquake of March 27, 1964, and the discussion of Eichmann (*CP*, 379) seems indebted to Hannah Arendt's *Eichmann in Jerusalem*, which was published in 1963. Of course, the current event that looms largest is the assassination of John

F. Kennedy on November 22, 1963, less than six months before the moment marked near the beginning of *Language*:

> Smoke signals
> Like in the Eskimo villages on the coast where the earthquake hit
> Bang, snap, crack. They will never know what hit them
> On the coast of Alaska. They expect everybody to be insane.
> This is a poem about the death of John F. Kennedy.
>
> (CP, 377)

It's easy to see this and the three other references to Kennedy as an unhappy throwaway, or a somewhat lame performative joke: to declare the poem about John F. Kennedy thereby makes it about John F. Kennedy.[22] And to some extent the poem is such a joke, albeit a private one: the archives show that in early 1964 Spicer received a solicitation from Basic Books to contribute to an anthology on the death of Kennedy, and *Language* seems to register his hardly surprising response, given what would become his notorious opposition to "political poetry" as expressed in his various lectures.[23] In these, Spicer objects to political poetry as being fundamentally at odds with the principles of dictation, which necessitate that the poet abandon the poem as an instrument for achieving precise, defined goals. Among Spicer's examples of "the bad thing" is wanting to say in a poem "I think that the Vietnam crisis is terrible" (H, 6); for that sort of message, Spicer suggests, "the thing to do is to write a letter to the editor" (H, 14).[24] But more to the point in this context is that Spicer would have seen such an anthology as a crassly commercial and opportunistic endeavor, and his response is to write a "poem about the death of John F. Kennedy" that the anthology on the subject would choose not to print. In this way, he exactly anticipates what will become the governing conceit of the *Book of Magazine Verse*, a work itself political in Spicer's view, since for him the politics of the poetry community is the proper space of intervention for the poet qua poet: "There are bosses in poetry as well as in the industrial empire . . . Your enemy is simply something which is going to try to stop you from writing poetry" (H, 153). If Spicer's politics can be puerile at times, he is anything but in his recognition of the institution of the magazine as a properly political and social space, which renders the *Book of Magazine Verse* a thoroughly political intervention: "Sure *Poetry* magazine will pay you . . . But a magazine is a society. I think *Open Space* proved that" (H, 157) Spicer opines, before concluding that he doesn't read *Poetry* because "I don't believe in the society that it creates" (H, 157).

Presumably, Spicer would also object to the "society" created by the Basic Books anthology, and in *Language* Spicer ostentatiously eschews presenting Kennedy's death as an important "theme" to be mined for poetic capital – hence its presentation in the guise of a gratuitous add-on. At the same time, however, he refuses to confine such a "topical" concern to the realm of the "non-poetic" against which a disinterested "pure poetry" might be measured, and even posits its centrality to his book in a manner which doesn't seem to be simply ironic. This is because Spicer distrusts the valorization of "authentic feeling" or the "personal" as a motor for poetry just as much as he does the socially important "issue." For Spicer, seriality is a means to put both of these under pressure, and in *Language* more than any other of Spicer's books, seriality works by way of the sporadically diaristic, valorizing the unfinishedness of the moment as opposed to its ideal enclosure within an artistic frame. *Language* in this way is not unlike the work of James Schuyler in "The Morning of the Poem" or "A Few Days," and we have seen throughout how Spicer's poetics imply a certain contingency, a refiguring of the occasion as the accidental, in both its everyday and metaphysical acceptations.[25] The poem, then, lets Kennedy's death enter the timescape which *Language* traverses, and, as John Vincent has noted, implicitly suggests a different way a poem can be "about" a subject. In this respect, Spicer's project not only echoes the diverse practices of post-war avant-garde artists such as Cage or Smithson, but also stretches clearly back to Whitman: we have here various versions of a kind of inclusivity which resists the idea of the non-poetic as such. Yet concurrently, *Language* also conceives of poetry as quite the opposite: explicitly critical in every sense, by which I mean related to crisis in its etymological meaning of decision; a determinate intervention.[26] This a tension under which poetry threatens to explode, or by way of which Spicer makes poetry explode, as in this poem from "Thing Language":

1st SF Home Rainout Since. Bounce Tabby-Cat Giants.
    Newspapers
Left in in my house.
My house is Aquarius. I don't believe
The water-bearer
Has equal weight on his shoulders.
The lines never do.
We give equal
Space to everything in our lives. Eich-
Mann proved that false in killing like you raise wildflowers.
    Witlessly
I
Can-
not
accord

sympathy
to
those
who
do
not
recognize
The human crisis.

(CP, 379)

Under the guise of a quasi-random process of association, this poem
charts public and private, political and personal, in fascinating ways.
Spicer moves from the ephemera of San Francisco newspapers' sports
headlines to other current affairs which the institution of journalism
could be seen to juxtapose as if equivalent: "We give equal / Space
to everything in our lives." Yet it is in relation to just such "spacing"
(which *Language* is at pains to record) that poetry on its most formal
level intervenes, through the radically different "weights" lines are made
to bear in this poem, as the poem pointedly refuses such "equality."
Meanwhile, the word "house" functions at once as a contingent space
of domesticity, itself receiving or breached by the public discourse of
the newspapers, and as the trans-individual characterological destiny
implied by the zodiac (Spicer was born on January 30). And in this
poetry so open to the contingent, Eichmann – the "Mann" cut off by
the line break, making Eichmann in some way everyman or anyone,
the German "Man" – reveals the fundamental nihilism of the sort of
reified "equality" which renders all tasks and objects equivalent, be
they gardening or killing, wildflowers or humans. To "recognize" this
by way of language means to break with the general uniformity of the
Whitmanian line and to foreground language and rearticulate it down
to the very spaces it charts on the page and by way of syntax, in lines
and sentences. It means to insist on a poetic crisis to match the human
one, where every line and where it breaks implies choice for both poet
and reader. And this also means to decide, or take sides, to abjure the
"witless" indiscrimination of Eichmann: "Dare he / Write poetry /
Who has no taste of acid on his tongue / Who carrys his dreams on his
back like a packet? / Ghosts of other poets send him shame / He will be
alive (as they are dead) / At the final picking" (*CP*, 388). It is here the
negative, destructive power of poetry, its burning acidity, that allows
the poet to enter the ghostly community of poetry, to die properly, to
cease mere life, as Spicer joins Blake's Devil, writing the Proverbs of Hell
with "corroding fires" (xvii). And for Spicer, "recognition" in the form
of registration is also decision, because, as the poetics of dictation insist,

one's own "marks" arrive in a manner analogous to all the others that come from the other "outside," and the poet's job consists precisely in routing them to and on the page. So writing is inevitably itself a reading and interpretation because to "mark" is to route, to produce graphemes which themselves flow out of the swelling tide of overabundant marks through which the poet swims, bearing along voice, body, ears, eyes, and page. In this way, the newspaper, archive and library all echo the ocean, and reading mirrors listening:

Intermission 1

"The movement of the earth brings harmes and fears.
Men wonder what it is and what it meant."
        Donne
In the next line
Contrasts this with "the celestial movement of the spheres."
        Rhyme soothes. And in a book I read in college fifteen years
        ago it said that this was an attack on the Copernican theory
        and a spidery hand had penciled in the margin
        "Earthquake."
Where is the poet? A-keeping the sheep
A-keeping the celestial movement of the spheres in a long,
        boring procession
A-center of gravity
A-(while the earthquakes of happiness go on inside and outside
        his body and the stars in their courses stop to notice)
Sleep.

                                                    (*CP*, 387)

"Earthquake," penciled into a book Spicer would have withdrawn from the UC Berkeley library, localizes Donne, and makes him a poet of California and the Pacific Rim, an unsettled space of shock and violence, which itself mirrors the violence of Kennedy's sudden and unforeseeable assassination. This literally "marginal" reading reinstates Donne as a poet of crisis and disturbance, resisting the official text's positioning of him as a poet of the "center" in every sense; indeed, as a poet opposing a theory which would decenter the human in relation to the universe. Thus critically and anonymously reclaimed by a marginal, wavering hand, Donne is recast as the model of the poet which Spicer will follow throughout *Language*: the one who notes the rupturing earthquakes within and without and agrees not to know their meaning as they hit (like the Eskimos), as opposed to the academic custodian of rhymes herded like sheep to bolster gravity and the cosmic order, as enshrined by the institutional authority of the printed, bound page.[27] Listening to poetry against and alongside the ocean's roar, seeing the tremulous signs in the margins, quaking inside and out: these are the elements of the poetic insomnia in the night's intermission that shrug off the sleep of gravity and control, and allow the poet to enter death, tear hell, receive dictation, become, by degrees, a ghost among ghosts.

But whereas Donne uses the conceit of a compass drawing a circle to figure and measure affective distance in his "Valediction," Spicer invokes phonemes, which he fully recognizes as phenomenal and not acoustic in nature, and therefore themselves established through distance and difference, a distance at once internal and external, rendering the personal inevitably the Outside, when heard aright.[28] So, with "Graphemics" 10, *Language* ends:

> Love is not mocked whatever use you put to it. Words are also
>   not mocked.
> The soup of real turtles flows through our veins. Being a [poet]
>   a disyllable in a world of monosyllables. Awakened by the
>   distance between the [o] and the [e]
> The earth quakes. John F. Kennedy is assassinated. The dark
>   forest of words lets in some light from its branches.
>   Mocking them, the deep leaves
> That time leaves us
> Words, loves.
>
> (CP, 402)

This poem condenses and restates *Language* to a considerable extent. The first line insists on the homology between words and love which has been central to the entire book, and the relation of earthquakes and the Kennedy assassination to both should by now be evident. But in addition to the phenomenal poetic "awakening" this poem celebrates, the ending of *Language* also subtly but carefully calls out again for awareness of the "human crisis." "Graphemics" 9 tells the story of a German postage stamp depicting a chapel and an oak tree, in which some German citizens detected a likeness of Hitler. "The / Oakman grows behind every chapel. / The fine / Print on the contract" (CP, 402) the poem lets drop mystifyingly, until one remembers that "Oakman" is a plausible English rendering of Eichmann, lurking there to be seen if one reads closely enough. This gives rise to the warning, ostensibly in reference to the postage stamp, that "Graphemes should not be looked at so minutely" (CP, 402), but taken in a larger sense it's a message that comes both to underwrite and undercut the affirmational ending of *Language*, is itself the fine print on the contract which Spicer asks the reader to sign, without reading. This is the reader's Faustian bargain that Spicer's impossible demand entails: to wakefully quake to every grapheme he marks down, no matter how slight its semblance and no matter its dictated origin, yet also to love Spicer unconditionally, on faith, beyond the legible.[29] Indeed, this reading of Oakman as Eichmann is largely supported by minute graphemic overdetermination in the preceding section, where the "Eich" morpheme is reintroduced through a complicated play on the English first-person pronoun, "I," the German "Ein" or "one," and an "Eich" which means "oak" but here seems also to function as a slippage between "Ein" and the German for "I": Ich. When the poems states "Ein / Eichenbach steht einsam" (*CP*, 401), it seems that a lonely oak tree here comes to stand for a fantasy of independent self-sufficiency and coherence that tempts the subject: "I – / lands of thought within thought within thought. Those cold spaces. / I within I within i etc. / Flowering, all-one" (*CP*, 401).[30] This would be a version of Eliot's crucial take on Bradley in *The Waste Land*, "each in his prison / Thinking of the key, each confirms a prison" (*Collected Poems*, 69) problematized by Spicer's insistence on "I" as no more than grapheme, mark: "I am I – both script i and cursive i" (*CP*, 401).[31] Meanwhile, the "fine print" of the last three lines of *Language* continue to disturb syntactic routings, and in ways that are strictly speaking insoluble, because within the phrase "Mocking them" both the implied subject of the verb and the antecedent of the object pronoun are left unspecified. However, it doesn't seem coincidental that the most compelling syntactic routing is the most problematic semantically: it is tempting to suggest that "light" is the implied subject of "Mocking" and that "them" refers to the "deep leaves," post-positioned, and in apposition with "Words, loves." This means it is light which mocks the "deep leaves" of "Words, loves," and that, of course, gives us a conclusion which directly contradicts line one of this poem. Which explains poetry, and also continues the book's habit of cancelling its affirmations, which was announced as early as the very first poem. Alongside this problem, however, the poem ends by once again affirming temporality as the driver of both poetry and eros. And finally, the "dark forest of words" cannot but evoke the "dark forest where we wander amazed at the selves of ourselves" of "Morphemics" (*CP*, 392), Dante's "selva oscura" punned into the space of a journey inward, where we roam wakefully between [o] and [e], or maybe find ourselves with Charlie Parker, who "dances now in some brief kingdom (Oz) two phonemes / That were never paired before in the language" (*CP*, 395). One listens to poetry, finally, as much as words, loves, are mocked. This side of Oz, or after the brief kingdom, we have only the erasures of time; islands, histories, archipelagos of loss for birds to shit on: "No love deserves the death it has" (*CP*, 393), mocked or not.

*

The *Book of Magazine Verse* is to a large extent a collection of overwhelming bitterness, and its emblem is the lemon:

> "Limon tree very pretty
> And the limon flower is sweet
> But the fruit of the poor lemon
> Is impossible to eat"
> In Riverside we saved the oranges first (by smudging) and left
>   the lemons last to fend for themselves. They didn't usually
> A no good crop. Smudge-pots
> Didn't rouse them. The music
> Is right though. The lemon tree
> Could branch off into real magic. Each flower in place. We
> Were sickened by the old lemon.
>
> (CP, 406)

A smudge pot is an oil-burning heater meant to protect fruit trees from frost, developed in precisely Spicer's region of southern California; this poem for "*Poetry* Chicago," (written when Chicago, not Los Angeles, was America's "second city") begins by insisting on specifically Californian provincial, regional practice and terminology, as it describes how lemons are sacrificed in favor of the more attractive orange. The question the "Six Poems for *Poetry* Chicago" ask is how, then, to branch into the "real magic" that the lemon tree also promises, according to Spicer's reading of the folk song his poem starts by citing?[32] In poem 4 of the sequence, Spicer identifies the lemon's husk as the problem. Unlike the orange, "a fruit easily to be eaten" (CP, 407), "The Rind (also called the skin) of the lemon is difficult to understand / It goes around itself in an oval . . . / It's the shape of the lemon, I guess that causes trouble. It's ovalness, it's rind. This is where my love, somehow, stops" (CP, 407). What's surprising here is that these qualities of the lemon – emphasized by the apostrophes which indicate identity rather than attribute – stop love for Spicer, rather than foster it. After all, the orange, "easily to be eaten," recalls the poems that are "easily laid" from *After Lorca*, whereas the lemon, wound in on itself and difficult to open, seems an image of the more difficult poems which Spicer values.[33] Of course, the lemon itself is a crucial word and image throughout *After Lorca*, figuring for the Spanish poet too a resistance or negativity he esteems.[34] But this section of the *Book of Magazine Verse* seems to revisit and perhaps repudiate those elements of *Lorca*, here proposing an ideal skinlessness if love and magic are to start: "Could we get / Out of our skins and dance?":

> With
> Out

Skin.
A good dream. The
Moment's rest.

(CP, 408)³⁵

Much of the mournfulness of the *Book of Magazine Verse* stems from its fatigue with many of the restlessly defensive and aggressive positions Spicer's poetics had sketched so insistently ever since *Lorca*, as if at this late date Spicer would reinvent himself as a poet of the sweet and inviting: "Well, I'm trying to become an orange" (*H*, 121), he quipped in Vancouver, discussing this sequence. He couldn't, or wouldn't: "You can lead a horse to water but you can't make him drink":

> The horse, lead or not lead to water is still there. Refusing
> Bare sustenance.
> Each of us has inside of him that horse-animal
> Refusing the best streams or as if their thick water flowing were
>   refusing us. After
> Miles and miles of this, horse and rider,
> What do you say? How come
> Love isn't as great as it should be?

(CP, 410)

These lines are particularly important because they also can be taken as a self-criticism of the entire *Magazine Verse* project, with Spicer cast as the refusing "horse-animal" pretending that it is the magazines, or the stream, which are refusing him. The loveless lemon will not be peeled, and the bitterness of rejection morphs into recognition of the extent to which it has been programmed by the poet, to culminate in melancholic self-reproach as Spicer sorts out his failure with the "captains" of poetry, sex, and love which he lists early on in the book (*CP*, 405). These are the three arenas of defeat that Spicer explores throughout this last work.

In the midst of this, the poems also take the measure of the two trips Spicer made to Vancouver the last year of his life, in January and again in May and June. Canada looms large not only by way of the "Seven Poems for the Vancouver Festival" but also in "Three Poems for *Tish*," the latter a Canadian poetry magazine. Indeed, it is the last poem of that section which is cited above, and it is possible to read it as at least allegorizing how Spicer, through increasingly self-destructive behavior, refused the new Canadian future which dropped into his lap in 1965.³⁶ Likewise, the second "Poem for the *Vancouver Festival*" seems to represent Vancouver as more a terminal destination than the site of a new beginning. Interestingly, it maps the latter not against the Bay Area of Spicer's adult life, but rather the Los Angeles of his childhood, here the "south" balanced against the Canadian "north" in the poem's refrain: "You are going south looking for a drinking fountain / I am going north looking for the source of the chill in my bones" (*CP*, 417). This then might leave the Bay Area itself as the site of the crossing the poem evokes, as Spicer and an unspecified "you" pass by as they move in opposite directions, the latter towards sunny climes of oranges and lemons, perhaps in search of a "drinking fountain" to be assimilated to the fountain of youth in contrast with the poet's "age":

> Our hearts, hanging below like balls, as they brush each other in our
>   separate journeys
> Protest for a moment the idiocy of age and direction.
> You are going south looking for a drinking fountain
> I am going north looking for the source of the chill in my bones
>
>   (*CP*, 418)

In the fifth poem, Spicer again lets drop a comment which it's tempting to extend to the entire Vancouver experience:

> Vancouver parties. Too late
> Too late
> For a nice exit.
>
>   (*CP*, 419)

However, in the first of the *Vancouver Festival* poems Spicer still does gesture at creating a new, ideal city, using as his allegorical model the geometry of the baseball diamond: "We shall build our city backwards from each baseline extending like a square ray from each distance" (*CP*, 417). Baseball is pivotal in the *Book of Magazine Verse*, providing a way for Spicer to link his sense of poetry to that of the city, as well as to talk about God, which he does here more explicitly than in any of his poetry since the *Imaginary Elegies* and *Fifteen False Propositions Against God*. By way of God and baseball, Spicer worries a question which increasingly supplemented his insistence on the necessity of poetic "death": that of the human, in relationship to poetry and community, or "words, loves." This is stressed in the poems for the Catholic magazine *Ramparts*, and those for the *St. Louis Sporting News*. The last poem for *Ramparts* is one of the most important in the *Book of Magazine Verse*.

> Mechanicly we move
> In God's Universe, Unable to do
> Without the grace or hatred of Him.
> The center of being. Like almost, without grace, a computer center. Without
>   His hatred

A barren world.
A center of being – not the existence of robots.
If He wanted to, He could make a machine a Christ, enter it in
        its second person which is You.
Why he bothered with man is a mystery even Job wondered.
God becoming human, became a subject for anthropologists,
            history, and all the other wretched itchings of an animal
            that had suddenly (too suddenly?) been given a soul.
When I look in the eyes and the souls of those I love, I
            (in a dark forest between grace and hatred) doubt His wisdom.
Cur Deus Homo, was the title of St. Anselm's book. Without question
    marks.
Grace!

                                                                (CP, 413)

Here, Spicer begins with an almost Nietzschean critique of God's relationship to our space of action, seeming to insist on our need of either
grace or damnation as arbiter of our movements – our need, as Nietzsche
might have put it, for our suffering to have a *meaning*. Yet Spicer seems
at the same time to suggest that the role of the Divine as purveyor of
meaning is undermined by God as program or law, in some way as
mechanical as the world He created. This is picked up in the final poem
for the *Sporting News*: "God is a big white baseball that has nothing
to do but go in a curve or a straight line ... / Given these facts the
pitcher, the batter, and the catcher all look pretty silly ... / Off seasons
/ I often thought of praying to him but could not stand the thought of
that big, white, round, omnipotent bastard. / Yet he's there. As the game
follows rules he makes them. / I know / I was not the only one who felt
these things" (CP, 416). Obviously, such lines, pointing as they do to
an omnipotent, impassible, unreachable God, can evoke the Calvinist
strain in Spicer which many readers, most notably Robert Duncan,
find to be foundational for his poetry. In his very helpful account of
this issue, Norman Finkelstein isolates the most important elements of
Spicer's "Calvinism" in two phrases about Spicer from Robin Blaser:
his "passionate sense of god as 'entirely Other'" and his acceptance of
the "dualism" implying "the absolute otherness of complete meaning"
(cited in Finkelstein, 162, 161).[37] Yet the poem for *Ramparts* cited
above laments not the distance between the human and the divine but
their proximity – *Cur Deus Homo* is usually translated as "Why God
Became Man," and that is the question Spicer asks here, suggesting that
a machine – a computer or robot – would have made a better Christ,
while humans stagger through their lives stunned by the souls they aren't
equipped to manage. In other words, in the *Book of Magazine Verse*
Spicer, characteristically, doesn't seem to choose between Catholicism

and Calvinism. Instead, he presents at *once* the terrifying distance and "otherness" of the Calvinist God *and* the frightening intimacy of the Catholic insistence on the incarnation. At the same time, "complete meaning" is defied by the baseball diamond's divided function as the arena of community and communality, and also of human loneliness against the divine. That loneliness is also the poet's, as the *Sporting News* poems figure the poet as a "catcher" throughout, terrified and hapless before both the Divine white baseball flying according to laws the knowledge of which make it no easier to grasp, and the Outside here figured as a wild and haunted knuckleballer throwing "Junk" pitches (*CP*, 414) which seem "scientifically impossible" (*CP*, 415) despite God's rules.[38]

On June 17, 1965, when Spicer delivered his last lecture in Vancouver, the *Book of Magazine Verse* had progressed no further than the third poem of "Seven Poems for the Vancouver Festival." This means the remaining four poems of that section, and the "Ten Poems for *Downbeat*" which follow, chart the very last days of Spicer's life: he collapsed in his apartment elevator on July 31, and was largely delirious and often comatose over the seventeen days he managed to live on (*P*, 356–60). If Vancouver weighs heavily in much of the *Book of Magazine Verse*, the final poems return Spicer to Berkeley, and specifically the Berkeley Poetry Conference of mid-July, where he gave a reading and delivered his notorious "lecture" on Poetry and Politics.[39] The Conference featured many of the leading poets from Donald Allen's *New American* anthology and Spicer's entourage, including Olson, Duncan, Creeley, John Wieners, and Ginsberg, to name only a few. Not surprisingly, Spicer greeted his inclusion in such an august affair not as a consecration, but with rage, misgiving, envy, resentment, and sorrow. These emotions work themselves through over the final poems Spicer was to write, but not to the exclusion of all else. The poems for *Downbeat*, a music magazine, justify themselves as submissions to that outlet by referring to and citing songs, mostly folk and country, while continuing to dialogue with the Vancouver poems by sketching a specifically Pacific coastal regional space.[40] The folk song "Sweet Betsy from Pike," a Gold-Rush era ditty detailing a couple's migration to California, signals a shift from the North–South travels evoked in the poems for the Vancouver Festival to a more expected pattern of westward travel along the frontier and to the ocean. Thus, the first poem for *Downbeat* begins with a line from the song and a reference to the archetypal Olsonian locale of Gloucester Harbor in New England (which Spicer renders "Glouchester"), to end with western motifs: Chinese labor on the transcontinental railroad, Donner Party cannibalism, and the postulation of a

Pacific edge culture: "West coast is something nobody with sense would understand . . . / We are a coast people / There is nothing but ocean out beyond us. We grasp / The first thing coming" (*CP*, 421).[41] Spicer moves from an implicitly conservative New England groundedness to the negativity he usually associates with the West Coast, but additionally, by way of the all-American folksiness of "Sweet Betsy from Pike" and "The Wreck of the Old 97" (alluded to in the fourth poem for *Downbeat*), Spicer questions the relationship of Canada to the American discourse of Manifest Destiny which inextricably ties a certain form of cultural authenticity to the frontier, westward migration, and imperialism. So he tells "Dennis" (presumably Wheeler) "you don't have to hear any / Of the mountain music they play here" (*CP*, 422) before concluding "British Columbia / Will not become a victim to Western Imperialism if you don't let it. All those western roads. Few of them / Northern" (*CP*, 422). The emphasis on specifically American imperialism is why the "Ten Poems for *Downbeat*" then shift their focus from one form of "national" music – indigenous folk songs – to a different sort: the national anthem, as emblem of a falsely imposed and ultimately destructive form of collective identity, as opposed to the communally produced and shared folk materials exemplified by the songs. The fifth poem, "For Huntz," is crucial to the entire sequence:

> I can't stand to see them shimmering in the impossible music of the Star
>   Spangled Banner. No
> One accepts this system better than poets. Their hurts healed for a few
>   dollars.
> Hunt
> The right animals. I can't. The poetry
> Of the absurd comes through San Francisco television. Directly
>   connected with moon-rockets.
> If this is dictation, it is driving
> Me wild.
>
> (*CP*, 423)

At the outset, the poem seems to continue the equivalence of poets with baseball players mobilized previously, as "them" in the first line could refer to players seen on television standing in respect under the stadium lights during the playing of the national anthem, as is the case before every game played in America. This could be the "poetry of the absurd" beamed into the living room or bar, and "Directly connected with moon-rockets" because the first commercial telecommunications satellite was launched on April 6, 1965.[42] Meanwhile, this indictment of careerist poetic aspiration crystallizes around three words beginning in / h / yoked together by an insistent alliteration somewhat unusual in

Spicer: "hurts," "healed," and "Hunt." Poets, it would seem, are like baseball players: motivated more by money than love of their craft, succeeding by cynically choosing easy poetic prey, unlike Spicer who can't "Hunt / The right animals." At the same time, the dictation he stays faithful to seems increasingly difficult to disentangle from all the other absurd broadcasts beaming down. Still, if dictation is driving him "wild" this is not necessarily a bad thing; in fact, it could be what makes him the right sort of animal, as opposed to the poets domesticated by the "system."

This poem's legibility as a familiar Spicerian complaint about the "whorship" of poetry might be why the next one begins: "The poem begins to mirror itself. / The identity of the poet gets more obvious" (*CP*, 423). Here, Spicer eschews the emphasis on music that has concerned him in this section until now: "Why can't we sing songs like nightingales? Because we're not nightingales and can never become them" (*CP*, 423). The next poem returns to a sound Spicer compared and opposed to the language of poetry as far back as *Troilus*, and as recently as in the opening of *Language*: the ocean's surf. Against the inevitable significations of language and the systemic, ordered coherence of musical scales is the supplemental "breaking noise" of the Pacific Ocean's surf pushing through the windows at Stinson Beach: "I wish / I were like an ocean, loud, lovable, and with a window ... / It makes its noises surfacing while I and everybody make mine, only / Its beaches we've starved on. Or loved on. It roars at me like love" (*CP*, 424). But neither a nightingale or an ocean, in his last three lyrics Spicer concentrates on the noises that poets make, within the "system" which permits them, of which the magazines, as Spicer suggests here, are finally only a part. Spicer's final works are about the condition of starving, and this investigation culminates in his famous settling of accounts with Ginsberg, the addressee of his final poem:

> At least we both know how shitty the world is. You wearing a beard
> as a mask to disguise it. I wearing my tired smile. I don't see
> how you do it. One hundred thousand university students
> marching with you. Toward
> A necessity which is not love but is a name.
> King of the May. A title not chosen for dancing. The police
> Civil but obstinate. If they'd attacked
> The kind of love (not sex but love), you gave the one hundred
> thousand students I'd have been very glad. And loved the
> policemen. Why
> Fight the combine of your heart and my heart or anybody's
> heart. People are starving.
>
> (*CP*, 426)

The background to this poem is well known. Blaser explains: "The North Beach story of the meeting behind the poem is this: Allen arrived at Jack's table in Gino & Carlo's Bar and said he'd come to save Jack's soul. Jack replied that he'd better watch it or he'd become a cult leader rather than a poet" (*The Fire*, 139). More specifically, as both Michael Davidson and Killian and Ellingham point out, Spicer is responding to Ginsberg's poem "Kral Majales," which recounts Ginsberg's visit to Prague, where as he tells it in his own notes he was "elected May King by 100,000 citizens" (775) before being harassed by police and ultimately deported by the displeased Czechoslovakian government.[43] Spicer attacks Ginsberg for lines like these: "And I am the King of May, which is the power of sexual youth, / and I am the King of May, which is Kral Majales in the Czechoslovakian tongue, / . . . . and I am the King of May, which is old Human poesy, and 100,000 people chose my name" (353). What Spicer seems to object to most vociferously here is the cult of personality which Ginsberg has allowed to grow about him, a formation whose impulsion comes not from love but only a "name," and which is inherently violent or even militaristic, as evidenced by the students depicted as "marching" rather than "dancing." The danger inherent in the "name" as Ginsberg deploys it is one Spicer had reflected on in the curious eighth poem for *Downbeat*, where he considers a phrase presented as cited: " 'Trotskyite bandits from the hills,' Churchill called 'em long after Trotsky had been assinated [*sic*]" (*CP*, 425). The poem harps on the non-coincidence between the bandits so demarcated and their "namesake" – "Name sook, name not sought"; "If they didn't / Know about Trotsky his name was there" (*CP*, 425) – as the putative identification is manipulated even more by Churchill than by the "bandits" themselves: "Certain anyway / To die anyway" (*CP*, 425). Finally, the poem seems to suggest that the appellation "Trotskyite" in effect renders those so called ultimately "nameless" and therefore "an excellent target for bazookas. Name- / Less figures, T. and Churchill called them" (*CP*, 425). Spicer seems to say that the necessity of the "name" can only lead to an appropriative violence, on both sides. Yet the poem to Ginsberg begins not on the note of aggressive opposition, but rather of shared, guilty complicity, the complicity of those who know the shitty truth about the world. This poem is Spicer's final admonition, where he tries to coax Ginsberg into seeing the Spicer hiding beneath his own beard; where he holds up, as distorted mirror, his own face. Where the poets differ, however, is in Spicer's willingness to display his shameful inadequacy in the face of the shit, as opposed to Ginsberg's need to obscure it behind his beard, or his offer of "love." Spicer's final line seems a response to these from Ginsberg's poem:

and the Capitalists drink gin and whiskey on airplanes but let Indian brown
   millions starve
and when Communist and Capitalist assholes tangle the Just man is arrested
   or robbed or had his head cut off

(353)

But it would be hasty to read Spicer as upbraiding Ginsberg for his celebratory narcissism in the face of the bare realities of a world where "brown millions" are starving, because Spicer's final line – the last line of his entire poetic output – is also an auto-citation. The first poem for the *Sporting News* concludes:

"Learn
How to shoot fish in a barrell," someone said,
"People are starving."

(*CP*, 414)

What this implies is that it is precisely because people are starving that appealing to their need or "necessity" is as easy as shooting fish in a barrel, which Ginsberg would be doing poetically, when he asserts himself as their champion; that because they're so hungry, they'll always be happy to gobble down fish shot in the barrel you produce. Spicer suggests that Ginsberg, like himself, knows the world is cause for shame, and insists that the ethical position is to display your shame and that of others, and not shamelessly, like Ginsberg, to pretend you are able to satiate their starving need, or salve their want. In his final poem, Spicer insists on a poetry of lack, on a song of the beaches we've starved on; not indiscriminate, Whitmanian "love," but the wheat and the chaff threshed by each heart's combine, or more probably, the love the heart has rigged like a baseball game that's been fixed, as "combine" can also mean a criminal organization.

Hostility, anger, violence, and complicity govern the book's penultimate lyric too. It begins by reformulating Spicer's unease with political poetry:

They've (the leaders of our country) have become involved in a network of
   lies.
We (the poets) have also become [*sic*] in network of lies by opposing them.

(*CP*, 425)

No poet, however, could be less convinced than Spicer by such a feeble gesture towards a purity to be obtained at the cost of withdrawal from engagement with the powers of destruction. These cannot be dodged, in poetry or elsewhere. In the *Book of Magazine Verse*, however, Spicer comes close to naming what is opened by his constant attacks, aggression, and rhetorical destruction of both self and other, what ultimately counts, and stands behind it:

> What we kill them with or they kill us with (maybe a squirrel rifle) isn't
>   important.
> What is important is what we don't kill each other with
> And a loving hand reaches a loving hand.
> The rest of it is
> Power, guns, and bullets.

(CP, 425)

A political poem, if anyone ever wrote one.

Notes

1. See *P* for the details of this information, especially the chapter "The Long Silence," and pp. 255–8 for the car crash and its aftermath. The Blaser–Duncan correspondence of this period contains a good deal of concern and even more annoyance about Spicer. In March 1963, for example, Blaser went so far as to inform Duncan, "I believe Jack is insane and I'm coming round to the indifference which is my only defense" ("Robin Blaser Papers": BANC MSS 79/68). See Jarnot, pp. 215–20, for the major Spicer–Duncan falling out of 1962.
2. It's not clear to what extent this was simply a bureaucratic maneuver to get rid of a not entirely productive Spicer, as the project was relaunched under a different form the following year (*P*, 287).
3. *P* speculates that most of his income during this time came from his mother (322).
4. Silliman's article is a truly indispensable reading of *Language*, to which I am enormously indebted, and a healthy corrective to what he dubs a "mythic" tendency of reading Spicer's work as ever increasing in intensity, and culminating in the *Book of Magazine Verse*. I fully subscribe to his reservations regarding this trajectory. While the essay was first published in 1985, I mostly refer to the slightly emended version published in *The New Sentence* in 1987.
5. Joseph Conte makes a similar point about the implications of the cover of *Language*, while casting the opposition in terms of the "finite structure" of "langue" as opposed to the "infinite number of transformations" offered by "parole" (105). Critics routinely refer to the importance of linguistics for Spicer's poetry, and frequently specify the article published in the journal whose cover Spicer appropriated, "Correlation Methods of Comparing Idiolects in a Transition Area," co-authored with his project director at Berkeley, David Reed. The article explains the methodology Reed hoped to use in his Linguistic Atlas of California, and there is no question that Spicer's regionalism was highly attuned to questions of regional dialect,

usage, and oral tradition, as *Language* and the *Book of Magazine Verse* as well as his Vancouver lectures make clear. The article itself, however, is almost exclusively concerned with methodological issues of quantitative, statistical analysis rather than language per se. In terms of the linguistics which informs *Language*, it is the Stanford project which is decisive.

6. This was not purely a conceit. The Spicer Papers at the Bancroft Library contain an undated rejection slip from Denise Levertov at *The Nation* for "Two Poems for *The Nation*" and "Ten Poems for *Downbeat*," as well as another from M. L. Rosenthal on *Nation* letterhead referring to unspecified works.

7. See Chapter 2 of the present study for a full account of the poetics of address in *Admonitions*.

8. *Open Space*, edited by Stan Persky, was very much a coterie publication of the San Francisco poets, with a submissions box at Spicer's favorite bar, Gino & Carlo, yet it was hardly precious or pretentious. It was printed cheaply in very small runs, and distributed free of charge; Spicer frowned on its circulation beyond the Bay Area. An editorial statement from the "Taurus Issue" gives a sense of both the intentions and the tone: "'Open Space' is actual working place, is free, is for the city – it isn't meant for manuscript collectors or bookdealers who sell it as valuable merchandise – if I find anyone doing that I'll take bloody action." For more on *Open Space*, see Clay and Phillips, *A Secret Location on the Lower East Side*, pp. 60–1, and *P*, especially pp. 278–80. In his Berkeley lecture of July 14, 1965, Spicer declares quite simply, "I couldn't have written *Language* without it" (*H*, 166).

9. Aside from the occasional minor difference in orthography. The final poems of "Graphemics" were not published in *Open Space*.

10. I have replaced the dash which separates "morpheme" and "cence" in the second line quoted above in the *Collected Poems* with a hyphen. This follows the text as printed in *Open Space* and seems to make, shall we say, sense: I believe the grapheme in question is not a piece of punctuation governing syntax, but a mark indicating that the morpheme "cence" arrives in a terminal position; a similar hyphen following "inn" indicates that it, on the contrary, is initial.

11. The rules in question refer to principles of probability and regularity in the combinations of free and bound morphemes, but I haven't found any place in the notes where they are stated as clear propositions.

12. I thank Kevin Killian for sharing with me information he tracked down on the "Stanford-Brentwood Computer-Assisted Instruction Laboratory," without which this chapter could not have been written.

13. The very first word of the poem is a demonstrative: "This ocean . . ." (*CP*, 373), indicating that not just any ocean is in question here. That the book *Language* opens with a deictic, inscribing the subject of enunciation and therefore the mark of the personal into its concerns from the very first word, is hardly inconsequential, as Ron Silliman has pointed out (*New Sentence*, 150). I will rely on Silliman's bravura reading of the poem throughout my own account of it.

14. Spicer's troping of the ocean in this connection goes all the way back to his play *Troilus* of 1955, in which Cressida calls the ocean "Just a cold dark

fact that no metaphor could make significant. It didn't even mean to be meaningless" (143).

15. As we saw in Chapter 3, Silliman considers "overdetermination" and its tendency to contradiction to be the central element of Spicer's poetry (149). The casting of "overdetermination" as blithely unresolved logical contradiction is no more notable in Spicer than in Stevens, probably one of the main places Spicer learned it: "It was Ulysses and it was not," Stevens wrote in "The World as Meditation" (442), to give one example.

16. Spicer's terminology here seems to derive from Chomsky's transformational grammar, which arrived on the scene after Spicer's foundational training in linguistics. As evidenced in these poems, his engagement with Chomskyan linguistics seems slight. See Chapter 4 of this study for an analysis of "Transformations II."

17. "Die Ferne" is German for "distance."

18. "no distant" asks to be corrected to "no more distant"; however, none of the printed versions of the poem give such a reading. In the only recording of Spicer reading *Language* he reads the poem as printed, though he does seem to stumble.

19. In this respect and several others, the poem is a re-writing of Spicer's early masterpiece "We find the body difficult to speak." See Chapter 1 for an extended reading of that poem.

20. Such a reading would take us uncannily close to Derrida's more or less contemporary investigation of the sign in Husserl in *Speech and Phenomena*.

21. Spicer's predictions for both leagues were inaccurate, as the St Louis Cardinals won the National League pennant and went on to beat the New York Yankees in the World Series. The hometown San Francisco Giants finished fourth, however, as Spicer had forecast, only three games behind the Cardinals, and three victories shy of a mark Spicer had deemed "impossible" (*CP*, 382). Spicer and his friend George Stanley seem to have had an annual tradition of exchanging baseball predictions, and in the third issue of *Open Space* Stanley's predictions are published next to Spicer's, underneath a large, baseball-themed drawing by Fran Herndon titled "Predictions."

22. For example, Anita Sokolsky writes that this poem makes what seems "the palpably false claim that its subject is the recent presidential assassination" (203), though her subsequent analysis of how this forces us to consider "how to parse a truth claim" (204) leads her to questions not altogether different from mine. I agree with John Vincent, who suggests this gesture asks either to be taken as a joke or a "comment on the notion of thematics itself"; he rightly specifies that these two options "are not mutually exclusive" (*Queer*, 162).

23. The letter, dated February 6, 1964, attaches a long list of "poets contacted" which includes a wide array of establishment poets but also the entirety of Donald Allen's *New American Poetry* anthology, as well as Pound, Eliot, Auden, and Zukofsky, among many others. The anthology was published as *Of Poetry and Power: Poems Occasioned by the Presidency and by the Death of John F. Kennedy*, edited by Erwin Glikes and Paul Schwaber, Basic Books, 1964.

24. As Peter Gizzi points out in his annotations, Spicer frequently wrote such letters himself, and Gizzi reproduces one which objects to the *San Francisco Chronicle*'s reporting of the Vietnam War (*H*, 45, n. 24). At the Berkeley conference, Spicer also signed an anti-Vietnam War petition circulating among the participating poets (*P*, 349).
25. For more on this, see the section on "Birdland, California" in Chapter 1.
26. As Christopher Nealon puts it, "Spicer wants to be vigilantly alert to crisis, almost seeming at times to want to trigger it" (107).
27. Spicer's intuition regarding "A Valediction: forbidding Mourning," which he misquotes slightly, is borne out by at least one contemporary editor: in his Penguin edition of Donne, A. J. Smith glosses the relevant line as referring to earthquakes too (406). Spicer had been pushing such a line ever since his graduate school paper on Donne's "Geographical Lore." Meanwhile, the "Valediction" is itself a poem about distances, and the device that measures them: the circle-drawing compass.
28. The last poem in "Phonemics" describes consonants as "A pattern for imagination" and phonemes as "Constructs / Of the imagination" (*CP*, 396). The indispensable analysis of the Saussurian insistence on the non-empirically phonic character of the phoneme is found in Part 1, Chapter 2 of Derrida's *Of Grammatology*, "Linguistics and Grammatology." See above all pp. 44–65. Derrida cites Saussure to the effect "It is impossible for sound alone, a material element, to belong to language ... The linguistic signifier ... is not [in essence] phonic but incorporeal ..." (53).
29. Spicer's editorial collaborators confirm that the theory of dictation entailed an analogous paradox: on the one hand Spicer was "casual with errors" out of alleged respect for the poem's form as dictated, but this same respect implied that every textual alteration, no matter how slight, was potentially disastrous to the integrity of the work (*P*, 335).
30. The German refers to a folk song (hence the poem's lisping conclusion: "Old / Senses in new thongs" (*CP*, 401)) "Ein Eichbaum," which posits an oaktree growing in splendid isolation and seeming to exist "only for itself" (thanks to Richard Sieburth for tracking this down and helping with the German). The origin of Spicer's "Eichenbach," which is not a German word, is mysterious. Editorial notes in the archives, possibly in Blaser's hand, indicate this might have been a printer's error.
31. The relevance of these lines from Eliot is clearer when one remembers his footnote to them, which cites F. H. Bradley to this effect: "My external sensations are no less private to myself than are my thoughts or my feelings. In either case my experience falls within my own circle, a circle closed on the outside ..." (75).
32. The folk song Spicer refers to was covered by Peter, Paul, and Mary in 1962, but Spicer clearly has the Trini Lopez version of 1965 in mind. Lopez distinguishes the vowel in the compounds "lemon tree" and "lemon flower" from that in the single word precisely as Spicer phonetically transcribes it in the *Book of Magazine Verse*, and discusses it in the Vancouver lectures (*H*, 121). In the song, the refrain Spicer cites is presented as an allegory for the inevitable disappointment behind the enticements of love, of why "Love isn't as great as it should be" (*CP*, 410). There's no mention in the song of "magic," though it is beneath the tree's branches that the

couple spends a summer of love before the girl leaves the sadder but wiser singer of the tale.

33. "Some poems are easily laid. They will give themselves to anybody and anybody physically capable can receive them . . . The quiet poems are what I worry about – the ones that must be seduced . . . properly wed, they are more beautiful than their whorish cousins" (*CP*, 138).

34. For example, "I carry the No you gave me / Clenched in my palm / Like something made of wax / An almost-white lemon" (*CP*, 135).

35. I quite agree with James Liddy's suggestion: "In saying the rind is also called the skin, Spicer declares that he is talking about human fruits" (263).

36. On his two trips to Vancouver, Spicer's readings and lectures were well attended, enthusiastically received, and even rewarding financially, and he suddenly found himself at the very center of a burgeoning poetic and artistic scene. On the strength of the impression he made during these visits he was even offered a full-time position at Simon Fraser University in Vancouver, where he would have started in the autumn of 1965, had he not stopped for death instead. See *P*, pp. 317–65, for details of Spicer's last months.

37. I agree with both Finkelstein and Blaser that these issues, and not homosexual guilt as Duncan argues, are the most important elements of Calvinism for Spicer.

38. For an indispensable account of baseball in Spicer, see Gizzi, "Enter the Diamond" (*H*, 192–9). In baseball jargon, "junk" pitching is as Spicer describes it: a technique relying on guile and unusual, often unpredictable ball movement, rather than power, speed, and control. Of all junk pitches, the knuckleball is the most notoriously difficult for catchers to handle. It is a particularly apt figure for dictation, as it is the only pitch in baseball whose placement, movement, and effect are unknown even to the pitcher when it is released. Spicer's "lecture" on the *Book of Magazine Verse* examines the baseball allegory at some length, to the point where it becomes muddled even for Spicer: "I think our baseball thing has gotten all confused" (*H*, 128).

39. See *P*, pp. 345–50, for more on the Conference. The "California Lecture" is reprinted in *H*, pp. 149–72.

40. Spicer's interest in folk music was long-standing. He even had his own weekly folk music show on alternative Berkeley radio station KPFA in 1949, which was cancelled after a forty-week run due to listener complaints about the bawdy lyric variants he and his co-hosts tended to introduce. See *P*, p. 30.

41. The "heathen Chinee" the poem mentions are also the popular title of a Bret Harte poem, "Plain Language from Truthful James." This work would have been resonant to Spicer for several reasons: Harte was a northern Californian author and an important element of the Californian literary history which always interested him, but beyond this the story of the poem's reception echoes Spicer's concerns in the *Book of Magazine Verse* in important ways. Meant to be a satire attacking anti-Chinese racism directed at the immigrants competing for jobs, the poem was widely read literally and used as a powerful tool in support of the very phenomenon the socially progressive Harte had meant to throw into disrepute.

42. Against the reading I offer here, Blaser suggests that the poem depicts the projection of the American flag onto the moon. However, American astronauts didn't place it there until 1969 (*The Fire*, 125). Working from Blaser, Michael Davidson posits the flag and the song as backdrop to "the shimmering television images of the first unmanned moon landing" (*San Francisco*, 169). As there were real-time television broadcasts of images transmitted from Ranger 9 on March 24, 1965, this is entirely plausible, and it would certainly be another instance of the American imperialism Spicer is concerned with in this section. Given the way the book is put together, however, I think the baseball resonances are "there," whatever Spicer, or what spoke through him, was thinking. Peter Gizzi also hears baseball behind this reference to the national anthem (*H*, 193).

43. See *P*, p. 355, and *San Francisco Renaissance*, pp. 169–71.

Coda: 1958

1958 looked to be an exciting year for Spicer. 1957 had seen the great success of the "Poetry as Magic" workshop in San Francisco, as well as the publication of his first book, *After Lorca*. The autumn had also borne witness to the famous *Howl* obscenity trial, which Spicer attended, there meeting Russell Fitzgerald, with whom he shared what seems to be his longest lasting romantic relationship, tumultuous though it was. The trial also brought San Francisco to national attention as the center of the presumably nascent counter-culture "Beat" movement, a phenomenon which caused some ambivalence in Spicer on two counts: first, he felt the Beats, largely relocated from the East Coast, had unfairly thrown into the shadows his truly local, poetically superior entourage; second, the Beat poet Bob Kaufman emerged as an ultimately terminal rival for the affections of Russell Fitzgerald.[1] Sometime late in 1957, this constellation of circumstances and the crucial addition of financial pressure led Spicer to undertake the writing of a detective novel, set in the San Francisco counter-culture now so prominent in the national media. Ostensibly, this would allow him both to land some punches and to profit financially from the limelight into which the Beats had thrown his city, but a reading of the unfinished novel (dubbed *The Tower of Babel* by its editors) quickly dispels any sense that it could have been a significant commercial success: though there is a murder, the real mysteries are those of poetics, as the book's main character returns from the East Coast where he has allowed himself to become an "academic" poet, in the hope that the new San Francisco scene he has read about will allow him to re-engage with those poetic energies that spurred him to write when he himself was a young man in the area. Unable to find a publisher willing to pay an advance, Spicer gave up at what seems more or less the half-way point, having provided a tour of the Bay Area demi-monde replete with significant hints that the married Ralston's poetic awakening can only come as a sexual one too: his most important encounter is with the seductive young man and poet, Rue Talcott. Near the end of the portion of the novel which Spicer did complete, however, comes a poetic "breakthrough" for Ralston which, in this very Jamesian novel, one imagines Spicer had projected as entirely ironic, given the theories of dictation that were emerging at this time: "It was one of *his* poems. A little alien perhaps . . . but *his* . . . I am myself, Ralston thought with surprise, and my poems are my poems" (152–3).[2] Coming on the heels of *After Lorca*, it's hard to imagine Spicer endorsing this poetics of identity and propriety or to see how this can be reconciled with his late declaration "I really honestly don't feel that I own my poems" (*H*, 15).

The work on the detective novel, however, fed into Spicer's poetry quite materially: interspersed in the notebook in which he was writing the novel, one finds lyrics from *Admonitions*, and subsequently from *A Book of Music* along with early drafts of *Billy The Kid*, as if these works grew out of the prose project as it emerged. And clearly, as Spicer narrativized and allegorized his poetic theories in the often fascinating *The Tower of Babel*, he put them to the test in the works mentioned above, notably seeing the last two as in dialogue, as this unpublished 1958 letter to Blaser attests, in a language which also challenges Ralston's claims:

> The Book of Music was written by a poet (not myself any longer) who wanted to explore the way that the contradictions of words and sounds ("indefiniteness is an element of the true music") make themselves felt in the twin worlds of the intellect and the emotions. The lines of the poem do not progress. One must be willing to read them forwards and backwards, to become trapped in them.
>
> My new book "Billy The Kid" is different. Its shape is the contradiction between speech and poetry and between sound and sight. It offers the reader a sore dream. (*B*)

I believe this letter, so clearly pairing two books, points to a practice of which Spicer might not always have been deliberately aware, but which his Socratic and Hegelian dialectical thinking tended to follow: the production of pairs of books, which converse or argue with each other in a network in which each "contradicts the last," as he puts it earlier in the same letter. As we have seen, such pairs tend to emerge in the form of *After Lorca* and *Admonitions*, *A Red Wheelbarrow* and *The Holy Grail*, and above all, *Language* and *A Book of Magazine Verse*. If these contradictions often seem to come full circle and form parallels, that is because each individual book tends *also* to be in "contradiction" with itself, as the letter suggests. But specifically in reference to the books mentioned above, to a considerable extent the dialogue between the different contradictions Spicer mentions here becomes the conversational space of a major portion of his poetics for the rest of his life. This is the legacy of 1958.

As Stephanie Judy has pointed out (268) the "sentence by Poe" (*CP*, 171) cited above and on which Spicer "improvises" in the first poem of *A Book of Music* is a slight misquotation from Poe's *Marginalia*, where Poe writes of the "*indefinitiveness*, which is, at least, *one* of the essentials of true music" (138, Poe's italics). Poe's line comes in the midst of reflections on writing words for songs, and leads him to postulate that "brief poems" written to be set to music need to be seen as separate from "ordinary literature" and "independent of merely ordinary proprieties" (136) in their embracing of an "indefinitiveness" which would be much less desirable in other forms of verse. Spicer's hope to explore the contradictions of "words and sounds" is in keeping with such concerns, and the broader desire to sort out sound, word, speech, and poetry echoes Pound, who divided poems into those meant to be spoken, sung, or chanted.[3] But Spicer also is addressing an older question of aesthetics, which goes back to Pater, Schopenhauer, and beyond, and has to do with music as the ideal art, in that it is autotelic and auto-referential, beyond reason and argument. In this respect, *A Book of Music* treats music as a kind of danger to poetry; as the poem "Cantata" puts it: "Ridiculous / How the space between three violins / Can threaten all of our poetry. / We bunch together like Cub / Scouts at a picnic. There is a high scream. / Rain threatens. That moment of terror. / Strange how all our beliefs / Disappear" (*CP*, 172). This opposition between music and belief is one Spicer had been thinking about for at least three years. In his play *Troilus*, Spicer has his eponymous character say, "I like music. You don't have to believe anything to hear it" (93–4). Such a statement points to the well known, well worn, and yet inevitable sense of the ultimate aesthetic autonomy of music, most famously expressed by Walter Pater in the phrase "All art constantly aspires towards the condition of music" (106), as it is in music in which the "form" can "become an end in itself" (106). But such an "aspiration" is one with which Spicer is far from comfortable. In a letter to his friend Graham Mackintosh, written during the composition of *Troilus*, Spicer remarks:

> That is why music is the art most popular with war-children [Spicer refers here both to the Trojan War and World War II]. One can understand a piece of music without reference to the past, without reference to anything but the music itself. That is why poetry, the exact opposite of music, is least popular with war-children. They live, the most gifted and most sensitive of them, in two dimensions instead of three. They can't dig time – and this causes them to be more intense within the limits of their two dimensions than a three-dimensional person could possibly be. (112)

In *A Book of Music* Spicer is interested in poetry as the "exact opposite" of music in these senses, yet as both a trained linguist and an extremely skilled technician, Spicer is well aware that poetry is also fundamentally an aural medium. These are the contradictions he examines throughout. The "Book" begins, therefore, with the opposition of music to meaning. A seagull "cawing its head off" is "As absolutely devoid of meaning / As a French horn" (*CP*, 171). And it is by way of meaninglessness that such cawing can reach the true music, as all that might "stoop to definition" (*CP*, 171) is eliminated through a sort of phenomenological reduction of everything surrounding the seagull's cawing until nothing is left but the sound: "No fish / No other seagull, no ocean – the true / Music" (*CP*, 171). Yet these elements that have been removed – the pier, the fish, the ocean, the other seagull – are precisely what fill the poem and make it a surprisingly vivid seascape. This poem, then, is not music, in part by virtue of the very fact of being "about" it.

Spicer continues to dialogue with Poe in "Mummer." In support of "indefinitiveness," Poe had excoriated composers who use "*imitation in musical sounds*" (137, Poe's italics) to try to make their music mimic the actually occurring sounds of one's surroundings: birds chirping or cannons blasting, for example. "Mummer" presents the linguistically analogous phenomenon of onomatopoeia, in which a word's meaning derives precisely from the *sound* it mimics. Yet typically of Spicer, the onomatopoeia he proposes here is something of a special case, as he archly defines his title word thusly: "The word is imitative / From the sound mum or mom / Used by nurses to frighten or amuse children / At the same time pretending / To cover their faces" (*CP*, 174). This is different from, say, "sizzle," said to represent the sound of something frying, not the act of frying (unless we're speaking figurally), or "cock-a-doodle-doo," the sound a rooster makes, not the rooster itself. "Mummer," meaning actor or participant in a mime, has another sort of trajectory. It is thought to derive from the Old French *momer*, meaning "to mask oneself" or take part in a masquerade, as Spicer's lines register with their reference to covering one's face. However, this French word in turn is said to imitate the muffled and distorted sounds uttered by people wearing masks. In this way, what is being mimicked is not a natural sound but the sound of a particular kind of talking, or more precisely, the sound of a talking in which the meaning cannot be distinguished, is "indefinite." Certainly, there are many imitative words for sounds we make as humans – to hem and to haw, and even, perhaps, to moan. But here we have an imitative word said to *derive* from a sound, but representing not the making of that sound but the very act of imitation itself. This is both frightening and funny, just as it is in Spicer's joke etymology not to know if the nurse mums the mom or if Mom herself is always a mum – filling the space created by the word that names her, rather than giving rise to it. Harping on the same root, this is what the poem mumbles. At the same time, to be "mum," of course, is to be silent. In all these cases, what might seem the ultimate form of linguistic "definiteness" – onomatopoeia, where the word shares the sound of what it names – veers off into what joins the two "enemies," poetry and music: an ultimate resistance to imitation, to the natural as matrix.

This parallel is taken up in "Duet for a Chair and a Table." Here, the naming capacity of language, rather than being opposed to music, is troped as being a form of it: a "symphony" or a "song." The sense of music proposed here is not as the absence of meaning, but rather as a system of relations. Just as a musical scale is a system which gives the "meaning" to any note within it – which shifts and organizes the notes through the intervals it permits – so language is a system which, according to Spicer, encloses us, names us, and shifts us about like furniture. As the first lines remind us, in terms of semantics "Nothing / is less important" than "The sound of words as they fall away from our mouths" (*CP*, 176). Yet without these sounds, astonishingly, the semantic doesn't happen. Speech here is a kind of magic, a conjuring act – very explicitly a performative in which it is only through that unimportant sound that: "We / Can learn our names from our mouths / Name our names" (*CP*, 177) – not our *selves*, but our *names*, in a form of mummery, a mumbling imitation of the sounds we make saying "mom" and "I." In this way, the names become things, they shift and are shifted, above all that famous shifter "I" which anybody can take up and use, no matter his or her name: "Words make things name / themselves / Makes the table grumble / I / In the symphony of God am a table," like us, "Who in the same music / Are almost as easily shifted as furniture" (*CP*, 177).

A Book of Music is Spicer at his most Poe-like, his most metaphysical, which, as William Carlos Williams could have told him, might well be Spicer at most his American.[4] *Billy The Kid* is about another way of being American, through local legend, lore, and historically and regionally locatable forms of speech; at the same time, it considers authenticity as an effect of the reproduction of imagos. The poem begins by insisting on Billy as mediated by a whole series of representations that give or create news of him, by way of a figure that is not incidental to Spicer's poetics, if not yet as central as it will soon become: "The radio that told me about the death of Billy The Kid" (*CP*, 185). This is not just the Outside dictating, but also an evocation of the sort of radio program Spicer would undoubtedly have listened to in his childhood – programs which were frequently "serial" and which favored popular genres like the western.[5] Similarly, Michael Snediker has shown just how many cinematic treatments there were of Billy the Kid in the 1930s, 1940s, and 1950s, arguing that in this way Billy "himself" is also "serial," like the poem that houses him.[6] His reading also strongly suggests Spicer's familiarity with ostensibly "historical" sources, such as accounts by the wonderfully named John Poe, and Walter Noble Burns.[7] This is especially likely as Spicer's interest in nineteenth-century western Americana is well established. If Billy's story takes place in Arizona, closer to home in several ways is the somewhat analogous tale of the California outlaw, Joaquín Murieta, the subject of a book of poems by Spicer's companion Ronnie Primack, *For the Late Major Horace Bell of the Los Angeles Rangers*, brought out by Spicer's publisher, White Rabbit Press, in 1963. Primack recounts that this work was instigated by Spicer having lent him the 1881 memoir of Horace Bell – the man who finally tracked and killed Murieta (*P*, 252).[8] Primack's book, heavily indebted stylistically to Spicer's *Billy The Kid*, is also illustrated with a gorgeous, fold-out map, the work of Cathy Mackintosh, then married to Spicer's former correspondent Graham, by now the publisher of White Rabbit Press. The prominence of the map and Primack's subject matter suggest a possible link between this project and Spicer's *Map Poems*, whose locations can be keyed to important sites of the Murieta tale.[9] The *Map Poems* might well wend their way back to *Billy The Kid*, by way of Primack's intervention in his Murieta piece.

As Spicer's letter to Blaser indicates, *Billy The Kid* often veers off into the flattest, most casual demotic, which hovers on the edges of the entire work: "Billy The Kid / I love you / Billy The Kid / I back anything you say (*CP*, 191). These instances tend to foreground the subject of enunciation, and thus, what Spicer in his letter to Blaser calls "speech" – "What I mean is / I / Will tell you about the pain" (*CP*, 187) – but without pretensions to mimetic representation, as the figures this speech proffers push against the downhome phraseology and tone: "It was a long pain / About as wide as a curtain / But long / As the great outdoors" (*CP*, 187). Rather than meditate on the relationship between sound and representation, as did *A Book of Music*, *Billy The Kid* warily circles an overdetermined topos of Americana it refuses to corner and track, only to end with a close-up to which the whole poem has been leading: "Billy The Kid / (In spite of your death notices) / There is honey in the groin / Billy" (*CP*, 191). If Billy is everywhere recognized as a mythic stereotype of the western genre, this never leads to his transformation into a mythologized archetype, as images crystallize only to be erased or fail to cohere in this collage-like poem which denies its status as such (*CP*, 185–6). The sparse, jagged, laconic language echoes the arid landscape and the conventions of cowboy talk, in a play on idiom and genre grounded entirely differently from the theoretical speculations on language as representational vehicle in *A Book of Music*. To a considerable extent, Spicer's feeling that *Billy The Kid* is a poem about the prosaic and the image rather than sound and sense in their uncanny relationship, is borne out. What joins these two works is that they are both also to a very large degree love poems, like the vast majority of Spicer's best work, and again characteristically, elegiac ones. More than this, added to theorizations of the Outside, haunting, and the "book" in *After Lorca* and *Admonitions* as well as the poetics of address both those works bring into play, the contrasting maneuvers and rhetorics of *A Book of Music* and *Billy The Kid* very largely round out the palette that Spicer will rely on henceforward, and finalize the transition first undertaken in the pivotal works of 1957.

However, some of these poems are also found in a site even more unlikely than the *Tower of Babel* notebook. For around this time, Spicer was also compiling a manuscript for a projected "selected poems," and many of the poems from *A Book of Music* figure within it. This means that well after the rousing letter to Blaser in *Admonitions* excoriating the individual lyric, Spicer was still seriously considering putting together a collection of them, and refusing to abandon a project whose inadequacy he himself had so passionately argued. One has to imagine that an ultimate commitment to the "book," perhaps solidified by *Billy The Kid*, is what prevented the "selected poems" from ever seeing the light of day, but in the wake of *Admonitions* it's hard to see how Spicer could have continued to work on such a project without serious misgivings and a sense of bad faith. This might be why the bad faith of the poet is at the heart of the unpublished lyric he chose to close the "selected poems," called, appropriately enough, "Poet."[10] It begins,

> He knocks upon our doors un-
> Cannily
> As if the only test
> Were some way of being right
> That a poem can give one
>
> (B)

This is a literally dialectical poem, as the line break negates the negation of "uncannily," separating the poet from the haunted and haunting voice of the ghost, and revealing him as no more than a clever, manipulative, "canny" trickster. Poetry is here reduced to a paltry "way of being right," while as for the poet himself: "He is like an an- / Droid constructed of all our emotions" (B) – no more than a simulacrum of a person, a composite of the emotions of others which, it would seem, have been objectified, fossilized, turned into poetic parts or "converted into poetry" like foreign currency. This sort of mechanical morcellation is of course echoed formally, as the line breaks split words into morphological elements, representing language as a kind of android or perhaps cyborg itself – half human, half a machine made of combinatory elements – in moves which clearly look forward to *Language*. At the same time, the "poet" is not only an "android" but for the space of a line also an "an" – the indefinite article, indicating this ultimately unacceptable form of "negative capability" which allows the poet to become anything at all – any and all of our emotions, thrown together in the poetic mummery of the human. Though Spicer never published this poem, he never dismissed as trivial the risks it presents, never wrote as if there were somewhere a poetry so authentic that it could simply throw them off.

As early as 1966, Gilbert Sorrentino captured the significance of Spicer in a statement which also brilliantly doubles the contradictory workings of Spicer's own poetics: "Spicer achieved that rare and difficult feat – he created an art which was at once subservient to, and dominant over, a set of ideas" (55). The older brother of a legendary debating champion, Spicer fashioned poetry, letters, and poetics which often seem to follow the possibility of disagreement for its own formal beauty, in a serious game in which winning is only an epiphenomenon: "George / Said to me that the only thing he thought was important in chess was killing the other king. I had accused him of lack of imagination" (*CP*, 331).[11] At the same time, Spicer's "set of ideas" implied a problem which was in some ways insoluble. Robin Blaser has stressed how for Spicer language

> had to be poised in the middle – between things, and among things. It did *not* belong either to Jack or to the Outside . . . I think the reason that he chose to join himself to Olson in those last weeks [of his life] was the sense that Olson had, where the poet is among things, not in charge of them . . . Because Spicer did not think he was in charge of, but that he was among things. There is a world out there. (*P*, 338–9, Blaser's italics)

A world which, Blaser reminds us, Spicer always "reaffirms," even as he marks its terror and violence (*P*, 339). Spicer's poems, in the end, are not proud enough to hate the readers at their gate, unable not to tear Hell. What Blaser makes clear is that if they stand on the other side, it is the other side of the Outside too. From there we hear them, "Crying out against the inelegance / Of all that is not sacred" (*CP*, 59).

Notes

1. For biographical details, see *P*, pp. 118–39. Lisa Jarnot's recent biography of Duncan discusses how around this time the poets in his circle and Spicer's began to think of themselves as explicitly "anti-beatnik" (172).
2. For more on the novel, see the editors' "Afterword," John Vincent's "Pinnacle of No Explanation," and my *American Modernism's Expatriate Scene*, pp. 140–8, which explores this episode in greater detail.
3. "for there are three kinds of *melopoeia*: (1) that made to be sung to a tune; (2) that made to be intoned or sung to a sort of chant; and (3) that made to be spoken; and the art of joining words in each of these kinds is different . . ." (*Literary Essays*, 28).
4. For Williams, Poe is more "American" than Hawthorne precisely because he refuses to transpose a fundamentally European descriptive and narrative paradigm to his "own milieu," as does Hawthorne, heeding instead the "local necessities" that imply a "*beginning* literature . . . that must establish its own rules, own framework" (*American*, 228–9, Williams' italics). Such positions should lay to rest the association of Williams' "Americanness" with homespun.
5. See Gizzi's "Afterword" in *H*, pp. 187–8, for an excellent account of these aspects of the radio.
6. See *Queer*, pp. 126–67 for an excellent, detailed reading of the book, and pp. 132–4 for the cinematic history of the Billy story. I follow Snediker's assertion that Spicer's Billy derives "authenticity" from forms of reproduction which can be mechanical, but I don't agree that a Benjaminian "aura," even as modulated by Snediker (244, n. 2) is as pertinent as the sedimentation of generic convention in the establishment of this effect. In terms of the films on the subject, Snediker is right to point to the decisive intervention of Arthur Penn's *The Left Handed Gun* of 1958, featuring a homoerotic screenplay by Gore Vidal and Paul Newman as Billy.
7. See *Queer*, pp. 158–62. Burns is the source of the surprising "fact" that Billy had an associate whose alias was "Alias," something Spicer clearly picked up on.
8. If, as Primack asserts, Spicer "knew pretty much everything about California" (*P*, 252) he also would have known that the Murieta (or Murietta, as it is sometimes spelled) tale gave the plot to *The Life and Adventures of Joaquín Murieta, the Celebrated California Bandit*, by Yellow Bird, a.k.a., John Rollin Ridge. Published in 1854, this work is one of the first novels written in California, and thought to be the first published in the United States by a Native American.
9. Gizzi and Killian explain that a box of facsimile road maps found in Spicer's papers bear page numbers that correspond to the numbers which serve as titles to the *Map Poems* (*CP*, 452). Collation of the maps and perusal of the poems situate "111" just outside Sacramento, "137" at Mount Shasta, "185" with the "Golden Gate," that is, the entrance to San Francisco Bay, and "217" with Eureka, as the first four words also indicate. Spicer seems to have mistranscribed as "155" what is in fact map 153, showing Stockton, California. Mount Shasta, the Sacramento Valley, and Stockton

all figure in Murieta's wanderings, as he runs from the law in Yellow Bird's telling.
10. Or "A Portrait" in some variants.
11. See *P*, p. 362, on Holt Spicer's achievements in university forensics.

Bibliography

Adorno, Theodor. *Minima Moralia: Reflections from Damaged Life*, trans. E. F. N. Jephcott. New York: Verso Press, 1997.

Allen, Donald (ed.). *The New American Poetry: 1945–1960*. Berkeley: University of California Press, 1999.

Arendt, Hannah. *The Human Condition* (second edition). Chicago: University of Chicago Press, 1998.

Auden, W. H. *Selected Poems*, ed. Edward Mendelson. New York: Vintage Books, 1979.

Beckett, Samuel. *Disjecta: Miscellaneous Writings and a Dramatic Fragment*, ed. Ruby Cohn. New York: Grove Press, 1984.

Bersani, Leo, and Adam Phillips. *Intimacies*. Chicago: University of Chicago Press, 2008.

Blake, William. *The Marriage of Heaven and Hell*, ed. with Intro. and Commentary Geoffrey Keynes. London: Oxford University Press, 1975.

Blaser, Robin. *The Fire: Collected Essays of Robin Blaser*, ed. Miriam Nichols. Berkeley: University of California Press, 2006.

—. *The Holy Forest: Collected Poems of Robin Blaser*, ed. Miriam Nichols. Berkeley: University of California Press, 2006.

Butts, Mary. *The Taverner Novels: Armed with Madness and The Death of Felicity Taverner*. Kingston, NY: McPherson, 1992.

Chamberlain, Lori. "Ghostwriting the Text: Translation and the Poetics of Jack Spicer," *Contemporary Literature*, vol. 26, no. 4 (1985): 426–42.

Clarkson, Ross. "Jack Spicer's Ghosts and the Immemorial Community," *Mosaic*, vol. 34, no. 4 (2001): 199–211.

Clay, Steven, and Rodney Phillips. *A Secret Location on the Lower East Side: Adventures in Writing, 1960–1980*. New York: New York Public Library and Granary Books, 1998.

Conte, Joseph. *Unending Design: The Forms of Postmodern Poetry*. Ithaca, NY: Cornell University Press, 1991.

D'Emilio, John. *Making Trouble: Essays on Gay History, Politics, and the University*. New York: Routledge, 1992.

Damon, Maria. "Jack Spicer's Ghost Forms," in *After Spicer: Critical Essays*, ed. John Emil Vincent. Middletown, CT: Wesleyan University Press, 2011.

—. *The Dark End of the Street: Margins in American Vanguard Poetry*. Minneapolis: University of Minnesota Press, 1993.

Davidson, Michael. *Guys Like Us: Citing Masculinity in Cold War Poetics.* Chicago: University of Chicago Press, 2004.

—. "Incarnations of Jack Spicer: Heads of the Town up to the Aether." *Boundary 2*, vol. 6, no. 1 (Autumn, 1977): 103–34.

—. *The San Francisco Renaissance: Poetics and Community at Mid-Century.* Cambridge: Cambridge University Press, 1991.

DeBord, Guy. "Theory of the Dérive." *Situationist International Anthology: Revised and Expanded Edition*, ed. and trans. Ken Knabb. Berkeley: Bureau of Public Secrets, 2006.

Decker, William Merrill. *Epistolary Practices: Letter Writing in America Before Telecommunications.* Chapel Hill, NC: University of North Carolina Press, 1998.

Derrida, Jacques. *Of Grammatology*, trans. Gayatri Chakravorty Spivak. Baltimore, MD: Johns Hopkins University Press, 1976.

Dickinson, Emily. *The Poems of Emily Dickinson*, ed. R. W. Franklin. Cambridge, MA: Harvard University Press, 1998.

Donne, John. *The Complete English Poems*, ed. A. J. Smith. London: Penguin Books, 1996.

Doolittle, Hilda (H. D.). *Helen in Egypt.* New York: New Directions, 1961.

Duncan, Robert. *Caesar's Gate: Poems, 1949–50*, with paste-ups by Jess [Collins]. Berkeley: Sand Dollar, 1972.

—. *The First Decade: Selected Poems 1940–1950.* London: Fulcrum Press, 1968.

—. *The H. D. Book*, ed. and Intro. Michael Boughn and Victor Coleman. Berkeley: University of California Press, 2011.

—. "Robert Duncan Papers" (BANC MSS 78/164c), Bancroft Library, UC Berkeley.

Eliot, T. S. *Collected Poems: 1909–1962.* New York: Harcourt, Brace, & Co., 1991.

—. *Selected Prose*, ed. Frank Kermode. New York: Farrar, Straus, & Giroux, 1975.

Eshelman, Clayton. "The Lorca Working," *Boundary 2*, vol. 27, no. 1 (1977): 31–49.

Faas, Ekbert. *Young Robert Duncan: Portrait of the Poet as Homosexual in Society.* Santa Barbara, CA: Black Sparrow Press, 1983.

Finkelstein, Norman. "Spicer's Reason to 'Be- / Leave," in *After Spicer: Critical Essays*, ed. John Emil Vincent. Middletown, CT: Wesleyan University Press, 2011.

Freccero, John. *Dante: The Poetics of Conversion*, ed. Rachel Jacoff. Cambridge, MA: Harvard University Press, 1986.

Fredman, Stephen. *Poet's Prose: The Crisis in American Verse* (second edition). Cambridge: Cambridge University Press, 1990.

García Lorca, Federico. *In Search of Duende*, ed. Christopher Maurer. New York: New Directions, 1998.

—. *Selected Verse: A Bilingual Edition*, ed. Christopher Maurer. New York: Farrar, Strauss, & Giroux, 1997.

Ginsberg, Allen. *Collected Poems 1947–1980.* New York: HarperPerennial, 1984.

Gizzi, Peter. "Afterword: Jack Spicer and the Practice of Reading," *The House that Jack Built: The Collected Lectures of Jack Spicer*. Hanover, NH: Wesleyan University Press, 1998.

Goar, Jim. "Jack Spicer's 'The Book of the Death of Arthur,'" *Jacket*, no. 37 (2009).

Hatlen, Burton. "'Crawling into Bed with Sorrow': Jack Spicer's *After Lorca*," *Ironwood*, vol. 14, no. 2 (1986): 118–35.

Hawkey, Christian. *Ventrakl*. New York: Ugly Duckling Press, 2010.

Herd, David. *John Ashbery and American Poetry*. Manchester: Manchester University Press, 2003.

Hlibchuk, Geoffrey. "From Typology to Topology: On Jack Spicer," *Contemporary Literature*, vol. 51, no. 2 (Summer 2010): 310–40.

Holt, Kelly. "Spicer's Poetic Correspondence: 'A Pun the Letter Reflects,'" in *After Spicer: Critical Essays*, ed. John Emil Vincent. Middletown, CT: Wesleyan University Press, 2011.

Howe, Susan. *The Birth-mark: Unsettling the Wilderness in American Literary History*. Hanover, NH: Wesleyan University Press, 1993.

Imbriglio, Catherine. "'Impossible Audiences': Camp, the Orphic, and Art as Entertainment in Jack Spicer's Poetry," in *After Spicer: Critical Essays*, ed. John Emil Vincent. Middletown, CT: Wesleyan University Press, 2011.

Jarnot, Lisa. *Robert Duncan: The Ambassador from Venus*. Berkeley: University of California Press, 2012.

Judy, Stephanie A. "'The Grand Concord What'": Preliminary Thoughts on Musical Composition in Poetry," *Boundary 2*, vol. 6, no. 1 (Autumn, 1977): 267–85.

Jung, C. G. "On the Relation of Analytical Psychology to Poetry," in *The Portable Jung*, ed. Joseph Campbell. New York: Viking Penguin, 1971.

Katz, Daniel. *American Modernism's Expatriate Scene: The Labour of Translation*. Edinburgh: Edinburgh University Press, 2007.

Kaufmann, Vincent. *L'équivoque épistolaire*. Paris: Editions de minuit, 1990.

Keenaghan, Eric. "Jack Spicer's Pricks and Cocksuckers: Translating Homosexuality into Visibility," *The Translator*, vol. 4, no. 2 (1998): 273–94.

Killian, Kevin. "Spicer and the Mattachine," in *After Spicer: Critical Essays*, ed. John Vincent. Middletown, CT: Wesleyan University Press, 2011.

—. "Under the Influence," *Exact Change Yearbook*, no. 1, 1995.

Levinson, Stephen. *Pragmatics*. Cambridge: Cambridge University Press, 1983.

Liddy, James. "A Problem with Sparrows: Spicer's Last Stance," *Boundary 2*, vol. 6, no. 1 (Autumn, 1977): 259–66.

Malory, Thomas. *Works*, ed. Eugène Vinaver. Oxford: Oxford University Press, 1971.

Mayhew, Jonathan. *Apocryphal Lorca: Translation, Parody, Kitsch*. Chicago: University of Chicago Press, 2009.

Mellors, Anthony. *Late Modernist Poetics: From Pound to Prynne*. Manchester: Manchester University Press, 2005.

Middleton, Peter. "An Elegy for Theory: Robin Blaser's Essay 'The Practice of Outside,'" in Miriam Nichols (ed.), *Even On Sunday: Essays, Readings, and*

Archival Materials on the Poetry and Poetics of Robin Blaser. Orono, ME: National Poetry Foundation, 2001.

Motherwell, Robert (ed.). *The Dada Painters and Poets: An Anthology* (second edition). Cambridge, MA: Harvard University Press, 1989.

Nealon, Christopher. *The Matter of Capital: Poetry and Crisis in the American Century*. Cambridge, MA: Harvard University Press, 2011.

Nichols, Miriam. *Radical Affections: Essays on the Poetics of Outside*. Tuscaloosa, AL: University of Alabama Press, 2010.

O'Hara, Frank. *The Collected Poems of Frank O'Hara*, ed. Donald Allen. Berkeley: University of California Press, 1995.

Olson, Charles. *Collected Prose*, ed. Donald Allen and Benjamin Friedlander. Berkeley: University of California Press, 1997.

—. *The Maximus Poems*, ed. George Butterick. Berkeley: University of California Press, 1983.

Parkinson, Thomas. "The Sun and the Moon in Yeats's Early Poetry," *Modern Philology*, vol. 50, no. 1 (August, 1952): 50–8.

Pater, Walter. *The Renaissance: Studies in Art and Poetry*. Berkeley: University of California Press, 1980.

Paton, Lucy Allen. *Studies in the Fairy Mythology of Arthurian Romance*. Boston: Athenaeum Press (Radcliffe College Monographs), 1903.

Perloff, Marjorie. *The Poetics of Indeterminacy: Rimbaud to Cage*. Evanston, IL: Northwestern University Press, 1981.

Poe, Edgar Allan. *The Complete Works of Edgar Allan Poe, Volume XVI, Marginalia, Eureka*, ed. James A. Harrison. New York: AMS Press, 1965 (reproduced from 1902 New York edition).

Pound, Ezra. *Literary Essays of Ezra Pound*, ed. T. S. Eliot. New York: New Directions, 1968.

—. *Selected Prose: 1909–1965*, ed. William Cookson. New York: New Directions, 1973.

Primack, Ronnie. *For the Late Major Horace Bell of the Los Angeles Rangers*. San Francisco: White Rabbit Press, 1963.

Rabaté, Jean-Michel. *Language, Sexuality and Ideology in Ezra Pound's Cantos*. Albany, NY: SUNY Press, 1986.

Rasula, Jed. "Spicer's Orpheus and the Emancipation of Pronouns," *Boundary 2*, vol. 6, no. 1 (Autumn, 1977): 51–102.

Rickels, Laurence. *The Case of California*. Minneapolis: University of Minnesota Press, 2001.

Riley, Peter. "The Narratives of *The Holy Grail*," in *Boundary 2*, vol. 6, no. 1 (1977): 163–90.

Rimbaud, Arthur. *Œuvres complètes*, ed. Antoine Adam. Paris: Bibliothèque de la Pléiade, Editions Gallimard, 1972.

Schwabsky, Barry. "Between the Dead and the Living: Jack Spicer's Second Life," *The Nation Online*, December 17, 2008.

Shakespeare, William. *Hamlet*, New Cambridge Shakespeare. Cambridge: Cambridge University Press, 1989.

Silliman, Ron. "Spicer's Language," in Bob Perelman (ed.), *Writing/Talks (Poetics of the New)*. Carbondale, IL: Southern Illinois University Press, 1985.

—. *The New Sentence*. New York: Roof Books, 1987.

Smith, Simon. *Mercury*. Cambridge: Salt Publishing, 2006.

Smithson, Robert. *The Collected Writings*, ed. Jack Flam. Berkeley: University of California Press, 1996.

Snediker, M. D. "Prodigal Son (Midway along the Pathway)," *Criticism*, vol. 51, no. 3 (Summer 2009): 489–504.

—. *Queer Optimism: Lyric Personhood and Other Felicitous Persuasions*. Minneapolis: University of Minnesota Press, 2009.

Sokolsky, Anita. "Character Assassination in the Poetry of Jack Spicer," in John Emil Vincent 9ed.), *After Spicer: Critical Essays*. Middletown, CT: Wesleyan University Press, 2011.

Sorrentino, Gilbert. *Something Said (second edition)*. Chicago: Dalkey Archive, 2001.

Spicer, Jack. *The Collected Books of Jack Spicer*, ed. Robin Blaser. Santa Barbara, CA: Black Sparrow Press, 1980.

—. *Jack Spicer's Detective Novel: The Tower of Babel*. Hoboken, NJ: Talisman House, 1994.

—. "Letters to Allen Joyce," *Sulfur*, 10 (1987): 140–53.

—. "Letters to Graham Mackintosh," *Caterpillar*, 12 (1970): 83–114.

—. "Letters to Robin Blaser," *Line*, 9 (1987): 26–55.

—. *One Night Stand and Other Poems*, ed. Donald Allen, Pref. Robert Duncan. San Francisco: Grey Fox Books, 1980.

—. "Selected Letters from the Spicer/ Duncan Correspondence," *Acts*, 6 (1987): 13–30.

—. *Troilus*. No: A Journal of the Arts, no. 3 (2004): 77–153.

Starkie, Enid. *Arthur Rimbaud* (new and revised edition). London: Hamish Hamilton, 1947.

Stevens, Wallace. *Collected Poetry and Prose*, ed. Frank Kermode and Joan Richardson. New York: Library of America, 1997.

Tiffany, Daniel. *Radio Corpse: Imagism and the Cryptaesthetic of Ezra Pound*. Cambridge, MA: Harvard University Press, 1995.

Vanderborg, Susan. *Paratextual Communities: American Avant-Garde Poetry Since 1950*. Carbondale, IL: Southern Illinois University Press, 2001.

Vincent, John Emil (ed.). *After Spicer: Critical Essays*. Middletown, CT: Wesleyan University Press, 2011.

—. "Before *After Spicer*," in *After Spicer: Critical Essays*. Middletown, CT: Wesleyan University Press, 2011.

—. "Pinnacle of No Explanation: Jack Spicer's Exercise of the Novel," in John Emil Vincent (ed.), *After Spicer: Critical Essays*. Middletown, CT: Wesleyan University Press, 2011.

—. *Queer Lyrics: Difficulty and Closure in American Poetry*. New York: Palgrave, 2002.

Walsh, John K. "A Logic in Lorca's 'Ode to Walt Whitman,'" in Emilie Bergmann and Paul Julian Smith (eds), *¿Entiendes? Queer Readings, Hispanic Writings*. Durham, NC: Duke University Press, 1995.

Weston, Jessie. *From Ritual to Romance*. New York: Anchor Books, 1957.

White, Jared. "Jack Spicer on Mars," *Open Letters Monthly: An Arts and Literature Review*, January, 2009. Online at: http://www.openlettersmonthly. com/january-2009-jack-spicer/.

Whitman, Walt. *Complete Poetry and Collected Prose*, ed. Justin Kaplan. New York: Library of America, 1982.

Williams, William Carlos. *Imaginations*. New York: New Directions, 1970.

—. *In the American Grain*. New York: New Directions, 1956.

—. *Paterson*. New York: New Directions, 1963.

—. *Pictures From Brueghel and Other Poems*. New York: New Directions, 1967.

Yao, Steven G. *Translation and the Languages of Modernism: Gender, Politics, Language*. New York: Palgrave Macmillan, 2002.

Yeats, William Butler. *The Poems*, ed. Daniel Albright. London: J. M. Dent (Everyman Editions), 2003.

—. *A Vision: A Reissue with the Author's Final Revisions*. New York: Collier Books, 1965.

Index